WEBER'S
AMERICAN BBQ
A MODERN SPIN ON THE CLASSICS

JAMIE PURVIANCE

FOOD PHOTOGRAPHY BY
TIM TURNER

LIFESTYLE PHOTOGRAPHY BY
MICHAEL WARREN

hamlyn

CONTENTS

SPECIAL FEATURES }

AMERICAN-MADE
KOREAN BARBECUE

38

NOUVEAU 'CUE
RIBS

80

WHAT'S NEW IN BARBECUE?

Jamie Purviance

> **WHAT WAS ONCE A STYLE OF FOOD ROOTED IN THE RURAL SOUTH IS NOW ALMOST EVERYWHERE, EVEN IN BIG CITIES, AND, IN TURN, THOSE CITIES ARE INFLUENCING THE FOOD.**

Barbecue. Surely you've heard of it, but what exactly is it? I used to think I knew. It was supposed to be spice-rubbed pork ribs glistening with sauce, or tender slices of smoked brisket dripping juices on paper or succulent shreds of pork shoulder piled high on soft white buns. Those were supposed to be the epitome of barbecue – an American institution that has held tightly to strict principles since the first days of our nation. At least that is what I thought. Several years ago I accidentally offended a fellow student at the Culinary Institute of America by inviting him to a weekend 'barbecue' where I intended to grill hamburgers and sausages. He was raised in North Carolina with more than a little local pride, and so he responded indignantly, 'That's not barbecue. Real barbecue is cooked in a pit with wood, not on a grill.' Then he schooled me about serious regional differences in barbecue. Maybe you have heard of these. In the Piedmont of North Carolina, barbecue means pit-cooked and chopped pork served in a tomato-tinged vinegar sauce with slaw and hush puppies on the side. No beef is allowed. But in Texas proper, barbecue *is* beef – especially brisket and hefty beef ribs – and pit masters there are likely to protest at anyone coating it with sauce or trying to eat it with a fork. On and on my classmate went, pounding his fists on the table and telling me you can't possibly cook barbecue with gas. You have to do it like third-generation pit master Sam Jones at Skylight Inn BBQ in Ayden, North Carolina, where a billboard outside the legendary restaurant clearly states, 'If it's not cooked with wood it's not BBQ.' Well, okay, I assumed my red-faced classmate had sufficient credentials that I should believe him. I filed away his lesson about what 'authentic' barbecue means, and for years I tended to agree with it. While writing this book, however, I felt compelled to check his facts and to dig a little deeper. Among other things, I wanted to know about the origins of American barbecue. It turns out that American barbecue's starting point was *barbacoa*, which dates to the 1500s: a framework of green branches and sticks elevated high over a fire for cooking. That's how barbecue was practised in a region that is now the West Indies and along the south-eastern coast of North America, including Florida. Just to be clear, those Indians were not cooking racks of baby back ribs or smoky briskets to be sliced for barbecue sandwiches. No, no, no. They were cooking fish, turtles, iguana, alligator and snakes – pretty much anything they could catch and slaughter. So if you really want to talk about authentic American barbecue, maybe we should forget the pulled pork sandwiches and think instead about how to roast an alligator over a campfire.

In fact, maybe we should forget the whole question of what's authentic. Clearly, with barbecue, the food evolves over time with cultural changes. Today, brisket seems like it is permanently enshrined along with beef ribs and sausage as part of the 'holy trinity' of Texas barbecue meats. Historically speaking, however, brisket is a relatively new thing, and soon it might be replaced (check out the timeline on the facing page). What was once a style of food rooted in the rural South is now almost everywhere, even in big cities and, in turn, those cities are influencing the food. At Hometown Bar-B-Que in Brooklyn, New York, pit master Bill Durney is a lot more creative than he ever would be in Central Texas where he did his barbecue training. On Durney's menu you will find sweet Korean sticky ribs, a Vietnamese-style lamb belly banh mi sandwich with crunchy daikon and spicy jerk baby back ribs. Why? The people in Brooklyn, some of them from Korean, Vietnamese and Caribbean backgrounds, like their distinctive international flavours in their barbecue.

Barbecue competitions, including the ones on reality television shows, have made barbecue a sport that has launched winners towards fame and fortune. Lee Ann Whippen was a blue-collar caterer from Virginia who smoked her way to the top at some major competitions. When a restaurateur from Chicago saw an opportunity to take barbecue upmarket, he recruited Whippen to be the executive chef at Chicago q, a fine-dining restaurant in the city's Gold Coast neighbourhood. In a space that looks more like a private country club than an old-school barbecue joint, Whippen is wowing diners with her competition-style ribs, blackened alligator, and a brunch menu with eggs Benedict on prime-grade brisket. Brunch at a barbecue restaurant? Yes! Why not?

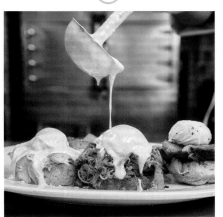

Doug Adams grew up near Texas barbecue country and took the food for granted until he moved to Portland, Oregon, to attend cooking school. Today this Top Chef finalist cooks at the high-end Imperial restaurant, where his menu draws from a wood-burning grill and tastes from his childhood. Adams' food caters to Portland's funky eclectic culture, but still he shows traces of barbecue everywhere. 'I am obsessed with smoke,' he says. 'I try every piece of meat or produce that comes into the kitchen on the wood grill before it goes anywhere else.' At first glance his dish of green beans with smoked elk tongue, kimchi and a deep-fried egg seems to have no traditional roots at all. 'Yeah, I know that dish sounds weird,' admits Adams, 'but to me it is so Texas. It is smoked meat and pickles. As for the egg, we deep-fry almost everything in Texas. If you break down my food, you see a lot of barbecue. As a chef I am always asking myself how can I build on barbecue but do it differently.'

Traditionalists don't need to worry about these changes. Just because someone asks 'what if?' or 'why not?' we are not threatening barbecue; we are broadening it. Gradual change has been part of its nature since the days of *barbacoa*. In our food-obsessed, Internet-connected, melting-pot nation, change is happening faster than ever, and it's no coincidence that the popularity of barbecue is surging. My respect

for the classic dishes is deep and permanent, and I have shared many of those recipes with you in this book. I have also shared recipes and stories inspired by the classics but freed by the creativity at play today. I hope you cook them and make them your own. Each time we bring our own styles and stories to the experience, we contribute something real to this ever-expanding phenomenon called American barbecue. So get into it. Barbecue like you mean it and ask yourself, 'What's next?'

IN OUR FOOD-OBSESSED, INTERNET-CONNECTED, MELTING-POT NATION, CHANGE IS HAPPENING FASTER THAN EVER, AND IT'S NO COINCIDENCE THAT THE POPULARITY OF BARBECUE IS SURGING.

AMERICAN BARBECUE
OVER TIME

1600s

By the 1600s settlers in the New World were using various spellings to describe the style of cooking that they had adapted from the Indians. Terms such as 'borbecue' and 'barbecu' were meant to signify that their ways were more civilised than the 'savage' techniques they had witnessed. That's funny because the settlers' barbecues often devolved into rowdy brawls among drunken men.

1700s

Political candidates in the 1700s used barbecues as a tactic for drawing big crowds, plying undecided voters with bourbon, rum and roasted meat. George Washington wrote in his diary that he attended six barbecues between 1769 and 1774. Later, after he had set in place the cornerstone of the United States Capitol building in 1793, he hosted a meal featuring a 500-lb (227-kg) barbecued ox.

1800s

During the 1800s, barbecue thrived in the South and expanded westward, too, along with the settlers. By midcentury, railroad promoters used barbecues to lure citizens into supporting railway construction: have a free meal, buy shares in a rail company. On national holidays like the Fourth of July, settlers gathered, cleared the land if needed and pooled whatever each family had to offer – hogs, ox, venison, turkeys and even squirrels. People ate, drank and danced to the music of fiddlers well into the night.

The emancipation of slaves in 1865 meant that for the first time, African-American pit masters were free to run barbecue joints for their own profit. Henry Perry was born near Memphis in 1875 and worked for much of his young life in steamboat kitchens moving up and down the Mississippi River and Missouri River. In the early 1900s he moved to Kansas City and started selling smoked meat wrapped in newspaper for 25 cents a slab. Eventually he opened the first real barbecue restaurant in Kansas City, and his menu included beef, woodchuck, raccoon and opossum. When Henry died, a former employee, Charlie Bryant, took over the restaurant and then sold it to his brother Arthur. You can go to Arthur Bryant's restaurant in Kansas City today (in a new location), but don't ask for opossum. That was old American barbecue.

1900s

In the early 1900s butchers at Central Texas meat markets bought whole forequarters of beef from local ranchers, carved off the best cuts to display in the meat case, and put the less desirable ones, like chuck and shoulder, on a smoker to prevent them from going to waste. Over time their barbecued meats proved to be more popular and profitable than fresh meats, so many butchers specialised in selling barbecue. In the 1960s, though, intensive farming and refrigerated transport made beef a national industry, and meat markets could order whatever pre-butchered, shrink-wrapped cuts they wanted. Most of them chose brisket because it was so inexpensive. Today, with brisket prices much higher than they were a decade ago, some Texas pit masters predict that they might need to find something cheaper.

2000s

By the year 2000, barbecue had expanded well beyond roadside stands and restaurants. Weber had grown from a small, midwestern company to the world's largest manufacturer of barbecue grills. Today, Weber grills are sold in nearly every town in the US, and Americans are able to recreate many traditional barbecue dishes in their own backyards. Increasingly, barbecue cooks are riffing on tradition and shaping new, multicultural styles. See page 18 for the Top Five Barbecue Trends Today.

IT'S ALL ABOUT

FIRE

I doubt we will ever reach a consensus in America about what barbecue is and what it isn't. Fans can be downright dogmatic in their loyalties, claiming that if you are not making their kind of barbecue you are not making real barbecue. That's okay. It means we have a great diversity of styles. New American barbecue encompasses all styles, with a unifying element that has been present since the days of barbacoa: fire. Broadly speaking, barbecue means cooking over a fire. With that in mind, if we are going to get better at barbecue, we should get better at controlling fire.

WOOD

When you introduce enough heat and oxygen to wood, it burns. Molecules in the logs get hot enough that they break apart and rearrange themselves into gases. All that activity of breaking apart and rearranging produces heat and light, or in other words, fire...and smoke. In the early stages, while the wood is dehydrating with a lot of hissing and sizzling, the smoke is pretty dark and sooty because the wood is burning off impurities. At higher temperatures (370–540°C/700–1000°F), the wood starts to release a cleaner quality of smoke with a faint colour between white and blue rippling in the air. That's 'blue smoke,' the kind that holds soft woodsy aromas associated with great barbecue.

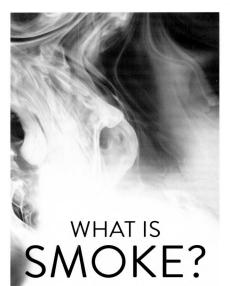

WHAT IS SMOKE?

Smoke combines three types of matter in one. The smoke you see in the air is made of tiny solid particles and droplets of liquid. What you don't see are the invisible gases that are more responsible for making barbecue taste good. Those gases hold magically aromatic wood compounds that make us say *yum*.

When we barbecue we should be trying to capture those invisible gases, not so much the thick visible smoke. If you see a fire pushing dark smoke out of the vents like a freight train, the solid and liquid particles are far too big. They are piling up on the surface of the meat, probably creating a sooty taste.

If a fire has plenty of oxygen (from airflow through the vents) and the fuel is dry, temperatures rise to the point that you get lovely aromatic compounds in tiny little particles. At this point the temperature inside the fire is usually over 400°C/750°F, but that's almost impossible to measure, because we shouldn't put probes into burning embers; instead, we need to watch the colour and density of the smoke.

CHARCOAL

Charcoal is essentially burnt wood – at least partially burnt. In a process known as pyrolysis, nearly all the water, gases and many of the organic compounds in the wood have been incinerated in the process of making charcoal. What's left then is almost pure carbon.

Hardwood lump charcoal is a perfect example. These are black, irregularly shaped lumps of thoroughly charred wood. You can still see the wood grain in some pieces. When lump charcoal is made from scrap timber, it looks more like broken planks, only black. Either way, the wood has been burned at very high temperatures (about 540°C/1000°F) in a very low-oxygen environment.

Today there are more than 75 types of hardwood charcoal, including many from a certain 'varietal' of wood, like mesquite or hickory. Each type of wood has its own range of aromas and heating potential. For example, mesquite has more lignin (aromatic alcohols) than hickory, so it burns hotter and leaves a sharper taste in the food. When manufacturers rely on hardwood scraps from timberyards and building supply operations, you really can't be sure of the wood's origin, and usually the aromas are generic and unimpressive.

The main reasons some cooks prefer lump charcoal are that it seems purer and more natural than briquettes, it lights easily, it burns hot, it produces a pleasant smoke and it leaves very little ash in your cooker (because it has

no fillers). Because the pieces are irregular, how and when they fall is a game of chance, and sometimes the distribution of heat shifts dramatically. One of the other challenges of cooking with lump charcoal is that it burns out pretty quickly, often within half an hour, so you need to be prepared to feed the fire continually. Otherwise, you are better off with briquettes.

Charcoal briquettes generate plenty of heat and sustain it for longer than lump charcoal. People debate whether or not briquettes add much flavour. I believe that many of them do, which is why I use them often. The flavour, of course, depends on the type of briquettes. The biggest manufacturer in America (Kingsford) started in the late nineteenth century as a way for auto man Henry Ford to use up the scrap wood left after making Model T cars. Today, when Kingsford makes briquettes, they start with sawdust that is cooked in airtight ovens. To the crushed wood they add limestone, boric acid, ground coal, sodium nitrate and a binder like cornflour. After that, the mixture is shaped into little pillows that are designed to allow air to flow easily around and between them.

With America's growing interest in natural products, some manufacturers are selling 100 per cent natural briquettes, avoiding the chemicals that make the briquettes easier to light and longer lasting. The all-natural briquettes are made almost entirely with crushed hardwood charcoal held together in the familiar pillow shape with a vegetable binder.

On the opposite end of the natural spectrum, some types of charcoal are saturated with petroleum chemicals for the sake of convenience. All you need to do is drop a lit match on these briquettes and presto – you have a fire. The fact that it smells like oil may or may not be a problem for you. I know people who grew up with so much lighter fluid on charcoal that they think their food *should* taste a little like oil. As with all things in barbecue, it's a matter of personal taste. Personally, I never use briquettes made with lighter fluid. It's so easy to light them with newspaper or Weber® lighter cubes.

WOOD CHIPS

AND CHUNKS

A fire made entirely of wood in a grill requires waiting about an hour for flames to burn down to a level that's right for grilling or smoking. Cooking over embers usually works much better than cooking over wildly dancing flames, but even then, managing mercurial embers is challenging. What a lot of people do instead is to create a fire with charcoal or gas, and then supplement it with wood. The wood is typically in the form of chips or chunks. I usually use wood chips in my grills and wood chunks in my smokers. In the end they can both add the same aromas and colours to your food. When to use one or the other is largely a matter of practicality.

Wood chips burn up faster. Even when soaked in water (as they should be), they burn quicker than wood chunks. I soak my wood chips in water for at least 30 minutes, sometimes much longer. As long as they are waterlogged, the length of time doesn't really matter. Then I lift them out of the water and shake off the excess. I wouldn't want to add handfuls of water that would cool off the charcoal. I scatter the wood chips – usually two or three large handfuls at a time – over the burning charcoal to turn the grill into a smoker immediately. The chips smoulder and smoke for somewhere between 20 and 30 minutes, depending on how hot the fire is and how much air is pouring through it.

Your gas grill can be a smoker, too, one that is even easier to control if it has a smoker box. This is usually a metal box with a hinged, perforated lid. In the most convenient scenario the smoker box sits right over a gas burner that you can control with its own dedicated knob. Fill the box with soaked, drained wood chips, turn the burner

on high to get the chips smoking within minutes, and then reduce the heat way down (or completely off) so that the chips smoke rather than catch fire. A nice thing about the hinged lid is that it allows you to replenish the wood chips and keep the smoke going for as long as you like. If the chips ever do catch fire, douse the flames with water from a spray bottle. That's true of flaming chips in a charcoal fire, too.

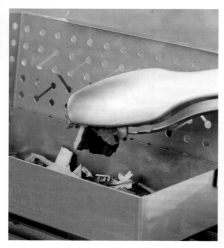

If your grill does not have a smoker box built over a dedicated burner, you can set a portable smoker box either under or on top of the cooking grate. Not surprisingly, the wood chips will light much faster when you set a box under the cooking grate and very close to one or two burners (do this *before* lighting the grill). The big limitation here is that you won't be able to replenish the chips with the box in that position. If you set a portable smoker box filled with wood chips on top of the grate, you will probably need to wait about 30 minutes with all the burners on high and the lid closed before you get a decent amount of smoke.

To reduce this wait time, some cooks start by putting dry wood chips on the bottom of the smoker box, and then filling the rest with damp wood chips so that the dry chips light a little faster and in turn ignite the damp chips.

When you are using a smoker, you are typically cooking for several hours, and adding wood chips every half hour or so might get tedious, so this is a good case for using wood chunks instead. They generate smoke slowly and steadily for hours. You don't even need to soak them in water. You could try, but trust me, the water doesn't penetrate into the wood very far. Drop the dry chunks on the burning charcoal.

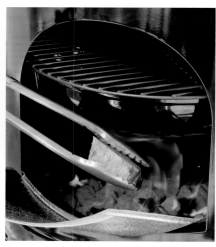

I usually start with four to six large handfuls. Sometimes one chunk is big enough for a handful. Sometimes you need three or more chunks to make a handful. The initial chunks of wood should last a few hours. After that, add a couple more handfuls at a time for a steady stream of smoke.

WOOD AS AN INGREDIENT

The barbecue world is swirling with opinions about which types of wood taste best with certain types of food. It used to be simpler. People smoked with whatever wood was plentiful and cheap. That's why hickory and pecan were so common with pork barbecue in the Carolinas. In Texas there was always post oak and mesquite nearby, so those were the types of wood pit masters used. One of the distinctive characteristics of Santa Maria-style barbecue out in California is the taste of a red oak tree that grows along the hillsides of Santa Maria County. So some regions have their rightful pairings. If you don't live in one of those regions, feel free to borrow one of their time-honoured pairings or make some new ones of your own. I recommend you start with what I call 'the big five'. These are the woods most readily available all over the country.

APPLE

MILD

One of the mildest woods, it has a nice sweet smoke that tastes great on seafood, poultry and pork.

CHERRY

MILD

This wood has a light fruity smoke similar to apple, but it also produces a rich, dark colour that is gorgeous on barbecued chicken or pork ribs.

BEECH

MODERATE

An all-purpose wood that generates a medium-strength smoke, beech goes well with fish, pork and game.

HICKORY

MODERATE

This one has a nutty taste that is similar to oak but it's a bit stronger, making it a good match with pork or beef. Pecan is close in flavour to hickory, so consider using that, too.

MESQUITE

STRONG

This south-western favourite is mighty strong, so much so that you might want to treat it like hot chillies. Using too much for too long would leave you with some bitter, pungent flavours. Try cutting the intensity of mesquite with something milder like apple or cherry.

BEYOND THE BIG FIVE

There are at least a dozen other wood choices. Alder wood is terrific with fish. Maple is a middle-of-the-road choice for poultry and pork. Walnut packs a punch almost as strong as mesquite, so use it sparingly and in combination with milder woods.

Whatever wood you choose, it must be seasoned, meaning the wood has dried in open air. If you buy your wood chunks or chips in a retail store, they will already be seasoned. If you want to try using wood from your garden, stack and dry it first. Freshly cut (green) logs hold as much as 50 per cent of their weight in water, so they would burn unevenly with a sooty smoke. Soft woods like pine and cedar are also problematic. They make lovely furniture, but their high sap content would make terrible barbecue, so stick to the hard (dense) woods.

HOW DO THEY } WORK?

What equipment you use to barbecue is often a matter of what you already happen to have. If your cooker can hold the temperatures you need and allow wood smoke to waft over your food, you're in business. However, each type of cooker does have its own advantages based on the way it works. Water smokers are designed to hold very low temperatures for several hours (even overnight) with little involvement required from you. A charcoal grill can do just about anything a water smoker can do (and more), but it requires frequent tending of the fire, especially for long cooking sessions. A gas grill is the easiest of these three for maintaining precise temperatures, and having the flexibility to create different zones of heat opens up a lot of possibilities. Some gas grills have built-in smoker boxes for wood chips, making it simpler than ever to barbecue.

EXHAUST
DAMPER

CONVECTION
HEAT

WATER
PAN

LIT
CHARCOAL

INTAKE
DAMPER

WATER SMOKER

A water smoker operates in some of the same ways as a kettle charcoal grill. Oxygen enters from below and feeds the charcoal that is raised on a grate for quick combustion. The heat radiates upwards, conducts somewhat through the cooking grates and circulates around the cooking chamber with smoke. The big difference is that the heat is almost always low (110–140°C/225–275°F) because the amount of oxygen entering a smoker is less than what typically enters a kettle grill. The heat is also always indirect because of a water pan that sits between the charcoal and the food. The pan deflects the direct heat around the food, and the water absorbs much of the heat. The more water you pour into the pan, the more heat it absorbs. The water slowly releases heat and humidity into the cooking chamber. When you lift the lid, a lot of heat escapes, but the thermal mass of water continues to hold enough heat that the smoker can return quickly to the ideal smoking temperature.

CHARCOAL GRILL

A charcoal kettle grill is a culinary multitasker – an amazingly efficient tool for cooking many different ways, including searing, roasting and smoking, depending on how you arrange the fire and the food in relation to one another.

In a kettle grill, the charcoal gets the oxygen it needs mostly through the damper on the bottom of the bowl. With the charcoal raised on a grate, plenty of oxygen can move under and around the individual briquettes or other pieces, causing temperatures to rise quickly. Heat radiates off the charcoal and hits the food directly, just like the sun's heat travels to earth, losing strength as it gets further from the source. The heat also conducts through the metal cooking grate, searing whatever else is on the hot grate. And the heat circulates under the closed lid, travelling with the air that moves inside the grill. The damper on the lid allows some hot air to escape through the vents, creating a vacuum that is filled by fresh air entering at the bottom of the grill. This airflow moves heat and smoke around the food continuously in a convectional pattern. The bigger the openings in the dampers, the faster the convection happens, and the higher the temperatures climb.

EXHAUST DAMPER
CONVECTION HEAT
WOOD CHIPS
LIT CHARCOAL
INTAKE DAMPER

GAS GRILL

COOKING GRATE
BURNER TUBE
KNOB
REGULATOR
PROPANE GAS

A gas grill is really a horse of a different colour. Its fuel is obviously very different and so is the way the fuel burns. In most cases the fuel comes in a portable tank filled with pressurised liquid propane. As you release liquid propane from the tank, it immediately vaporises into a gas that is ignited by a spark. The spark comes from a push button igniter that makes a single loud click, or a button that operates a battery-powered igniter that goes tick-tick-tick. Gas is forced through the area where the spark(s) occur and it ignites. A gas grill's regulator is that round metal device that looks like a flying saucer between the tank and the valves. Its job is to control the pressure of the gas releasing from the tank. The gas flows through a hose to valves operated by control knobs. As you turn a knob from low to medium to high, more gas is released towards the burner tubes and a blue flame above the burner becomes larger.

Metal bars above the burners radiate heat upwards to cooking grates, which transfer the heat to the food being grilled. As the food cooks, drippings fall on to hot surfaces inside the grill and vaporise into smoke. With the lid closed and air entering from the bottom of the cooking chamber, heat and smoke circulate around the food imparting that distinctive barbecued flavour. You can add wood-smoke flavour using techniques described on page 10.

Fuels such as natural gas and propane burn cleanly and completely, leaving no smoke or ash behind. Natural gas is piped from a local utility. Propane gas is compressed into a liquid that is easy to transport in tanks. When it comes to cooking, natural gas and propane deliver almost identical results, but you need a different type of grill for each type of gas. Many barbecue restaurants, including some of the most acclaimed, cook with gas-powered smokers that burn wood for flavour. The fire and flavour are easier for the cooks to control, and a similar arrangement could be easier for you, too.

⊙ LIGHTING CHARCOAL

▼

A chimney starter is an upright metal cylinder with a handle on the outside and a wire rack inside. Fill the space under the wire rack with a few sheets of wadded-up newspaper or a few Weber® lighter cubes, and then fill the space above the rack with charcoal briquettes.

▼

Once the charcoal is lit, some impressive thermodynamics channel the heat evenly throughout the fuel, meaning all of the pieces burn evenly and you can start cooking with consistent temperatures all the way across your charcoal fire.

▼

When the briquettes are lightly covered with grey ash, put on two insulated barbecue mitts or oven gloves and grab hold of the two handles on the chimney starter. The swinging handle is there to help you lift the chimney starter and safely aim the coals just where you want them.

LIGHTING A GAS GRILL
⊙

Lighting a gas grill, in most cases, is as simple as lifting the lid, turning on the gas and igniting the burners (follow your Owner's Guide for lighting instructions). Here's how to do it: after you've opened the valve on your propane tank all the way (or turned on the gas at the source), wait a minute for the gas to travel through the gas line, and then turn each burner to high. Close the lid and preheat the grill to about 260°C/500°F.

DIRECT AND INDIRECT HEAT

People often ask me for my single most important tip about grilling and barbecue. It's a hard question to answer because most of the important tips relate to a specific type of food, like a steak or a pork shoulder or a rack of beef ribs. So the answer I usually give is something like this: if you learn how to create and control the differences between direct and indirect heat, you increase your chances of success dramatically. If you limit yourself to just one type of heat or the other, you are missing opportunities for control. A great griller masters the fire, not the other way around.

Simply put, when you are cooking right over a fire, you are using direct (grilling) heat. When the fire is off to the side of the food, or the food is somehow shielded from direct heat, you are using indirect (roasting) heat.

Foods that do best over direct heat are small and tender – things like hamburgers, steaks, seafood of all kinds and vegetables. In a matter of minutes, direct heat can char

the outside of the food and penetrate far enough inside that the centres are cooked, too. If you use direct heat only with big, tough cuts of meat like a pork shoulder, the outsides will burn long before the centres are cooked, let alone tender. An indirect fire works best for larger, tougher foods that need gentle circulating heat and longer cooking times, such as roasts, whole chickens and ribs.

> *A GREAT GRILLER MASTERS THE FIRE, NOT THE OTHER WAY AROUND.*

BASIC } SET-UPS

⊙ INDIRECT COOKING

For a charcoal grill, the lit briquettes are split apart on the charcoal grate so that you have two separate zones of direct heat on opposite sides of the food and one of indirect heat in the middle. You can use baskets to hold the briquettes or you can pour the briquettes right on to the charcoal grate in two even beds. Sometimes it helps to have a foil tray in the middle. Filling that tray about halfway with water weighs it down and provides some humidity inside the grill, which is useful for maintaining temperatures.

On a gas grill, the most common way to set up for indirect cooking is to have the outside burner(s) on and the inside burner(s) off. If you have a three-burner grill, turn all the burners on and preheat the grill for about 10 minutes. Then turn off the burner in the middle and adjust the other two burners to the level of heat you like. If you have a six-burner grill, preheat it with all six burners on for about 10 minutes. Then turn off one or two burners in the middle.

OFF

MEDIUM

⊙ DIRECT COOKING

Set up your charcoal grill for direct cooking by spreading lit charcoal in a single layer all the way across the charcoal grate. This creates one wide zone of direct heat. If the food you're cooking is likely to flare up, it's helpful to keep a small part of the charcoal grate clear of briquettes as a safety zone of indirect heat.

Using direct heat on a gas grill is simply a matter of cooking the food right over lit burners.

HIGH

SMOKER } SET-UP

Smokers come in an amazing array of designs. I could show you dozens of smokers that look almost nothing like each other even though they are designed to do the same thing.

There are cinderblock pits with a wood fire on the bottom or to one side. There are barrel smokers (shaped like an oil barrel or pipeline on its side) with a firebox to one side so the fire and smoke flow horizontally over the food. There are rotisserie smokers with electric-powered spits rotating racks of meat. There are pellet smokers in the shape of a refrigerator with a firebox to the side where an electric augur pushes tiny sawdust pellets on to a burner. There are kamado-style smokers made of ceramic material in the shape of a giant oval urn with the fire on the bottom and a plate in the middle to deflect the rising heat.

That's just an abbreviated sampling of what's out there. You could spend days looking at all the smoker options and comparing various features and costs. Whatever type of smoker you choose, the key is that you are able to gain control of how it cooks as soon as possible, rather than struggling with a lot of trial and error. That's one reason many barbecue cooks start with something simple like an upright water smoker. It's inexpensive, easy to control and very consistent from day one.

▼ TENDING TO YOUR SMOKER

A water smoker normally maintains temperatures in the range of 95–140°C/200–275°F for several hours with no added fuel, but there are at least a few ways to fine-tune the heat:

1. The easiest way to regulate the smoker's temperature is by adjusting the vents on the dampers. The less air you allow into the smoker, the lower the temperature will go. To raise the temperature, open the vents wider.

2. You can also raise the temperature in the smoker by adding more charcoal through the access door, although this is rarely necessary for recipes that cook in less than eight hours.

3. A third way is to adjust the amount of water in the pan positioned between the fire and food. The water regulates the temperature by absorbing heat and releasing it gradually. The more water you have in the pan, the lower the temperature will be. Adding more water will lower the temperature.

1 To set up a water smoker, first separate it into its three main sections: the charcoal bowl, the cooking chamber and the lid.

2 Lay the charcoal grate in the charcoal bowl and set the charcoal ring on top of the grate. The ring holds the charcoal in place and allows airflow through the holes for proper combustion.

3 Fill the ring about three-quarters of the way with charcoal briquettes. Fill a chimney starter with briquettes and light the charcoal in a safe place.

4 When the briquettes are lightly covered with grey ash, carefully pour the lit charcoal over the unlit charcoal.

5 Spread out the lit briquettes evenly with long-handled tongs. Over time the unlit charcoal will light and burn slowly, often extending the life of the fire for as long as eight hours without any additional fuel, although you can add that later if needed.

6 Make sure the water pan is empty and suspended inside the cooking chamber and the charcoal access door is closed. Set the cooking chamber over the charcoal bowl.

7 Immediately fill the pan about three-quarters full with water before the water pan gets too hot. Then set the two cooking grates in place inside the cooking chamber.

8 Now place the lid on top. A water smoker has vents on the bottom of the charcoal bowl and on the lid. At this point open the top vent completely and close the bottom vents about halfway. Wait until the smoker reaches the ideal smoking temperature range of 95–140°C/200–275°F.

9 Open the charcoal access door and add as many dry wood chunks as the recipe suggests. Add them either with long-handled tongs or wearing insulated barbecue mitts or oven gloves. Close the charcoal access door and wait a few minutes for the smoke to stream out of the vent on the lid.

TOP FIVE } BARBECUE TRENDS TODAY

1

BARBECUE IS GETTING PERSONAL

> Regional boundaries are giving way to loose individual riffs of barbecue that show as much free-spirited creativity as they do time-honoured traditions. Young chefs and backyard cooks are blending old-school techniques with fresh mixes of flavours inspired by their own imaginations to come up with recipes like pulled pork bo ssam lettuce cups and ribs with blueberry-chipotle barbecue sauce.

2

BARBECUE IS A FULLY-FLEDGED SPORT

> In the 1980s a few Midwesterners formed a little club for people who wanted to compete at making barbecue. Bragging rights were the only prizes. Since then, the Kansas City Barbecue Society (KCBS) has grown steadily in size and stature. It now has more than 21,000 members worldwide, and it sanctions more than 500 competitions each year, with more than $4.5 million awarded in prizes during 2014 alone.

3

BARBECUE IS COOKING WITH GAS

> In the old days, barbecue joints had a woodpile out back that was the only fuel for the pit, and a cook's primary tool was a shovel for the coals. Today, you are more likely to find barbecue chefs cooking with gas-powered, thermostat-controlled smokers with electric rotisseries turning racks of meat like a big wheel. The new smokers still burn wood, but much more for flavour than heat.

4

BARBECUE IS GETTING SWEETER

> It used to be that barbecue was all about the meat, which was sometimes basted with vinegar and spices. Today restaurants typically offer four to six styles of sauce at the table, most of them heavily sweetened with sugar, molasses, honey or agave. An average supermarket sells more than 20 kinds of barbecue sauce, and the bestselling ones are more than 50 per cent corn syrup or sugar.

> Barbecue restaurants are not museums; they are businesses adapting to what matters most to customers. More and more often, menus are highlighting expensive heritage meats and organic side dishes, not to mention craft beers and dozens of bourbons and ryes. Many joints still serve barbecue on paper, but there are a lot of fine dining touches out there, even pricey wine lists and valet parking.

5

BARBECUE IS MOVING UPMARKET

1
STARTERS

SEA BREEZE BARBECUED OYSTERS

SERVES: 4–6 | **PREP TIME:** 15 MINUTES, PLUS TIME TO SHUCK THE OYSTERS
GRILLING TIME: 3–4 MINUTES | **SPECIAL EQUIPMENT:** OYSTER KNIFE

24 large fresh oysters
1 large navel orange
12 fresh or frozen cranberries,
    thawed if frozen
2 tablespoons vodka
1 tablespoon fresh lime juice

Grapefruit juice is traditional in the quintessential New England cocktail; however, a new version of the Sea Breeze, with orange juice, has recently become the rage at beach resorts along the East Coast. That's something distinctive about American cuisine – it constantly morphs, with new flavours and techniques always in the offing. I've borrowed the flavours of this new take on the classic cocktail to create a fresh, summery relish for barbecued oysters. You can substitute half of a seedless grapefruit if you want the traditional flavour, but I think the orange pairs with oysters even better.

1 Grip each oyster, flat side up, in a folded tea towel. Find the small opening between the shells near the hinge and prise it open with an oyster knife. Try not to spill the delicious juices, known as the 'oyster liquor', in the bottom shell. Cut the oyster meat loose from the top shell, and then loosen the oyster from the bottom shell by running the oyster knife carefully underneath the body. Discard the top, flatter shell, keeping the oyster and juices in the bottom, deeper shell.

2 Prepare the grill for direct cooking over high heat (230–290°C/450–550°F).

3 Use a vegetable peeler to remove two strips of zest from the orange, each 7.5cm/3 inches long by 1cm/½ inch wide. Peel and supreme the orange (see caption and photo below). Place the zest strips, orange supremes, cranberries, vodka and lime juice in a blender. Cover and pulse until finely ground, almost puréed, scraping the inside of the blender jug a couple of times between pulses to achieve an even texture.

4 Spoon ½ tablespoon of the orange mixture on to each shucked oyster in its shell. Place the oysters on the cooking grate over **grilling/ direct high heat**, close the lid and grill for 3–4 minutes until the juices bubble. With tongs gripping one edge, transfer the oysters in their shells to a heatproof platter. Serve warm.

Supremes are more than backing singers for Diana Ross. They are also sections of citrus fruit with the membrane removed. To create orange supremes, peel the orange, removing as much of the white pith as possible. Cradle the fruit in one hand and hold it over a bowl as you use a paring knife to cut down along either side of the thin membranes between the segments, one at a time, removing the orange segments and leaving the membranes behind. Let the supremes drop into the bowl below as you make your way around the orange, removing the remaining segments.

CHARGRILLED OYSTERS
WITH BACON-BOURBON-GINGER BUTTER

SERVES: 4–6 | PREP TIME: 10 MINUTES, PLUS TIME TO SHUCK THE OYSTERS | CHILLING TIME: 2 HOURS
GRILLING TIME: 3–4 MINUTES | SPECIAL EQUIPMENT: OYSTER KNIFE

BUTTER
1 bacon rasher
115g/4oz unsalted butter, softened
1 tablespoon bourbon
2 tablespoons peeled, finely
    chopped fresh ginger
1 teaspoon chopped mint
¼ teaspoon sea salt

24 large fresh oysters

This recipe comes straight out of New Orleans, where chargrilled oysters are a big deal. The flavours of bacon, bourbon and butter are also big deals down there, so why not bring them all together in a Mardi Gras kind of moment? Once the butter has melted into the oysters, it's helpful to wear heavy-duty fire-retardant gloves for retrieving the oysters from the hot grill – or you can use long-handled tongs. Just don't lose all those buttery juices.

1   In a large frying pan over a medium heat, fry the bacon for 6–8 minutes until crisp, turning occasionally. Drain on kitchen paper, reserving 1 teaspoon of the rendered fat. Finely chop the bacon and place in a bowl with the reserved 1 teaspoon rendered fat and the remaining butter ingredients. Using a fork, whisk vigorously until well blended. Scoop the butter mixture on to a sheet of greaseproof paper, placing it on the edge closest to you. Fold the paper up and over and roll into a cylinder, smoothing as you roll. Twist the ends to seal, and wrap tightly. Chill until solid, at least 2 hours. Remove from the refrigerator 5 minutes before grilling time, and cut into ½- to 1-teaspoon chunks (depending on the size of the oysters).

2   Prepare the grill for direct cooking over medium-high heat (200–260°C/400–500°F).

3   Grip each oyster, flat side up, in a folded tea towel. Find the small opening between the shells near the hinge and prise it open with an oyster knife. Try not to spill the delicious juices, known as the 'oyster liquor', in the bottom shell. Cut the oyster meat loose from the top shell, and then loosen the oyster from the bottom shell by running the oyster knife carefully underneath the body. Discard the top, flatter shell, keeping the oyster and juices in the bottom, deeper shell. Place a chunk of the flavoured butter on top of each oyster.

4   Grill the oysters over **grilling/direct medium-high heat** for 3–4 minutes, with the lid closed, until the oyster liquor starts to bubble, the butter melts and the edges of the oysters just begin to curl. With tongs gripping one edge, transfer the oysters in their shells to a heatproof platter. Serve immediately.

When you are buying oysters to grill, choose big ones that will lie flat on the bars of the grate, like the three on the left of this photo. Avoid small ones that would shrivel up quickly and wobbly ones that would spill their 'liquor' in the grill, like the two on the right. Nobody likes an oyster that can't hold its liquor.

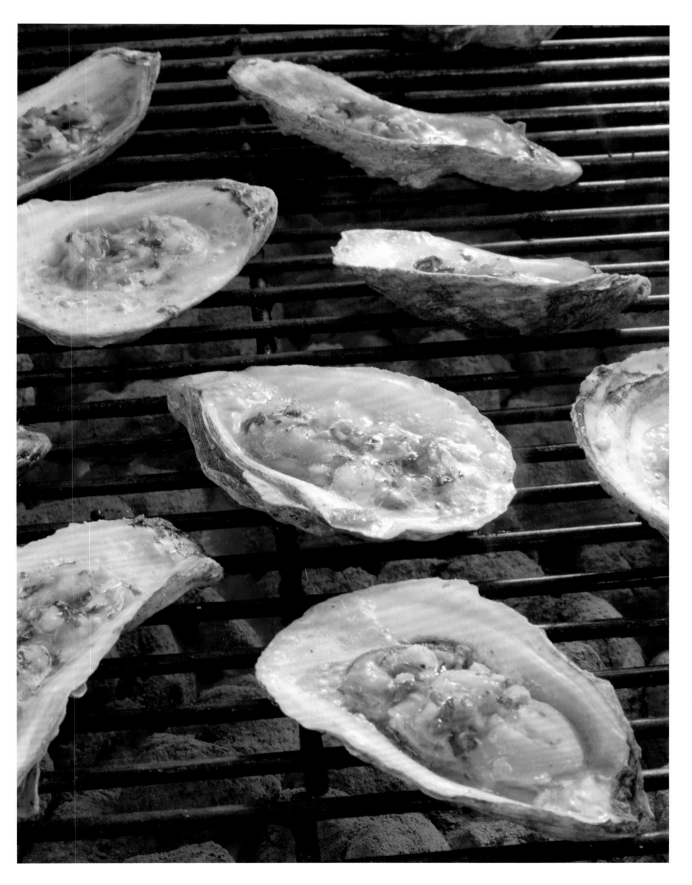

SMOKED SCALLOPS
WITH WHITE WINE BUTTER SAUCE

SERVES: 4–6 | **PREP TIME:** 10 MINUTES | **GRILLING TIME:** 8–14 MINUTES
SPECIAL EQUIPMENT: 1 LARGE HANDFUL PECAN WOOD CHIPS, 25-CM/10-INCH CAST-IRON FRYING PAN

12 scallops, each about 40g/1½oz,
    patted dry
½ teaspoon sea salt
½ teaspoon freshly ground black
    pepper
1 tablespoon rapeseed oil
85g/3oz unsalted butter
1 tablespoon finely chopped garlic
125ml/4fl oz dry white wine
2 tablespoons finely chopped tarragon
Zest of 1 lemon

Don't hesitate to use cast-iron frying pans right on the grill. It's a way of cooking that has worked wonders from the earliest days of American history, when settlers relied on frying pans to cook all kinds of food over live fires. Here some smouldering pecan chips give the scallops a touch of smoke. Often I grill scallops over very high heat to sear the outsides, but in this case I prefer the silky soft texture you get from gentle roasting. With a warm, nutty-tasting butter sauce spooned on top, the results are pretty decadent.

1   Soak the wood chips in water for at least 30 minutes.

2   Prepare the grill for direct and indirect cooking over medium heat (180–230°C/350–450°F).

3   Remove and discard the small, tough side muscle that might be left on each scallop, and then season evenly with the salt and pepper. Drain and add the wood chips to the charcoal or to the smoker box of a gas grill, following the manufacturer's instructions, and close the lid. When smoke appears, place a 25-cm/10-inch cast-iron frying pan on the cooking grate over **grilling/direct medium heat** and, without preheating the pan, swirl in the oil. Place the scallops in the frying pan and cook over **grilling/direct medium heat**,

with the lid closed, until lightly browned and just opaque in the centre, for 6–10 minutes, turning once. Remove the scallops from the pan (keep the pan on the grill) and keep them warm while preparing the sauce.

4   Add half the butter and the garlic to the frying pan and cook over **grilling/direct medium heat**, with the lid open, until the butter begins to brown, stirring constantly. Pour the wine into the pan, close the lid and cook for 2–4 minutes until reduced to about 3 tablespoons, stirring occasionally.

5   Slide the pan over **roasting/indirect medium heat** and add the remaining butter and the tarragon. Remove the pan from the grill, spoon the sauce over the scallops, garnish with the lemon zest and serve immediately.

Bigger is better for this recipe. Look for large scallops like the one on the far right. Assuming they are fresh, their texture will be superior to that of smaller scallops. They should glisten and smell sweet and their colour should be somewhere between light beige and pale pink, not bright white.

SPICY PRAWNS
WITH CHARRED POBLANO ROMESCO

SERVES: 4–6 | PREP TIME: 20 MINUTES
GRILLING TIME: 12–16 MINUTES

ROMESCO

2 poblano chillies, about
    225g/8oz total
15g/½oz fresh coriander sprigs
4 tablespoons sliced almonds, toasted
1 small jalapeño chilli,
    deseeded and chopped
1 tablespoon fresh lemon juice
1 garlic clove
¼ teaspoon freshly ground black pepper

Extra-virgin olive oil
Sea salt
1 teaspoon smoked paprika
450g/1lb large prawns, peeled and
    deveined, tails left on, patted dry

This green romesco sauce is less sweet and significantly spicier than a traditional roasted red pepper romesco, which is a Spanish vegetable sauce thickened with almonds. Remember that jalapeño chillies vary in heat from one to the next, so it is a good idea to taste them before adding them to a dish. If you like, you can even leave the jalapeño out of this recipe.

1 Prepare the grill for direct cooking over high heat (230–290°C/450–550°F).

2 Grill the poblano chillies over **grilling/direct high heat** for 10–12 minutes, with the lid closed, until blackened and blistered all over, turning occasionally. Place in a bowl and cover with clingfilm to trap the steam. Allow to stand for about 10 minutes. Remove and discard the charred skins, stalks and seeds, and then coarsely chop the chillies.

3 In the bowl of a food processor, combine the poblanos and the remaining romesco ingredients, including 4 tablespoons oil and ½ teaspoon salt, and process until well blended but some texture still remains. Transfer the sauce to a serving bowl.

4 In a bowl, whisk 1 tablespoon oil, ½ teaspoon salt and the paprika. Add the prawns and turn to coat in the mixture. Grill the prawns over **grilling/direct high heat** for 2–4 minutes, with the lid closed, until firm to the touch and just turning opaque in the centre, turning once.

5 Serve the prawns warm with the romesco sauce for dipping.

Burn, baby, burn. Grilling poblano chillies over high heat until they are blackened and blistered drives out the water and transforms their flavour into a smoky version of its former self. To loosen the skins, put the grilled chillies in a bowl, cover with clingfilm, and let them stand for about 10 minutes. Then you can remove and discard the burnt skins easily.

HOT-SMOKED SALMON
WITH WHIPPED HORSERADISH CREAM

SERVES: 6-8 | PREP TIME: 15 MINUTES | DRY BRINING TIME: 4-8 HOURS | GRILLING TIME: 40 MINUTES-1½ HOURS
CHILLING TIME: 2 HOURS (OPTIONAL) | SPECIAL EQUIPMENT: 3 LARGE HANDFULS ALDER WOOD CHIPS

DRY BRINE
100g/3½oz light brown sugar
4 tablespoons coarse sea salt
1 tablespoon coarsely ground
     black pepper
1 tablespoon finely grated lemon zest

1 salmon fillet (with skin), about
     900g/2lb, pin bones removed
2 tablespoons extra-virgin olive oil

HORSERADISH CREAM
125ml/4fl oz chilled whipping cream
1 tablespoon peeled, finely grated
     fresh horseradish or 2 teaspoons
     prepared horseradish
½ teaspoon finely grated lemon zest
⅛ teaspoon sea salt
⅛ teaspoon freshly ground black
     pepper
⅛ teaspoon hot pepper sauce

2 tablespoons finely chopped
     chives
Grilled lemon slices
Grilled baguette slices

We have all tasted thin slices of cold-smoked salmon with a texture that is fairly firm and dry because the fish is cooked at temperatures below 38°C/100°F in specialised commercial smokers. This recipe is a hot-smoked version that you can make at home. Start by soaking the salmon in a sweet, salty brine, and then smoking it with mild alder wood chips until the flesh is tender but still juicy so that it breaks apart into moist flakes. While the salmon is good eaten warm, the flavours develop even more while the fish chills in the refrigerator. Serve it at room temperature with creamy horseradish and a touch of tart lemon.

1   Combine the dry brine ingredients. Sprinkle one-third of the brine on the bottom of a large baking dish. Arrange the salmon fillet, skin side down, on top of the brine. Spread the remaining brine evenly over the salmon, pressing lightly to adhere. Cover with clingfilm and refrigerate for 4-8 hours.

2   Soak the wood chips in water for at least 30 minutes.

3   Rinse the salmon under cold water to remove the brine, pat dry with kitchen paper and brush both sides with the oil.

4   Prepare the grill for indirect cooking over low heat (as close to 130°C/250°F as possible).

5   Drain and add one handful of wood chips to the charcoal or to the smoker box of a gas grill, following the manufacturer's instructions, and close the lid. When smoke appears, grill the salmon, skin side down, over **roasting/ indirect low heat** for 40 minutes-1½ hours, depending on the thickness of the salmon,

with the lid closed, until firm and just slightly pink all the way to the centre, watching closely to prevent overcooking. Drain and add one handful of the wood chips to the charcoal or smoker box every 20-30 minutes until the wood chips are gone. If using a charcoal grill, add more briquettes as necessary to maintain the heat.

6   Remove the salmon from the grill and leave to cool to room temperature. Cover with clingfilm and refrigerate for at least 2 hours to allow the flavours to develop, if liked. Meanwhile, prepare the horseradish cream.

7   In the bowl of an electric mixer fitted with a whisk attachment, beat the cream until soft peaks form. Whisk in the remaining ingredients. Transfer to a serving bowl, cover and refrigerate until ready to use.

8   Garnish the salmon with the chives and serve at room temperature with the horseradish cream, grilled lemon slices and grilled baguette slices.

If you can, do yourself a favour and buy a piece of fresh horseradish for this recipe. Look for a blemish-free, firm root that feels heavy for its size. Clean and peel the outer layer with a vegetable peeler, and then grate the amount you need using a fine grater for a big pop of flavour. Wrap the unused portion in clingfilm and store in the refrigerator.

SMOKED CHICKEN NACHOS
WITH CHIPOTLE CREAM AND AVOCADO

SERVES: 6 | PREP TIME: 20 MINUTES | GRILLING TIME: 32–39 MINUTES | SPECIAL EQUIPMENT: 2 LARGE HANDFULS MESQUITE OR HICKORY WOOD CHIPS, LARGE GRILLPROOF PAN OR DISPOSABLE FOIL TRAY

CHIPOTLE CREAM
280ml/9½fl oz soured cream
1 canned chipotle in adobo sauce, finely chopped
1 tablespoon fresh lime juice
¼ teaspoon sea salt

RUB
2 teaspoons sea salt
1 teaspoon freshly ground black pepper
1 teaspoon ground cumin
1 teaspoon paprika
½ teaspoon ground cayenne pepper

4 chicken breasts (with bone and skin), each about 225g/8oz
350g/12oz corn tortilla chips
400g/14oz Monterey Jack or Cheddar cheese, coarsely grated
4 spring onions, cut into thin slices
2 tablespoons finely chopped jalapeño chillies
1 large avocado, cut into 1-cm/½-inch cubes
Juice of ½ lime
4 tablespoons roughly chopped fresh coriander
Shop-bought salsa (optional)

This is a fun way to use up leftover barbecued chicken or turkey. Who doesn't love some cheesy, meaty nachos with smoky soured cream and fresh avocado? It's worth smoking some spice-rubbed chicken breasts just for this recipe. Using bone-in rather than boneless chicken breasts requires a longer cooking time, but there's a dividend: the meat has more time to absorb the flavourful smoke.

1 Soak the wood chips in water for at least 30 minutes.

2 Whisk the chipotle cream ingredients, including any juices remaining from chopping the chipotle chilli. Refrigerate until ready to use.

3 Prepare the grill for indirect cooking over medium heat (180–230°C/350–450°F).

4 Mix the rub ingredients. Season the chicken breasts all over and between the skin and meat with the rub.

5 Drain and add the wood chips to the charcoal or to the smoker box of a gas grill, following the manufacturer's instructions, and close the lid. When smoke appears, grill the chicken, skin side down first, over *roasting/indirect medium heat* for 25–30 minutes, with the lid closed, until the juices run clear and the meat is no longer pink at the bone, turning once when the skin releases easily from the cooking grates. Remove the chicken from the grill and, when cool enough to handle, shred into pieces, discarding the skin and bones.

6 Increase the temperature of the grill to high heat (230–260°C/450–500°F).

7 Spread half of the tortilla chips into a large grillproof pan. Distribute half each of the cheese, spring onions, jalapeño and chicken over the chips. Repeat with another layer.

8 Place the pan with the nachos over *roasting/indirect high heat*, close the lid and cook for 7–9 minutes until the cheese is melted and the chips are tinged golden brown. Wearing insulated barbecue mitts or oven gloves, carefully transfer the pan to a heatproof surface. Top the nachos with the avocado and then drizzle with the chipotle cream and lime juice. Garnish with the coriander. Serve hot with salsa, if liked.

BARBECUED BUFFALO WINGS
WITH BLUE CHEESE DIP

SERVES: 6–8 | **PREP TIME:** 15 MINUTES | **GRILLING TIME:** ABOUT 20 MINUTES
SPECIAL EQUIPMENT: 1 LARGE HANDFUL MAPLE OR CHERRY WOOD CHIPS

SAUCE

4 tablespoons corn oil or groundnut oil
4 tablespoons hot pepper sauce
2 teaspoons sea salt
1 teaspoon ground white pepper
1 teaspoon freshly ground black pepper
½ teaspoon garlic powder

1.8kg/4lb chicken wings, wing tips removed, each split at the joint into 2 pieces

DIP

115g/4oz blue cheese, crumbled
125ml/4fl oz soured cream
4 tablespoons mayonnaise
2 tablespoons fresh lemon juice
½ teaspoon celery seeds
½ teaspoon sea salt
Hot pepper sauce

Who knew that buffalo have wings? Well, actually, these chicken wings are named for the city where they were crafted as bar food: Buffalo, New York. That story, like a lot of recipe origin stories, is disputed, but no matter how they came about, buffalo wings are fantastic at a picnic or wherever people appreciate spicy snacks that you can eat with your fingers.

1 Soak the wood chips in water for at least 30 minutes.

2 Prepare the grill for direct cooking over medium heat (180–230°C/350–450°F).

3 In a small saucepan, combine the sauce ingredients. Cook over a medium heat until warm, about 5 minutes, whisking occasionally. Set aside 4 tablespoons of the sauce. Pour the remaining sauce from the saucepan into a large bowl and add the wings. Turn the wings in the sauce to coat them evenly.

4 Drain and add the wood chips to the charcoal or to the smoker box of a gas grill, following the manufacturer's instructions, and close the lid. When smoke appears, grill the wings over **grilling/direct medium heat** for about 20 minutes, with the lid closed, until the juices run clear, turning occasionally (don't overcook or the wings will be dry). Transfer the wings to a large clean bowl and toss to coat with the reserved sauce.

5 In a bowl, combine the dip ingredients, including a few drops of hot sauce, and mix well. Serve the dip alongside the wings with extra hot sauce, if liked.

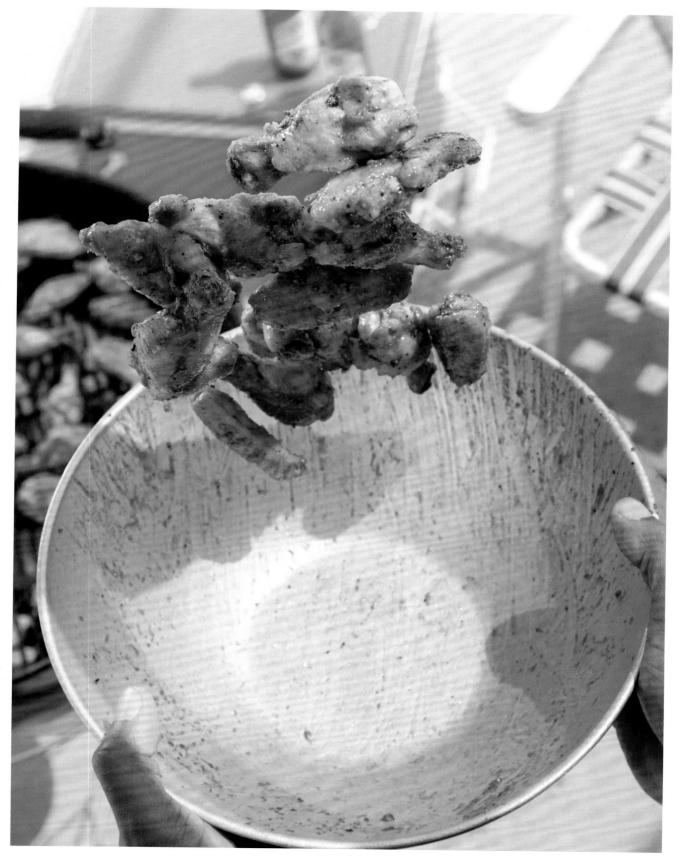

SMOKED LOUISIANA CHICKEN WINGS
WITH CAJUN RUB

SERVES: 6 | **PREP TIME:** 15 MINUTES | **GRILLING TIME:** ABOUT 30 MINUTES
SPECIAL EQUIPMENT: 2 LARGE HANDFULS HICKORY WOOD CHIPS

RUB

1 tablespoon brown sugar
2 teaspoons smoked paprika
1½ teaspoons sea salt
1 teaspoon onion powder
1 teaspoon dried oregano
¾ teaspoon garlic powder
½ teaspoon dried thyme
½ teaspoon freshly ground black
    pepper
½ teaspoon ground cayenne pepper

1.4kg/3lb chicken wings, wing tips
    removed, each split at the joint
    into 2 pieces

SAUCE

4 tablespoons tomato ketchup
4 tablespoons Louisiana-style
    or other hot chilli sauce
2 tablespoons brown sugar
2 teaspoons cider vinegar
1 teaspoon hot pepper sauce
½ teaspoon Cajun spice
    blend (optional)
40g/1½oz unsalted butter

Soured cream (optional)

This version of barbecued wings hails from the South, where a spicy Cajun rub meets hickory smoke and a pungent hot sauce. Serve with soured cream on the side just to take the edge off all that heat. The key to the chicken's texture is the combination of direct and indirect heat. Cooking the wings right over the fire renders out some fat and starts them on their way to being crispy. Finishing them to the side of the fire tenderises the meat while the sauce seeps inside.

1 Soak the wood chips in water for at least 30 minutes.

2 In a large bowl, combine the rub ingredients. Add the chicken wings and turn to coat. Allow the wings to stand at room temperature for about 30 minutes.

3 Prepare the grill for direct and indirect cooking over medium heat (180–230°C/350–450°F).

4 In a saucepan, combine all the sauce ingredients, except the butter, and bring to a simmer over a medium heat. Cook for 3–4 minutes until slightly thickened, stirring occasionally. Remove from the heat, add the butter, and whisk until the butter is melted.

5 Drain and add one handful of the wood chips to the charcoal or to the smoker box of a gas grill, following the manufacturer's instructions, and close the lid. When smoke appears, grill the wings over ***grilling/direct medium heat*** for 5 minutes with the lid closed, turning once. Move the wings over ***roasting/indirect medium heat*** and continue grilling, with the lid closed, for 10 minutes. Drain and add the remaining wood chips to the charcoal or smoker box. Brush the wings with some of the sauce, turn and grill for about 15 minutes more until crisp, deeply browned in spots and tender, brushing the wings one more time with the sauce. Remove the wings from the grill and serve warm with soured cream on the side, if liked.

Los Angeles is the stage not only for the Academy Awards and a galaxy of Hollywood stars, but also for the largest community of Koreans and Korean restaurants outside Seoul. Koreatown, or K-Town as locals know it, is a densely populated 2.7-square-mile metropolis of art deco architecture, pulsing nightlife and a red-hot culinary scene, where dozens of restaurants serve a special brand of barbecue over sizzling tabletop grills. This is elemental live-fire cooking, with thin strips of fatty pork and marbled beef in salty-sweet marinades crackling over smoky coals. Korean barbecue has swept all the way across America in recent years, but the trend started in Los Angeles, where traditionalists and innovators alike drew on rich, cultural heritage.

Meat, particularly beef, is expensive in Korea; in Los Angeles, however, a subculture of specialists with a cult following serve Wagyu, USDA prime and beef tongue at celebrity-heavy spots like Park's Barbeque and Genwa Korean BBQ. Brisket, short ribs, octopus and pork belly are also popular, as are fattier cuts that are often marinated and usually enjoyed after leaner beef slices. The well-seasoned grill racks at Soot Bull Jeep are about as old school as K-town gets, and here beef bulgogi and octopus sizzle over hardwood coals – smoke permeating everything from the scissor-cut, soy-marinated kalbi (short ribs) to customers' jeans. A packed room of loyal patrons raise glasses of soju and craft beer. Equally popular are the dome-shaped grills at Honey Pig, which guarantee that no part of the pork is wasted. Rendered fat from slices of *samgyeopsal*, or pork belly, drips down to lend its rich umami to a moat of kimchi (fermented vegetables and seasonings) and beansprouts, which are scooped up with salad and rolled in rice papers. At Sun Ha Jang, domed griddles sizzle slices of garlic and duck into crackling, and the reserved fat is spooned over rice. Dong Il Jang puts a twist on tradition by grilling marbled beef in butter over a griddle – what LA food critic Jonathan Gold calls 'the Korean equivalent of steak Diane'.

Small side dishes, called *banchan*, comprised of kimchi and pickled seasonal vegetables with crunchy and acidic flavours that balance the fatty meats, are every bit as crucial to the experience as what is on the grill. It's about the subtle layering of flavours – sweet and sour with fatty, spicy and rich. And nobody does this better than Genwa Korean BBQ, where 23 different banchan are served in a serene setting. Banchan offerings in LA restaurants almost always include a potato or macaroni salad, a decidedly American addition that you won't find back home in Seoul. Dipping sauces also reflect LA's booming Latino population. The popular garlicky soy sauce and pickled jalapeño dip that is spooned on to meats and wrapped in lettuce is as common in LA Korean barbecue joints as it is in taco bars in Mexico. In fact, today, Koreatown boasts almost twice as many Latino residents as Asian, and the Latin influence is inspiring the next generation of boundary-breaking Korean–American chefs.

LA native son Roy Choi is a pioneer in combining Mexican street food with Korean barbecue. Choi, who grew up in Los Angeles surrounded by Latino culture, revolutionised the food truck scene in 2008 when he and his business partner launched their wildly popular Kogi BBQ taco truck specialising in Korean short rib tacos. It's a craze that rippled east and back again, bringing Detroit brothers Brian and Steven Yeun to LA to launch The Bun Truck in 2011, a Korean–Mediterranean taco fusion that mixes Korean barbecued pork with Greek tzatziki, Sriracha and cucumber in a bao bun. Other American joints in the neighbourhood are serving up traditional fast food with a Korean twist featuring bulgogi on burgers, Philly cheesesteaks and pizza, while the nearby upscale French restaurant République is borrowing from Korean street food with kimchi fried rice adorned with soft-poached eggs. Koreatown, at its core, is pure Los Angeles: a melting pot of flavours, cultures and dreams.

AMERICAN
MADE
KOREAN
BARBECUE

WARM ARTICHOKE DIP
WITH PARMESAN CRUST

SERVES: 6 | **PREP TIME:** 15 MINUTES | **GRILLING TIME:** 23–30 MINUTES
SPECIAL EQUIPMENT: 1 LARGE HANDFUL APPLE WOOD CHIPS, 20-CM/8-INCH CAST-IRON FRYING PAN

400-g/14-oz can whole artichoke hearts packed in water, rinsed and drained, patted dry
175ml/6fl oz mayonnaise
175g/6oz cream cheese, softened
115g/4oz mozzarella cheese, grated
115-g/4-oz can chopped mild green chillies
4 tablespoons soured cream
2 teaspoons crushed garlic
1 teaspoon mustard powder
¼ teaspoon hot pepper sauce
¼ teaspoon freshly ground black pepper
Unsalted butter
40g/ 1½oz Parmesan cheese, finely grated
Grilled baguette slices or crisp flatbread

Artichoke dip is a classic in steakhouses and barbecue joints across the United States. Served with grilled bread slices or crisp flatbread crackers, it's a good way to start a meal, but it gets even better with the addition of a little smoke to highlight the sweet artichokes and a gratinéed crust of bubbling, nutty cheese on top.

1. Soak the wood chips in water for at least 30 minutes.

2. Prepare the grill for direct and indirect cooking over medium-high heat (200–230°C/400–450°F).

3. Drain and add the wood chips to the charcoal or to the smoker box of a gas grill, following the manufacturer's instructions, and close the lid. When smoke appears, grill the artichoke hearts over **grilling/direct medium-high heat** for 3–5 minutes with the lid closed, until warmed through, turning once. Remove from the grill and roughly chop.

4. Combine the mayonnaise, cream cheese, mozzarella, chillies, soured cream, garlic, mustard powder, hot sauce and pepper. Using a wooden spoon, smash the cream cheese against the inside of the bowl into a paste, and then stir the mixture until smooth. Stir in the artichoke hearts.

5. Lightly grease the inside of a 20-cm/8-inch cast-iron frying pan with butter. Transfer the artichoke mixture to the prepared pan, and then distribute the Parmesan evenly over the top. Cook over **roasting/indirect medium-high heat** for 20–25 minutes, with the lid closed, until browned and bubbling on the surface. Cool for 10 minutes before serving with grilled baguette slices or crisp flatbread.

Keep the dip on the chunky side by roughly chopping the smoked artichokes, and resist the urge to smooth the top of the dip in the frying pan. The peaks and valleys will create crisp golden edges that make people flip for this dish.

NEW PIMIENTO CHEESE SPREAD

SERVES: 8–10 | **PREP TIME:** 15 MINUTES | **GRILLING TIME:** ABOUT 35 MINUTES | **CHILLING TIME:** 2 HOURS
SPECIAL EQUIPMENT: 2 LARGE HANDFULS HICKORY WOOD CHIPS

1 red pepper, about 225g/8oz
1 teaspoon vegetable oil
340g/12oz mature Cheddar cheese,
    coarsely grated
125ml/4fl oz mayonnaise
3 tablespoons roughly chopped
    sweet pickles
2 tablespoons grated onion (use
    the large holes of a box grater)
1 teaspoon Worcestershire sauce
1 teaspoon Dijon mustard
1½ teaspoons finely chopped canned
    chillies in adobo sauce
½ teaspoon adobo sauce from the
    can, or to taste (optional)
1 garlic clove, finely chopped
Toasted bread
Celery
Carrots
Radishes

In the Carolinas, you may find an entire section of a grocery store devoted to various kinds of pimiento cheese, a spread whose main ingredients are preserved sweet red peppers (aka pimentos), grated cheese and mayonnaise. Here is a ramped-up recipe with contemporary flavours, including home-smoked red pepper to take it over the top. Not only is this a terrific party dish served with toasted bread and celery, but it is also a fine filling for grilled cheese sandwiches.

1 Soak the wood chips in water for at least 30 minutes.

2 Cut off the top and bottom ends from the pepper. Remove and discard the stalk. Stand the pepper upright and cut it down one side to create one long strip. Trim and discard the ribs and seeds (see the step-by-step below). Lightly coat the pepper strip and the end pieces with the oil.

3 Prepare the grill for direct and indirect cooking over medium heat (180–230°C/ 350–450°F).

4 Drain and add one handful of the wood chips to the charcoal or to the smoker box of a gas grill, following the manufacturer's instructions, and close the lid. When smoke appears, grill the pepper pieces, skin side down, over *roasting/indirect medium heat*, with the lid closed, for 10 minutes.

Drain and add the remaining wood chips to the charcoal or smoker box, and continue grilling for 18–20 minutes more, with the lid closed, until the skin is blistered. Move the pepper over *grilling/direct medium heat* and grill for 3–5 minutes, with the lid closed, until the skin is blackened all over. Place the pepper in a bowl and cover with clingfilm to trap the steam. Allow to stand for about 10 minutes. Remove and discard the charred skin, and roughly chop the pepper.

5 In a food processor, combine the pepper, cheese, mayonnaise, pickles, onion, Worcestershire sauce, mustard, chipotle chilli, adobo sauce (if using) and garlic. Pulse until the mixture is combined and the pepper and pickles are finely chopped. Transfer to a bowl, cover and refrigerate until cold, at least 2 hours. Serve cold or at room temperature with toasted bread, celery, carrots and radishes.

Sometimes knife skills make a big difference in a recipe. By cutting a pepper so that it lies as flat as possible on the cooking grate, you can improve how well it caramelises and chars, meaning you can achieve better flavours. Begin by trimming off the stalk and bottom ends. Stand the pepper up and cut an opening down one side. Put the pepper on its side and position your knife inside so you can make a cut between the inner wall of the pepper and the undesirable core and seeds. Go back and trim any whitish areas off the inner wall of the pepper. Now you have lots of surface area to lie flat on the hot cooking grate.

BACON-ONION-BOURBON SPREAD

SERVES: 10–12 | **PREP TIME:** 20 MINUTES | **GRILLING TIME:** ABOUT 1¼ HOURS | **CHILLING TIME:** 2 HOURS–3 DAYS
SPECIAL EQUIPMENT: 2 LARGE HANDFULS HICKORY WOOD CHIPS, 30-CM/12-INCH CAST-IRON FRYING PAN

This sweet and savoury spread is aimed straight at the heart of barbecue fanatics who have a thing for bourbon, bacon and brown sugar. The recipe makes about 1 litre/1¾ pints of spread, but it keeps well and it is quite versatile. Serve it with a soft cheese and crostini before dinner, spread it on a sandwich, or try it as a condiment for something simple that needs oomph, like a grilled chicken breast or pork chop.

GLAZE
75ml/3fl oz bourbon
75ml/3fl oz pure maple syrup
3 tablespoons light brown sugar
2 tablespoons black treacle
2 teaspoons finely chopped rosemary
    leaves

340g/12oz bacon rashers, cut
    crossways into 2.5-cm/1-inch
    pieces
900g/2lb yellow onions, quartered
    and cut into 5-mm/¼-inch slices
450g/1lb red onions, quartered and
    cut into 5-mm/¼-inch slices
6 garlic cloves, coarsely chopped
1 teaspoon sea salt
½ teaspoon freshly ground black
    pepper
1 tablespoon brown mustard
Grilled baguette pieces (optional)
Brie cheese (optional)

1. Soak the wood chips in water for at least 30 minutes.

2. Prepare the grill for direct and indirect cooking over medium heat (180–230°C/350–450°F).

3. Whisk the glaze ingredients. Set aside.

4. In a 30-cm/12-inch cast-iron frying pan over **grilling/direct medium heat**, fry the bacon for 10–12 minutes until crisp, stirring frequently. Using a slotted spoon, transfer the bacon to kitchen paper to drain. Pour off all but 3 tablespoons of the bacon fat. Add half each of the yellow and red onions to the pan and cook over **grilling/direct medium heat** for about 5 minutes, with the lid closed, until softened, stirring occasionally. Stir in the remaining onions, garlic, salt and pepper. Move the pan over **roasting/indirect medium heat**, drain and add the wood chips to the charcoal or to the smoker box of a gas grill, following the manufacturer's instructions, and cook the onion mixture for about 45 minutes, with the lid closed, until very tender and beginning to brown, stirring every 10 minutes.

5. Stir the glaze into the onions. Move the pan over **grilling/direct medium heat**, close the lid and cook for 10–15 minutes until the liquid is reduced and the bubbles begin to glisten, stirring often. Remove from the grill. Coarsely chop the bacon and reserve, and refrigerate 2 tablespoons for the garnish. Stir the remaining bacon and the mustard into the onion mixture. Cool, cover and refrigerate for at least 2 hours or up to 3 days. Remove from the refrigerator 1 hour before serving. Garnish with the reserved bacon, and serve on top of grilled baguette pieces with Brie, if liked.

SMOKED DEVILLED EGGS

SERVES: 6–12 | **PREP TIME:** 25 MINUTES | **COOKING TIME:** ABOUT 45 MINUTES | **CHILLING TIME:** ABOUT 30 MINUTES
SPECIAL EQUIPMENT: WATER SMOKER, 2 LARGE HANDFULS HICKORY WOOD CHUNKS, LARGE DISPOSABLE FOIL TRAY

If you have your smoker going for a big main course, why not make an unusual appetiser by smoking some eggs on the extra cooking grate. The hickory smoke adds great flavour and colour to traditional devilled eggs.

12 large eggs
3 bacon rashers
125ml/4fl oz mayonnaise
2 tablespoons finely chopped chives
2 teaspoons Dijon mustard
½ teaspoon smoked paprika
¼ teaspoon sea salt
¼ teaspoon freshly ground black
　　pepper

1　Prepare a water smoker for indirect cooking with very low heat (93–130°C/200–250°F). Add the wood chunks to the charcoal.

2　Place the eggs in a single layer in a large saucepan and add enough water to cover them by at least 2.5cm/1 inch. Place the saucepan (uncovered) over high heat and bring the water to the boil. Remove the saucepan from the heat, cover and leave the eggs to stand for 15 minutes. Drain the eggs and run cold water over them until cool to the touch. Peel the eggs and place them in a large disposable foil tray.

3　While the eggs are cooking, fry the bacon in a frying pan for 7–10 minutes until crisp, turning occasionally. Transfer the bacon to kitchen paper to drain. Crumble and set aside.

4　Smoke the eggs in the foil tray over **roasting/indirect very low heat** for about 45 minutes, with the lid closed, until they develop a smoky flavour, turning periodically to coat them evenly with a smoky hue. Transfer the eggs to a bowl and refrigerate for about 30 minutes until completely chilled. Then cut each egg lengthways in half, scoop out the yolks into a bowl and mash with a fork. Add the mayonnaise, chives, mustard, ¼ teaspoon of the paprika, the salt and pepper and mix until well combined. Spoon the mixture into the hollows of the egg whites and garnish with the bacon and the remaining paprika. If not serving immediately, cover and refrigerate.

SPINACH SALAD
WITH SMOKED VEGETABLES AND PIMENTÓN VINAIGRETTE

SERVES: 4 | PREP TIME: 15 MINUTES | GRILLING TIME: 25–35 MINUTES
SPECIAL EQUIPMENT: 2 LARGE HANDFULS OAK WOOD CHIPS, LARGE DISPOSABLE FOIL TRAY

400-g/14-oz can chickpeas, rinsed
    and drained
1 red pepper, about 225g/8oz,
    cut into 1-cm/½-inch dice
175g/60oz cherry tomatoes
Extra-virgin olive oil

VINAIGRETTE
2 tablespoons sherry wine vinegar
1 small garlic clove, crushed
½ teaspoon sea salt
½ teaspoon smoked paprika
¼ teaspoon freshly ground black
    pepper

140g/5oz baby spinach
½ small red onion, thinly sliced
115g/4oz thinly sliced Serrano or
    Parma ham, cut crossways into
    1-cm/½-inch strips
Freshly ground black pepper

This first course celebrates Spanish flavours with pimentón, or smoked paprika, garlic and olive oil, but it is the smoked vegetables that will make it a favourite. In fact, because it only takes about 30 minutes to smoke vegetables, you may find yourself adding them to other salads. Jamón serrano is Spanish dry-cured ham similar to Parma ham, which is a good substitute, but you could use another kind of Spanish charcutería, such as lomo or chorizo. For a vegetarian salad, substitute 85g/3oz grated Manchego cheese for the meat.

1 Soak the wood chips in water for at least 30 minutes.

2 Prepare the grill for indirect cooking over medium-low heat (as close to 180°C/350°F as possible).

3 In a large disposable foil tray, spread the chickpeas, pepper and tomatoes into three separate sections (it's okay if they touch). Drizzle each with 1 teaspoon oil, and then mix separately to coat evenly, keeping the sections separated.

4 Drain and add the wood chips to the charcoal or to the smoker box of a gas grill, following the manufacturer's instructions, and close the lid. When smoke appears, place the pan with the vegetables over ***roasting/indirect medium-low heat***, close the lid and cook for 25–35 minutes until the tomatoes begin to split and the chickpeas take on a light brown patina, stirring each ingredient once or twice during cooking. If the tomatoes start to collapse, remove them from the tray. Remove the tray from the grill and set aside to cool completely.

5 In a large bowl, combine the vinaigrette ingredients. Slowly add 75ml/3fl oz oil, whisking constantly to emulsify the vinaigrette. To the bowl, add the spinach, onion and the cooled chickpeas, pepper and tomatoes; toss to combine. Divide the salad evenly among four serving plates and top with equal amounts of the ham. Finish with a grinding of pepper. Serve immediately.

Be ready for anything. Ideally all the tomatoes, chickpeas and peppers will cook perfectly in the same amount of time, but they might not. Keeping them in separate piles allows you to remove any that are cooking faster than others.

CHARRED ICEBERG SALAD
WITH BUTTERMILK DRESSING

SERVES: 4 | **PREP TIME:** 15 MINUTES | **GRILLING TIME:** ABOUT 4 MINUTES
SPECIAL EQUIPMENT: 4–6 METAL OR BAMBOO SKEWERS

Sturdy, dense iceberg lettuce holds its shape on the grill while the outer leaves char, adding an extra smoky dimension to the traditional wedge salad. The tomatoes build on the charred flavours, and their warmth is a nice contrast to the cool buttermilk dressing.

DRESSING
4 tablespoons buttermilk
3 tablespoons soured cream
1 tablespoon fresh lemon juice
¼ teaspoon sea salt
¼ teaspoon freshly ground black
   pepper

340g/12oz yellow cherry tomatoes
Extra-virgin olive oil
⅛ teaspoon sea salt
1 head iceberg lettuce, outer leaves
   removed, cut through the core
   into quarters
12 baguette slices, each about
   1cm/½ inch thick
115g/4oz crumbled blue cheese
2 spring onions (white and light green
   parts only), thinly sliced

1 If using bamboo skewers, soak them in water for at least 30 minutes.

2 Whisk the dressing ingredients until smooth.

3 Prepare the grill for direct cooking over medium heat (180–230°C/350–450°F).

4 Thread the tomatoes on to skewers, lightly brush with oil, and season with the salt. Brush the cut sides of the lettuce quarters with oil, and brush the baguette slices on both sides with oil.

5 Grill the tomato skewers and lettuce quarters over **grilling/direct medium heat** for about 4 minutes, with the lid closed, until charred, turning the tomatoes as needed and the lettuce once to char the other cut side. During the last minute of grilling time, toast the baguette slices over direct heat, turning once.

6 Place the lettuce quarters on individual plates and arrange equal amounts of the tomatoes, blue cheese and spring onions around and over the lettuce. Pour as much dressing as you like over each salad and serve with the toasted baguette slices.

GRILLED TENDERSTEM BROCCOLI
WITH BUCATINI PASTA AND LEMON BREADCRUMBS

SERVES: 4 | **PREP TIME:** 30 MINUTES
GRILLING TIME: 3–5 MINUTES

Who knew tenderstem broccoli could be barbecued? Over a live fire, the outer leaves crisp and the stalks and heads char, adding a delightful smoky flavour and texture to this pasta dish, which benefits even more from a shower of toasted lemony breadcrumbs. Keep an eye on the crumbs while they toast to prevent burning.

70g/2½oz panko breadcrumbs
1 teaspoon dried oregano
¼ teaspoon crushed chilli flakes
115g/4oz pecorino cheese, finely grated
2 teaspoons finely grated lemon zest
Sea salt
Freshly ground black pepper
Extra-virgin olive oil
450g/1lb tenderstem broccoli, ends trimmed and stalks peeled
450g/1lb dried bucatini pasta

1 In a medium frying pan over a medium heat, toast the panko, oregano and chilli flakes for 3–5 minutes until the panko is golden, stirring frequently. Transfer to a bowl and cool for 5 minutes. Add the cheese, lemon zest, ¼ teaspoon salt and ¼ teaspoon pepper and stir to blend.

2 Prepare the grill for direct cooking over medium heat (180–230°C/350–450°F).

3 In a large bowl, whisk 1 tablespoon of oil with ½ teaspoon salt, and then add the broccoli, turning to coat. Grill the broccoli over **grilling/direct medium heat** for 3–5 minutes (depending on the thickness of the stalks), with the lid closed, until bright green in colour, charred in some spots, and crisp-tender, turning occasionally. Remove from the grill and, when cool enough to handle, cut off the florets and cut the stalks into 1-cm/½-inch pieces.

4 Bring a large pan of salted water to a rolling boil. Add the pasta and cook until al dente. Drain and reserve 250ml/8fl oz of the pasta water. Transfer the pasta to a serving bowl and toss with 1 tablespoon oil. Add the broccoli florets, stalk pieces and 175ml/6fl oz of the reserved pasta water and toss to combine. If liked, add more pasta water. Distribute the breadcrumbs on top. Serve warm, garnished with a generous grinding of pepper.

AUBERGINE PARMESAN
WITH TOASTED BREADCRUMBS

SERVES: 4–6 | **PREP TIME:** 25 MINUTES | **GRILLING TIME:** ABOUT 1½ HOURS
SPECIAL EQUIPMENT: PERFORATED GRILL PAN, 25-CM/10-INCH CAST-IRON FRYING PAN
OR 20-X-20-CM/8-X-8-INCH GRILLPROOF CASSEROLE

Extra-virgin olive oil
Sea salt
900g/2lb plum tomatoes,
    each cut lengthways in half
2 onions, chopped
3 garlic cloves, finely chopped
½ teaspoon dried oregano
¼ teaspoon crushed chilli flakes
 Freshly ground black pepper
25g/1oz fresh breadcrumbs
115g/4oz Parmesan cheese, finely
    grated
900g/2lb aubergines, ends trimmed
    and cut crossways into 1-cm/
    ½-inch slices
225g/8oz fresh mozzarella cheese,
    drained and thinly sliced
4 tablespoons chopped basil leaves
bread, to serve

This unexpected version of aubergine parmigiana gets a lot of help from the fire. Grilling the aubergine not only adds charred flavour to the gratin, it also eliminates the excess oil and fat from frying. The aubergine will continue to cook while baking in the gratin, becoming meltingly tender and rich. The results are particularly good when you barbecue this on a charcoal grill.

1 Prepare the grill for direct and indirect cooking over medium heat (180–230°C/350–450°F).

2 In a large bowl, whisk 2 tablespoons oil and ½ teaspoon salt. Add the tomatoes and turn to coat. Arrange the tomatoes, cut side up, on a perforated grill pan. Place the grill pan with the tomatoes over *roasting/indirect medium heat*, close the lid and cook for 25–30 minutes until reduced slightly in size and the skins shrivel. Remove from the grill and allow to rest until cool to the touch, about 10 minutes. Peel off and discard the skins, and then transfer the tomatoes to a food processor; process until smooth.

3 In a large saucepan over a medium heat on the hob, warm 1 tablespoon oil. Add the onions and cook for about 4 minutes until soft and translucent, stirring frequently. Add the garlic, oregano and chilli flakes and sauté until fragrant, about 1 minute. Add the tomatoes, 1 teaspoon salt and ½ teaspoon pepper. Simmer over a medium-low heat for 5 minutes, stirring occasionally. Remove from the heat.

4 Mix together the breadcrumbs, 3 tablespoons oil, half of the Parmesan cheese and ¼ teaspoon salt.

5 Brush the aubergine slices generously with oil, season evenly with ¾ teaspoon salt and ¾ teaspoon pepper, and then grill over *grilling/direct medium heat* for 8–10 minutes, with the lid closed, until softened and charred, turning once or twice.

6 Spoon a thin layer of the sauce into the bottom of a 25-cm/10-inch cast-iron frying pan. Arrange half of the aubergine slices over the sauce. Drop half of the remaining sauce by spoonfuls over each aubergine slice. Top with half of the mozzarella and the remaining Parmesan. Cover the cheese with the remaining aubergine slices in an even layer. Top with the remaining sauce and the remaining mozzarella. Spoon the breadcrumbs evenly on top. Grill over *roasting/indirect medium heat* for about 50 minutes, with the lid closed, until the breadcrumbs are golden. Serve warm with bread and garnished with the basil.

SMOKED OLIVES
WITH LEMON, CHILLIES AND THYME

Use whatever type of olives you like to eat, or mix up a few different ones. The green ones on top are Castelvetrano (buttery and mild). The middle ones are Kalamata (with a rich, pickled flavour). And the little ones on the bottom are Picholine (with a firm texture and tart 'green' taste).

SERVES: 8 | **PREP TIME:** 10 MINUTES | **GRILLING TIME:** 45 MINUTES–1 HOUR
SPECIAL EQUIPMENT: 2 LARGE HANDFULS HICKORY WOOD CHIPS, LARGE DISPOSABLE FOIL TRAY OR GRILLPROOF BAKING DISH

The strong flavours of briny olives can handle the robust aromatics of a wood like hickory, but do not cook these olives longer than an hour or their consistency will turn too soft. Properly cooked, the olives make a remarkable snack or appetiser, and if you have any left, how about some smoked martinis?

675g/1½lb assorted olives, such as Castelvetrano, Kalamata and Picholine
125ml/4fl oz extra-virgin olive oil
6 garlic cloves, each cut in half
2 red cherry chillies (pimiento chillies), each cut lengthways into halves or quarters
Zest of 1 lemon, shaved with a vegetable peeler
4 large sprigs thyme, each cut in half
4 teaspoons finely chopped thyme leaves

1 Soak the wood chips in water for at least 30 minutes.

2 Prepare the grill for indirect cooking over low heat (as close to 130°C/250°F as possible).

3 In a large disposable foil tray, combine all the ingredients except the finely chopped thyme.

4 Drain and add one handful of wood chips to the charcoal or to the smoker box of a gas grill, following the manufacturer's

instructions, and close the lid. When smoke appears, place the pan with the olives over **roasting/indirect low heat**, close the lid and cook for 45 minutes–1 hour until the olives are fragrant but still firm, stirring once or twice. After 20 minutes, drain and add the remaining wood chips to the charcoal or smoker box.

5 Transfer the olive mixture to a large bowl and toss with the chopped thyme. Serve warm or at room temperature.

HICKORY-ROASTED ALMONDS
WITH ROSEMARY AND SEA SALT

Presoaking almonds in water provides the necessary moisture for the hickory smoke to stick. Fresh rosemary, added after smoking, lends a beautiful herbaceous flavour.

SERVES: 12–16 | **PREP TIME:** 15 MINUTES | **GRILLING TIME:** ABOUT 45 MINUTES
SPECIAL EQUIPMENT: 2 LARGE HANDFULS HICKORY WOOD CHIPS, CHARCOAL GRILL, PERFORATED GRILL PAN

A grill pan with holes is an excellent accessory for this recipe, as it allows you to expose all the nuts to the smoke (without any falling through the cooking grate!). Taste them after 20 minutes of roasting. If you think they are smoky enough, don't add another chunk of wood. Make sure you are using raw nuts here, since toasted ones will dry out. Cashews would work well in place of almonds.

540g/1lb 3oz whole raw almonds
1 tablespoon fine sea salt
2 teaspoons chipotle chilli powder
2 teaspoons paprika
2 tablespoons extra-virgin olive oil
4 teaspoons finely chopped rosemary
    leaves

1. Soak the wood chips in water for at least 30 minutes.

2. Prepare the charcoal grill for indirect cooking over low heat (as close to 130°C/250°F as possible).

3. In a bowl or container, cover the almonds with water and allow to stand for 10 minutes; drain. Spread the almonds on a tea towel and pat until no longer wet but still damp. Place the almonds in a bowl with the salt, chilli powder and paprika. Toss to coat (the moisture will allow the spice mixture to adhere better to the almonds).

Transfer the almonds to a perforated grill pan.

4. Drain and add half of the wood chips to the charcoal and put the lid on the grill. When smoke appears, place the grill pan with the almonds over **roasting/indirect low heat**, close the lid and cook for 45 minutes until fragrant and smoky, stirring the almonds once or twice. After 20 minutes, drain and add the remaining wood chips to the charcoal.

5. Transfer the almonds to a bowl and add the oil and rosemary; toss well. Serve warm or at room temperature.

2

PORK

LESSONS FROM THE LEGENDS
PULLED PORK

I never thought I would find the world's greatest pulled pork sandwich on the streets of New York City, but then again, the man responsible for making it is no city slicker. Chris Lilly is a pit master from rural Alabama who, with his team, has won the American Royal Invitational in Kansas City, not to mention four Grand Championships at the Memphis in May competition. Each June he hauls his smokers to New York for The Big Apple Barbecue Block Party, a meat fest and charity fundraiser that attracts barbecue royalty from all over the country – and up to 125,000 visitors eager for the one-of-a-kind opportunity to taste dishes as fabulous as smoked lamb brisket from Tim Love in Texas, Jamaican jerk ribs from Bill Durney in Brooklyn, and, of course, Lilly's epic sandwich.

Sceptics might ask: What kind of pulled pork could possibly make it worth battling your way through such huge crowds? And isn't $12 a pretty hefty price tag for a sandwich? But just one bite of Lilly's creation tells you why he's a legend. His prowess with a live fire can transform a brawny pork shoulder into soft, moist shreds of meat mingled with outer edges of slow-smoked, seasoned bark, all with a tangy, mustard-laced snap. Put that into a soft roll and you have a lot more than a sandwich. It's a bold and savoury fistful of pure happiness.

TRIMMING

An entire pork shoulder weighs in at 6–10kg/ 12–20lb, which is nothing for a pit master to smoke and serve, but probably too much meat for a backyard barbecue. Instead, get yourself the top half of the shoulder, which usually weighs 2–4kg/8–16lb. In the US it goes by several names, and most of them include the term 'butt,' a misleading description at best because a pork butt has nothing to do with the back end of a pig. Regardless of the name, look for a roast with an even thickness of well-marbled meat from edge to edge and the shoulder blade still inside, because the bone adds flavour. The finest-tasting meat comes from heritage breeds such as Berkshire or Mangalica hogs; those breeds are what competitors often use to get blue-ribbon results.

Trim the fat down to a thickness of about 5mm/ ¼ inch so that it melts easily on the smoker, so the seasonings can get into the meat, and so you have a better chance of developing a gorgeous smoke ring. On the leaner side, remove as much fibrous silver skin as you can. Also remove any lymph nodes that could discolour the meat to a greenish hue. The folks at the processing plant usually remove these, but check anyway for light brownish masses, a little bigger than marbles, buried an inch or so within the meat.

DONENESS

After you have spent so many hours barbecuing a pork shoulder, all of the effort you poured into mixing a spice rub, trimming the meat and finessing the sauce could be wasted if you under- or overcook it. There are a few ways to know it's cooked right: the internal temperature should reach 88–90.5°C/190–195°F; you should be able to remove the bone easily from the meat, with the bone still looking moist (not chalky); and the meat should be so tender that you can break it apart into small pieces with just your fingers. If the meat is still quite warm, use forks or 'bear claws' to tear it apart, but do wait until the shoulder has rested for at least 20 minutes. The internal temperature should come down to about 60°F/140°F. If you break it apart and see steam rising, the meat is losing precious juices to evaporation and needs to rest longer.

THE SMOKE RING

The pinkish band of colour under the surface of some smoked meats strikes a thrill into the hearts of barbecue judges and backyard cooks alike. Achieving this handsome effect is a matter of encouraging the natural pink protein in the meat (called myoglobin) to react with gases carried in the smoke, specifically nitric oxide (NO) and carbon monoxide (CO). You can amplify the effect by making sure the meat is moist and cold when it first goes on the smoker, as the moisture will trap more NO and CO, and the cold temperature means you have a longer period of time for the myoglobin and gases to make their magic happen.

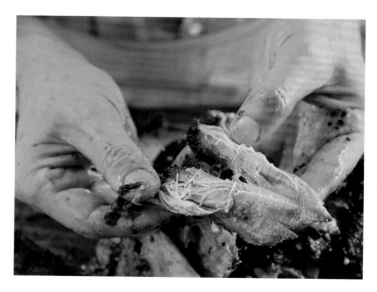

KANSAS CITY-STYLE
PULLED PORK

SERVES: 10–12 | **PREP TIME:** 30 MINUTES | **GRILLING TIME:** ABOUT 5½ HOURS | **RESTING TIME:** 1 HOUR
SPECIAL EQUIPMENT: CHARCOAL GRILL; 4 LARGE HANDFULS APPLE, CHERRY OR HICKORY WOOD CHUNKS;
LARGE DISPOSABLE FOIL TRAY; SPRAY BOTTLE FILLED WITH WATER; HEAVY-DUTY ALUMINIUM FOIL; INSTANT-READ THERMOMETER

In big cities, small towns and tiny neighbourhoods across America, pulled pork appears in styles as varied and multicultural as the people living there. One style that everyone seems to like (love, actually) hails from Kansas City, where generously spiced shoulder meat is barbecued to fall-apart tenderness and coated in a sauce of sweet and spicy complexity with a touch of smokiness. That's Kansas City-style: a little bit of everything delicious.

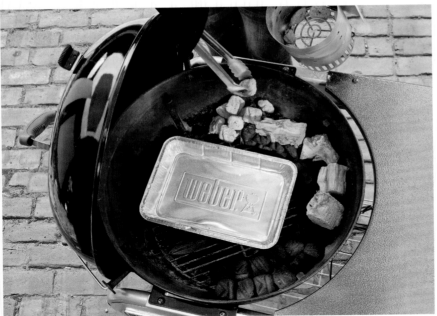

Don't rush it. The path to great pulled pork requires a fire that burns ever so slowly at temperatures between 110 and 130°C/225 and 250°F. If you cook it hotter than that, the muscles tend to seize up and push out moisture. If the temperature is consistently just right, the collagen in the meat will melt into juicy, delicious gelatine. That's what makes barbecued meat moist. One clever way of achieving this succulence is with the 'snake method' (for set-up instructions, see page 76). Essentially, you create an arc of charcoal briquettes and wood along one side of the grill and light the charcoal on one end of the 'snake' only. The briquettes and wood burn gradually over time, rather than all at once, so the fire never gets too high or too low and you shouldn't need to add any more fuel.

RUB

115g/4oz light brown sugar
4 tablespoons smoked paprika
4 teaspoons sea salt
2½ teaspoons mild chilli powder
2½ teaspoons garlic powder
2½ teaspoons onion powder
1½ teaspoons coarsely ground
   black pepper
½–1 teaspoon ground cayenne pepper

1 boneless pork shoulder, 1.8–2.3kg/4–5lb,
   trimmed of excess fat and silver skin,
   rolled and tied

SAUCE

3 bacon rashers
½ onion, finely diced
3 garlic cloves, finely chopped
125ml/4fl oz tomato ketchup
125ml/4fl oz golden corn syrup
125ml/4fl oz cider vinegar
4 tablespoons tomato purée
4 tablespoons mild chilli powder
2 tablespoons light brown sugar
1 tablespoon black treacle
1 tablespoon liquid smoke
1 tablespoon Worcestershire sauce
1 teaspoon celery salt
½ teaspoon sea salt

1   Mix the rub ingredients and then season the joint all over with the rub. Allow the meat to stand at room temperature for 30 minutes before grilling.

2   Prepare the charcoal grill for indirect cooking over very low heat (110–130°C /225–250°F) using the snake method (see photo at left and set-up instructions on page 76). When the temperature of the grill reaches 110°C/225°F, grill the roast, fat side down, over ***roasting/indirect very***

low heat, with the lid closed, for 4 hours, adjusting the top vent so the temperature of the grill stays as close to 110°C/225°F as possible. At the start of every hour, after the first hour, lightly spray the roast with water.

3   Meanwhile, make the sauce. In a heavy-bottomed saucepan over a medium heat, fry the bacon until browned and most of the fat is rendered out. Using a slotted spoon, remove the bacon. Leave 2–3 tablespoons of bacon fat in the pan. Eat the bacon or save for another use. Add the onion and cook for 3–4 minutes until soft and translucent, stirring occasionally. Add the garlic and cook for 1 minute, stirring occasionally to prevent it from burning. Whisk in the remaining sauce ingredients, bring to a simmer over a medium heat, and cook for 10–15 minutes, stirring

occasionally. Set aside to cool. Once the sauce has cooled, pour into a blender and blend until smooth. Separate the sauce into two containers. One half will be used for basting the roast before wrapping it in foil. The other half will be mixed with the pulled pork.

4   After 4 hours, use an instant-read thermometer to check the internal temperature of the roast. If it has not reached 70°C/160°F, continue cooking until it does. Once the roast has reached 70°C/160°F, remove it from the grill. Put the lid back on the grill to prevent heat loss.

5   On a large work surface, criss-cross two sheets of heavy-duty aluminium foil, each about 90cm/3ft long. Place the roast in the centre of the foil, fat side up.

Lightly brush the meat all over with the sauce. Bring the ends of the inner sheet together, folding on top of the meat. Then bring the ends of the outer sheet together, wrapping the roast tightly to trap the steam. Return the meat to the grill and cook over *roasting/indirect very low heat* for about 1½ hours, with the lid closed, until the internal temperature reaches 88–90.5°C/190–195°F. Remove from the grill and allow to rest, still in the foil, for 1 hour.

6   Unwrap the roast and, when cool enough to handle, pull the meat apart to shred it. Discard any large pieces of fat and sinew. Moisten the meat with as much sauce as you like. Serve immediately.

SMOKED PULLED PORK SHOULDER
WITH VINEGARY SLAW

SERVES: 12 | **PREP TIME:** 40 MINUTES | **COOKING TIME:** 8–10 HOURS
SPECIAL EQUIPMENT: WATER SMOKER; 6 LARGE HANDFULS APPLE,
CHERRY OR HICKORY WOOD CHUNKS; INSTANT-READ THERMOMETER

*In the Carolinas a lot of people are partial to a vinegary slaw with pulled pork.
The sharp, tangy flavours and crisp, fresh textures play balancing roles against
the rich slow-cooked meat. The slaw here has all the right hallmarks but it also
has a little twist to make it a bit different. You will find thinly sliced celery and
chopped fresh dill tossed with the standard ingredients. Save time by using a
mandolin or other shredder for the cabbage, but don't skimp on the time the slaw
sits in the refrigerator. It needs several hours to become almost pickled.*

SLAW
175ml/6fl oz distilled white vinegar
75g/3oz granulated sugar
2 tablespoons finely chopped dill
2 teaspoons sea salt
½ teaspoon freshly ground
    black pepper
1 head green cabbage, about
    675g/1½lb, cored and shredded
3 large celery stalks, very thinly sliced
2 carrots, peeled and
    grated through the large holes of a box
    grater
1–2 tablespoons finely chopped jalapeño or
    serrano chilli

PUSHING THROUGH 'THE STALL'
When you cook a big piece of meat like a pork shoulder, internal temperatures rise to about
65°C/150°F, and then curiously they stall or plateau for a while, sometimes hours, freaking
out backyard cooks. Don't freak. The reason for the stall is that the meat is cooling on the
surface as juices are evaporating. Just as sweat cools us when we get too hot, evaporating
juices cool meat on a smoker and prevent internal temperatures from climbing until the
surface of the meat dries out. You can wait patiently for all the moisture to evaporate or
push through the stall by wrapping the meat in foil to trap the heat and moisture.

RUB

2 teaspoons paprika
2 teaspoons sea salt
2 teaspoons freshly ground
  black pepper
1 teaspoon ground cumin
½ teaspoon onion flakes

1 bone-in pork shoulder roast, about
  3kg/6½lb, trimmed of excess fat
  and silver skin

SAUCE

500ml/18fl oz distilled white vinegar
240ml/8fl oz tomato ketchup
4 tablespoons light brown sugar
1 tablespoon Worcestershire sauce
2 teaspoons sea salt
½ teaspoon ground cayenne pepper

12 hamburger buns, split

1   In a large bowl, whisk the vinegar, sugar, dill, salt and pepper. Add the remaining slaw ingredients. Toss well, cover and refrigerate until ready to serve.

2   In a small bowl, combine the rub ingredients, and then massage the rub all over the pork.

3   Prepare the smoker for indirect cooking with very low heat (93–130°C/200–250°F). When the temperature reaches 110°C/225°F, add the wood chunks to the charcoal. Cook the meat, fat side down, over *roasting/indirect very low heat* for 8–10 hours, with the lid closed, until the internal temperature registers 88–90.5°C/190–195°F (not touching the bone) and the meat is so tender that it pulls apart easily. Check the smoker every hour and maintain an even heat. You may need to close some vents (partially) to lower the temperature or open some vents to raise the temperature. Also, you may need to add water to the water pan halfway through the cooking time, which will lower the temperature.

4   Meanwhile, make the sauce. In a saucepan, combine the sauce ingredients. Bring to the boil over a medium-high heat on the hob and cook for 8–10 minutes until the sugar is dissolved and the sauce is reduced to a ketchup-like consistency. Remove from the heat and allow to cool.

5   Remove the meat from the smoker and allow to rest for 10 minutes. Remove the bone (it should come out cleanly) and, when cool enough to handle, pull the meat apart to shred it. Discard any clumps of fat and sinew. Moisten the meat with as much of the sauce as you like. Pile the pulled pork on buns and top with the slaw, adding mayonnaise or mustard, if liked.

PORK SHOULDER
WITH SWEET CAROLINA MUSTARD SAUCE

SERVES: 12–16 | **PREP TIME:** 1 HOUR | **COOKING TIME:** 9–11 HOURS | **RESTING TIME:** 1–2 HOURS
SPECIAL EQUIPMENT: INJECTOR; WATER SMOKER; 6 LARGE HANDFULS HICKORY WOOD CHUNKS; SPRAY BOTTLE; LARGE DISPOSABLE FOIL TRAY; HEAVY-DUTY ALUMINIUM FOIL; INSTANT-READ THERMOMETER; DRY, INSULATED COOLER; BEAR CLAWS (OPTIONAL)

If your pulled pork aspirations include competition-worthy results, here are some tips to point you towards perfection.

1. Start with a large joint – 4–4.4kg/8–9lb of nicely marbled pork shoulder. A heritage breed of pork will give you excellent flavour, but even standard supermarket pork will barbecue better if the cut is bigger. The meat has to be able to stay on the smoker long enough to melt the connective tissue. If the roast is too small, it is likely to dry out before the connective tissue dissolves into succulent juices.

2. Give special attention to the 'money muscle,' a tube-shaped section of meat opposite the bone that has superior pork flavour and soft but not mushy texture. For competitions, some pit masters make a shallow cut to separate this muscle a little bit from the rest of the shoulder, exposing more surface area to smoke and making it easier to find after the shoulder is cooked. They inject the muscle carefully, puncturing it as few times as possible. Finally, they slice little medallions from it, rather than pulling/shredding the meat.

3. Inject the meat evenly with some fruit juice. This is not so much for flavour as for extra moisture. The meat will be on the smoker for so long that it is bound to lose at least one-third of its moisture. The more you have at the start, the more you can afford to lose. Alternatively, you could brine the meat for 24 hours in a solution of 500g/1lb 2oz sea salt dissolved in 4 litres/7 pints of water.

INJECTION
240ml/8fl oz unsweetened apple juice
115g/4oz unsalted butter
1 tablespoon Worcestershire sauce
1 tablespoon sea salt

RUB
2 tablespoons sea salt
2 tablespoons light brown sugar
2 tablespoons mild chilli powder
1 tablespoon paprika
2 teaspoons onion flakes
1 teaspoon ground cumin
1 teaspoon freshly ground
    black pepper

1 bone-in pork shoulder, 4–4.5kg/
    9–10lb, trimmed of excess fat and
    silver skin
125ml/4fl oz unsweetened apple juice

SAUCE
240ml/8fl oz American mustard
4 tablespoons unsweetened apple or
    white grape juice
2 tablespoons light brown sugar
2 tablespoons honey
2 tablespoons black treacle
1½ teaspoons garlic granules
1½ teaspoons onion flakes
1½ teaspoons mild chilli powder
1½ teaspoons freshly ground
    black pepper
½ teaspoon drinking chocolate powder

1. In a small saucepan, mix the injection ingredients. Bring to a simmer over a medium heat and cook until the butter is melted. Allow the injection to cool.

2. In a small bowl, mix the rub ingredients. Set aside 2 tablespoons of the rub for seasoning the pork later.

3   Inject the meat all over with the injection mixture, including the 'money muscle.'

4   Season the joint evenly with the rub left in the small bowl. Allow the meat to stand at room temperature while you prepare the smoker.

5   Prepare the smoker for indirect cooking with very low heat (93–130°C/200–250°F). When the temperature of the smoker reaches 110°C/225°F, add the wood chunks to the charcoal. Set the pork on the cooking grate, fat side down, close the lid and cook over *roasting/indirect very low heat* for 7–8 hours until the surface is dark brown all over, maintaining the temperature of the grill between 110 and 225°C/225 and 250°F throughout that time.

6   Fill a spray bottle with the 125ml/4fl oz apple juice.

7   Remove the roast from the smoker, spray it all over with juice, season evenly with the reserved 2 tablespoons rub, and place it, fat side down, in a large disposable foil tray. Cover the tray tightly with heavy-duty aluminium foil, crimping the edges.

8   Return the meat in the covered foil tray to the smoker and continue cooking for 2–3 hours more until the internal temperature

registers 88–90.5°C/190–195°F (not touching the bone) and the meat is so tender that it pulls apart easily. Check on the smoker every hour to maintain even heat. You may need to partially close some vents to lower the heat or open some vents to raise the heat. Also, you may have to add water to the water pan (this will lower the heat).

9   Set the meat, still wrapped in the tray, in a dry, insulated cooler and allow to rest for 1–2 hours. Meanwhile, make the sauce.

10 In a saucepan, whisk the sauce ingredients until smooth. Place the saucepan on the hob over a medium heat and bring to a simmer. Simmer for about 5 minutes, stirring often to prevent it from burning on the bottom. Remove from the heat.

11 Remove the pork from the tray. Remove and discard the bone from the joint (it should come cleanly out of the meat). Find the 'money muscle' and cut it away from the rest of the roast. Cut the money muscle crossways into 1-cm/ ½-inch slices. Pull apart the remaining meat using bear claws or two forks. Discard any clumps of fat and sinew. Pour the sauce over the meat and toss to coat evenly. Serve warm.

LEFTOVERS?

A big bone-in pork shoulder weighing 4–4.5kg/8–9lb makes a lot of pulled pork – enough for at least a dozen people. If you are not serving a big crowd all at once and you plan to have leftovers, make a double batch of the mustard sauce. Use half of it to sauce the meat right after it has been pulled. Use the other half as a sauce for these fried patties of pulled pork.

For every 450g/1lb of leftover meat, mix in 125g/4½oz panko breadcrumbs and 2 lightly beaten eggs. Shape into 12 patties, each about 7.5cm/3 inches wide and 2cm/¾ inch thick. Pour enough oil into a large frying pan to come 5mm/¼ inch up the side. Heat the oil over a medium heat, and then fry the patties (in batches) until golden brown and warm throughout, about 2 minutes per side, turning once or twice. Serve the patties warm with extra sauce and a fresh salad.

ROTISSERIE LECHÓN ASADO

SERVES: 6-8 | PREP TIME: 20 MINUTES | MARINATING TIME: 8-24 HOURS | GRILLING TIME: 2¼-2¾ HOURS
SPECIAL EQUIPMENT: 2 LARGE HANDFULS HICKORY WOOD CHIPS, LARGE DISPOSABLE FOIL TRAY, KITCHEN STRING,
ROTISSERIE, INSTANT-READ THERMOMETER

MARINADE
350ml/12fl oz fresh orange juice
125ml/4fl oz fresh lemon juice
125ml/4fl oz extra-virgin olive oil
1 onion, finely chopped in a food
    processor
20 garlic cloves, peeled, finely
    chopped in a food processor
1 tablespoon dried oregano
1 tablespoon sea salt

1 boneless pork shoulder,
    2.3-2.7kg/5-6lb, trimmed of
    excess fat and silver skin
1½ teaspoons sea salt
1 teaspoon freshly ground black pepper
1-2 tablespoons chopped oregano

When you roast this Cuban-style pork shoulder on a rotisserie that spins over a smoky fire, you can expect the internal juices to baste the meat from within while the aromas of wood seep into the savoury crust. Take the pork off the grill when it reaches about 77°C/170°F internally. At this temperature, it will be tender yet firm enough to slice.

1   Soak the wood chips in water for at least 30 minutes.

2   In a large bowl, combine the marinade ingredients. Make small slits all over the meat. Add the pork to the bowl with the marinade, and spread the marinade all over it. Cover and refrigerate for 8–24 hours, turning occasionally.

3   Prepare the grill for indirect cooking over medium-low heat (150–180°C/300–350°F). Place a large disposable foil tray in the centre of the charcoal grate between the two piles of charcoal or in the middle of the cooking grates of a gas grill.

4   Remove the meat from the bowl, reserve the marinade and allow the joint to stand at room temperature for 30 minute. Cover and refrigerate the marinade until needed in step 6. Season the meat. Using kitchen string, tie the joint to make the shape as uniform as possible. Slide one pronged fork on to the spit, with the tines facing inwards, about 25cm/10 inches from the end of the spit. Secure the fork, but do not tighten it yet. Slide the spit through the joint as close to the centre as possible, and gently push the meat into the fork tines so that they are deep inside. Add the other pronged fork to the spit with the tines facing inwards, and push firmly into the meat. Secure the fork, but don't tighten it yet. Place the spit into the rotisserie motor and centre the meat over the foil tray. Tighten the forks.

5   Drain and add the wood chips to the charcoal or to the smoker box of a gas grill, following the manufacturer's instructions. Close the lid and turn on the rotisserie motor. Grill the roast over ***roasting/indirect medium-low heat*** for 2¼-2¾ hours, with the lid closed, until an instant-read thermometer inserted into the thickest part of the joint registers 77°C/170°F. If using a charcoal grill, add more briquettes as necessary to maintain the temperature of the grill.

6   Meanwhile, in a saucepan over a medium-high heat, bring the marinade to the boil. Continue cooking at a low to medium boil for about 5 minutes until slightly reduced. This salty-sweet juice becomes the sauce for the meat. Pour the marinade through a sieve into a medium bowl and discard the solids. Allow to stand for about 5 minutes to allow the oil to rise to the surface. Skim off and discard as much of the oil as you like. Cover and refrigerate until just before serving.

7   Wearing insulated barbecue mitts or oven gloves, carefully remove the spit from the grill. Gently loosen the forks and slide the roast off the spit. Transfer to a carving board and allow to rest for 20–30 minutes. Cut the pork into slices and garnish with the oregano. Just before serving, gently reheat the sauce and serve it alongside the joint.

Trussing the joint with string will give the meat a uniform shape that allows you to secure it with all the tines of the rotisserie forks and to cook it more evenly.

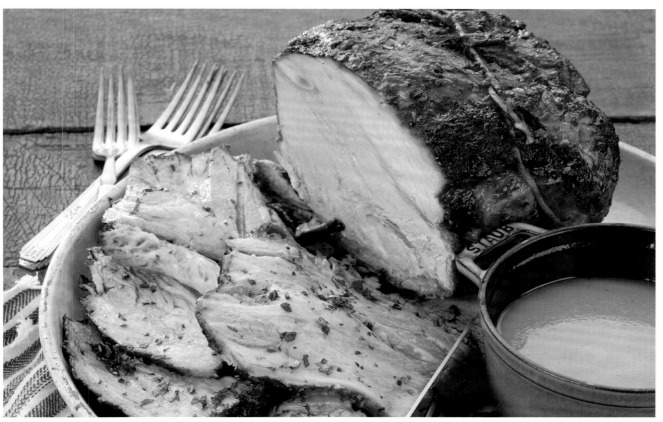

SLOW-ROASTED PORK BO SSAM
WITH CARROT-SPRING ONION-GINGER SLAW AND CHILLI SAUCE

SERVES: 6–8 | PREP TIME: 45 MINUTES | DRY BRINING TIME: 24 HOURS | GRILLING TIME: 4–4¾ HOURS
SPECIAL EQUIPMENT: 2 LARGE HEAVY-DUTY DISPOSABLE FOIL TRAYS

DRY BRINE
100g/3½oz granulated sugar
125g/4½oz sea salt

1 boneless pork shoulder 1.8–2kg/
   4–4½lb, trimmed of excess fat
   and silver skin
300g/10oz basmati rice

SLAW
10 spring onions (white and light green
   parts only), thinly sliced
1 carrot, 115–140g/4–5oz, coarsely
   grated
25g/1oz roughly chopped fresh
   coriander
2 tablespoons peeled, finely grated
   fresh ginger with juices
2 tablespoons vegetable oil
1 tablespoon unseasoned rice vinegar
1 tablespoon soy sauce

SAUCE
3 tablespoons sweet chilli sauce
2 tablespoons black bean garlic sauce
2 tablespoons vegetable oil
2 tablespoons unseasoned rice vinegar
1 teaspoon toasted sesame oil

4 tablespoons light brown sugar
1–2 heads round lettuce, leaves
   separated

The hardest part about this recipe for Korean-style barbecued pork is resisting the glorious aromas while the meat roasts over the fire for more than 4 hours. It's well worth the wait because the pork will develop a caramelised crust, thanks in part to a dry brine of sugar and salt that draws out some moisture that is then reabsorbed into the meat with seasoning. A last-minute crisping of the meat in a hot pan creates glistening edges for nice bits of crackling texture.

1 Twenty-four hours before grilling, dry brine the pork. In a large bowl, mix the sugar and salt. Place the joint in the bowl and rub the dry brine on all sides and crevices of the meat. Cover the bowl with clingfilm and refrigerate for 24 hours.

2 Prepare the grill for indirect cooking over medium-low heat (as close to 150°C/300°F as possible).

3 Remove the pork from the bowl and place it in a large heavy-duty disposable aluminium foil tray. Gently pat off any excess dry brine and juices with kitchen paper. Cook the roast over **roasting/indirect medium-low heat** for 4–4¾ hours, with the grill lid closed, until the meat is very tender and beginning to fall apart, turning the roast and basting with any pan juices every hour (there may only be a very small amount of juices to baste with). Remove the tray from the grill and transfer the meat to a chopping board. Discard the foil tray.

4 During the last hour of grilling time, cook the rice according to the packet instructions. In a bowl mix the slaw ingredients. In a small bowl, whisk the sauce ingredients.

5 Increase the temperature of the grill for indirect cooking over high heat (230–290°C/450–550°F).

6 Using two forks, shred the pork, discarding any large pieces of fat and sinew. Spread the pork in an even layer in the second large heavy-duty disposable foil tray. Sprinkle the brown sugar over the pork, and then grill over **roasting/indirect high heat** for 5–8 minutes, with the lid closed, until slightly browned and caramelised in spots, stirring occasionally. Transfer the pork to a serving bowl.

7 To assemble, spoon the rice and pork into a lettuce leaf, but do not overfill. Top with a spoonful of slaw and a drizzle of sauce. Roll up and eat.

PULLED PORK BREAKFAST BURRITOS
WITH EGGS AND CHEESE

SERVES: 6
PREP TIME: 25 MINUTES

2 tablespoons extra-virgin olive oil
565g/1¼lb leftover pulled pork (already tossed with sauce)
2 canned chipotle chillies in adobo sauce, finely chopped
3 tablespoons adobo sauce (from the can)
1 onion, thinly sliced
1 green pepper, thinly sliced
2 garlic cloves, finely chopped
8 large eggs
¾ teaspoon sea salt
¼ teaspoon freshly ground black pepper
25g/1oz unsalted butter
6 burrito-sized tortillas
225g/8oz Monterey Jack or Cheddar cheese, grated
4 tablespoons finely chopped fresh coriander
Shredded lettuce
Avocado slices
Shop-bought salsa (optional)
Soured cream (optional)

At the end of slow days, barbecue restaurants all over Texas and the South-west have leftover 'cue. Many places use their remaining pulled pork and other meats in clever ways, from salads to pastas, but one of my favourite ways is in breakfast burritos. What makes these so special is that you reheat the meat with chipotle chillies in adobo sauce, giving it a new layer of spiciness while you crisp up the edges.

1   In a large frying pan over a medium-high heat, warm 1 tablespoon of the oil. Add the pork, chipotle chillies and adobo sauce and cook for 7–9 minutes until the pork is crispy and hot, stirring occasionally. Reduce the heat to low and keep warm.

2   In a large, nonstick frying pan over medium-high heat, warm the remaining 1 tablespoon oil. Add the onion, green pepper and garlic. Cook for 8–9 minutes until softened and the onion just starts to brown, stirring occasionally. Stir the mixture into the pan with the pulled pork and keep warm.

3   Clean the nonstick frying pan and return it to a medium heat. Whisk the eggs, salt and pepper. Melt the butter in the pan and, when the foam subsides, add the eggs. Cook the eggs for 2–3 minutes, scraping the bottom of the pan occasionally with a flexible, heatproof spatula, until just set, or to your desired doneness.

4   Warm the tortillas according to the packet instructions. Place the tortillas on plates and divide the pork, eggs, cheese and coriander evenly among them. Top with lettuce and avocado. Roll up the tortillas, folding in the ends to hold in the filling. Serve with salsa and soured cream, if liked.

MEMPHIS PULLED PORK SPAGHETTI

The unusual sauce here picks up sweet mild chilli flavours from cubanelle peppers, also known as 'Cuban peppers,' which are light greenish in colour and tapered in their shape. If you can't find cubanelles, use Anaheim chillies instead, although they will taste a little hotter.

SERVES: 8–10 (MAKES 2.5 LITRES/4 PINTS SAUCE)
PREP TIME: 15 MINUTES, PLUS 35 MINUTES FOR THE SAUCE

Barbecue purists from the Carolinas may be shocked and dismayed to see the object of their great respect, pulled pork, in the company of anything so foreign and unrelated as spaghetti, but that's the way barbecue goes. Several restaurants in Memphis, Tennessee, are mixing soft and warm noodles with pulled pork and coating them with something that straddles the line between tomato sauce and barbecue sauce.

SAUCE
4 tablespoons extra-virgin olive oil
½ red onion, chopped
2 medium cubanelle peppers or Anaheim chillies, 75–115g/3–4oz each, stemmed, cored and chopped
4 teaspoons finely chopped garlic
1.6kg/3½lb canned tomatoes in juice
4 tablespoons black treacle
1 tablespoon mustard powder
1 teaspoon ground cinnamon
1 teaspoon sea salt
½ teaspoon freshly ground black pepper
675g/1½lb leftover smoked pulled pork, chopped

900g/2lb dried spaghetti
Chopped flat-leaf parsley
Crushed chilli flakes

1. In a large saucepan over a medium heat, warm the oil. Add the onion and peppers and cook until softened, about 4 minutes, stirring often. Stir in the garlic and cook for about 20 seconds until aromatic.

2. Add the tomatoes, treacle, mustard powder, cinnamon, salt and pepper. Bring the sauce to a low boil, and then reduce the heat to low. Simmer for about 20 minutes, uncovered, until slightly thickened to a marinara-sauce consistency, stirring occasionally.

3. Add the pulled pork to the tomato sauce. Simmer for about 10 minutes to warm through and blend the flavours. While the sauce is simmering, cook the pasta according to the packet instructions. Drain the pasta, transfer to a large serving bowl and then pour 1.5 litres/2½ pints of the sauce over the pasta, mixing gently to coat.

4. Serve the pasta in shallow bowls and garnish each with more sauce (about 4 tablespoons), parsley, chilli flakes and slices of crusty grilled bread, if liked.

Start with the meatiest ribs you can find. After you've dipped each rib in the egg mixture, allow the excess to drip back into the dish before coating with the polenta mixture. An excessively wet rib does not fry well. Also, have the ribs at room temperature to help keep the oil's temperature even.

SERVES: 8 | **PREP TIME:** 25 MINUTES
SPECIAL EQUIPMENT: DEEP-FRY THERMOMETER

In some Georgia barbecue joints, cooks have figured out how to combine chicken-fried steak and smoked ribs. (Finally!) If you want to try this at home, make sure the ribs have no sauce on them, or even any assertive rub, just the tender meat clinging to the bones. Coated with cornmeal-laced batter, the ribs fry up with a satisfying little crunch. Serve the ribs with Peachy Dipping Sauce – the recipe can be found on page 279.

250g/9oz unbleached plain flour
4 large eggs, at room temperature
4 tablespoons full-fat milk
50g/2oz polenta
2 teaspoons paprika
1 teaspoon sea salt
1 teaspoon freshly ground black pepper
Groundnut oil
2 racks leftover smoked baby back ribs, cut into individual ribs, at room temperature
Pickled jalapeño rings (optional)

1 Set out two shallow bowls and one deep bowl. Put half of the flour in the first shallow bowl. In the deep bowl, whisk the eggs and milk until uniform and smooth. In the second shallow bowl, combine the remaining flour, polenta, paprika, salt and pepper. Set the bowls in this order near the hob, with the second shallow bowl nearest to the burner.

2 Pour enough oil into a large, deep saucepan to come 5cm/2 inches up the side. Attach a deep-fry thermometer to the side of the pan. Heat the oil over a medium heat on the hob until the temperature on the thermometer registers 180°C/350°F.

3 Dip a rib into the flour, coating it lightly. Shake off any excess, and then dip in the egg mixture, coating well. Again, shake off any excess, and then dip into the polenta mixture, coating evenly. Set aside. After you've coated four or five ribs, slip them into the hot oil and fry until crisp and golden, 5–6 minutes, turning once or twice and adjusting the heat to keep the oil's temperature constant. Transfer the finished ribs to a wire rack set over a baking tray. Bring the oil's temperature back to 180°C/350°F and continue dipping and frying the remaining ribs in batches to prevent sogginess and overcrowding.

4 Serve the crispy ribs immediately, garnished with sliced pickled jalapeño rings, if liked.

LESSONS FROM THE LEGENDS

BABY BACK RIBS

Writing this book, I must have eaten my weight in baby back ribs. My first belt-busting research trip was to Pappy's Smokehouse in St Louis, where pit master Mike Emerson cooks about a ton of dry-rubbed ribs every day over apple and cherry wood. At Pappy's they have adopted the Memphis style of barbecuing ribs without sauce, although customers can choose from a few squeeze bottles of sauce on the tables. Just across town, a few miles from St Louis's graceful arch alongside the Mississippi River, chef Skip Steele, who used to cook at Pappy's, makes ribs with a different twist. For one thing, he finishes his racks with an apricot glaze and caramelises the sugars into the meat with a ferocious

blowtorch. What he achieves is a thin sheet of glistening, candy-like flavour that helps his barbecue stand out in the crowd.

This kind of distinction is the case in dozens of other cities and small towns I visited, especially outside big bastions of American barbecue like Memphis, Kansas City, the Carolinas and Texas. Traditionalists and innovators are barbecuing ribs in the same area but with different approaches, meaning that while long-standing traditions remain intact, there is plenty of room for the next wave of clever ideas.

CHOOSING THE RIGHT RACKS

1

Choose the meatiest ribs you can find. If you see any bones peeking through the meat (as in the photo above), it's a bad sign. We call those racks 'shiners,' and it means a butcher has cut the meat too close to the bone. Racks that weigh 1.1–1.4kg/2½–3lb usually have plenty of meat.

2

Choose racks with plenty of fat. Ideally the fat will be evenly distributed throughout the meat. Big clumps of jiggly fat lying on top should be trimmed off and discarded, as they do you no good. On the other hand, thin streaks of fat woven within the meat pack flavour and richness.

3

If you are fortunate you will find a strip of loin meat that runs horizontally on the meaty side of a rack. When the meat is fully cooked, you can pull off the whole strip and eat it by itself, and it's wonderful.

PULLING THE MEMBRANE

On the bone side of each rack is a thin, slick membrane that has a leathery texture when it's cooked; many pros remove it if the butcher hasn't done so already. To remove the membrane, start by finding a straight bone near the middle of the rack. Slide a blunt knife or your fingertips under the membrane at both the top and bottom of the bone and work your fingers under the membrane until they meet at the middle of the bone. You can now get a couple of fingers under the membrane and pull it straight up while holding the rest of the rack down with your other hand. The membrane often tears off in one whole sheet, but sometimes it requires a few separate pulls.

SMART SEASONING

The standard way to season ribs is to sprinkle a mixture of dried spices over both sides, especially the meaty side because it is most of what people eat. Some barbecue gurus like to add moisture to this step because they know that smoke dissolves into damp surfaces, so adding moisture improves the look of their smoke rings. A wet paste of dried spices with mustard or Worcestershire sauce is a clever way to get smokier ribs.

RIB FUNDAMENTALS

INDIRECT HEAT. The traditional way to barbecue baby back ribs is with roasting/indirect heat. That means the fire burns off to the side(s) of the racks on a gas or charcoal grill. On a smoker, a shield or water pan deflects the fire. A few barbecue joints, like Rendezvous in Memphis, cook ribs over direct heat, but I find it makes the meat dry.

BONE SIDE DOWN. Even though indirect heat circulates around all sides of the racks, the heat coming from the fire below is a little hotter. So start the racks bone side down to protect the meat on top from cooking too quickly. You need to give the connective tissue (collagen) in the meat enough time to melt slowly. That's when ribs taste juicy. Near the end of cooking, turn the rack over to collect juices that you use for basting.

SPRAY THE MEAT. Over time the surface of the meat will darken into a rich mahogany crust, but to prevent the crust from burning, especially on the ends, spray the meat on both sides with water. Be careful not to use so much water that you rinse away the spice rub.

ARE THEY DONE?

One way to check whether your ribs have reached the desired point of tenderness, without being mushy, is to push the tips of two exposed bones in opposite directions. The meat in between should begin to tear. The other way is with the bend (or bounce) test: lift a rack at one end and let it bend (or bounce) in the air. If the meat in the middle tears open, it's done.

PULLING CLEAN OFF THE BONE

Some folks like ribs to be so tender you could eat them without teeth, but most aficionados like a little chewiness in the meat. In fact, while I was training to be a KCBS certified barbecue judge, I was taught that if the meat slips off the bone with little effort, it's overdone. It should come clean off the bone, but only after you have taken a strong bite. At least that's what the pros say. You eat your ribs however you like.

One of the many unsubstantiated stories in barbecue folklore tells of a technique developed in Texas for steaming meat in foil after it has been smoked. The steam tenderises the meat, achieving the kind of tenderness that barbecue masters in other parts of the country can supposedly achieve without 'the Texas crutch.' Well, nowadays almost every barbecue team, countless barbecue restaurants and cookbook authors like me use it... because it works.

THE TEXAS CRUTCH

To try it yourself, brush smoked ribs (after they have achieved a dark brown crust) with juice, beer or barbecue sauce, and wrap each rack individually in heavy-duty aluminium foil, not the thin foil that could easily tear and leak. You must have a tight, unbroken seal to create enough steam.

Be careful not to cook the ribs too long in the foil. If you do, the precious crust on the surface will get soggy and the meat will turn both dry and mushy. Thirty minutes to one hour in foil is plenty of time. If the surface of the meat looks a little too wet coming out of the foil, set the ribs back over the heat without foil for 20 minutes or so to re-establish a crust.

BASIC BABY BACKS

SERVES: 4 | **PREP TIME:** 15 MINUTES | **GRILLING TIME:** 2–2¼ HOURS | **SPECIAL EQUIPMENT:** 3 LARGE HANDFULS HICKORY WOOD CHIPS, GAS GRILL WITH AT LEAST 3 BURNERS, METAL SMOKER BOX, SPRAY BOTTLE FILLED WITH WATER

PASTE
2 tablespoons American mustard
2 tablespoons Worcestershire sauce
2 teaspoons sea salt
2 teaspoons light brown sugar
2 teaspoons mild chilli powder
1 teaspoon garlic powder
1 teaspoon freshly ground black pepper

2 racks baby back ribs, each 1.1–1.4kg/2½–3lb
250ml/8fl oz shop-bought barbecue sauce

1 Soak the wood chips in water for at least 30 minutes.

2 Mix the paste ingredients, and then spread evenly all over the racks, spreading most of it on the meaty side.

3 Before lighting the gas grill, drain and add the wood chips to a metal smoker box. Set the smoker box under the cooking grate and over a burner on one side of the grill. Prepare the grill for indirect cooking over high heat (230–290°C/450–550°F), heating the wood chips in the smoker box. When the wood begins to smoke, lower the temperature of the grill to low heat, as close to 150°C/300°F as possible.

4 Lay the racks, bone side down and flat, on the cooking grates over *roasting/indirect low heat*. Close the lid and cook for 1 hour, maintaining the temperature of the grill as close to 150°C/300°F as possible. You may need to turn off one of the burners temporarily, especially on hot days. The wood chips should smoke for about 30 minutes. If they catch fire, spray a little water over the smoker box.

5 After the first hour of cooking, lightly spray the racks with water and swap their positions for even cooking. After 1½ hours of cooking, brush the racks on both sides with about half of the barbecue sauce. Continue cooking, bone side down, over *roasting/indirect low heat*, with the lid closed, until some of the meat has shrunk back from the ends of most of the bones by 5mm/¼ inch or more. They are completely done when you lift a rack at one end with tongs, bone side up, and the rack bends so much in the middle that the meat begins to tear easily. This may take 30–40 minutes more.

6 Remove the racks from the grill and, just before serving, lightly brush with more sauce. Cut the racks between the bones into individual ribs and serve warm.

TAMING THE FLAMES
Sometimes wood chips in a smoker box will dry out and catch fire. Don't panic. A few squeezes from a spray bottle filled with water will tame the flames.

BABY BACK RIBS
WITH SWEET AND SPICY BARBECUE SAUCE

SERVES: 4 | **PREP TIME:** 20 MINUTES | **GRILLING TIME:** ABOUT 3 HOURS
SPECIAL EQUIPMENT: CHARCOAL GRILL; 4–5 LARGE HANDFULS APPLE, CHERRY OR HICKORY WOOD CHUNKS;
LARGE DISPOSABLE FOIL TRAY; SPRAY BOTTLE FILLED WITH WATER; HEAVY-DUTY ALUMINIUM FOIL

One recent barbecue innovation is a low-maintenance way of sustaining a low temperature and steady smoke for hours and hours in a kettle grill. It's called the 'snake method' because charcoal briquettes are arranged in the shape of a snake that bends around the perimeter of the grill. The fire burns slowly from one end to the other, never getting too hot and never needing more fuel. Here is how to do it.

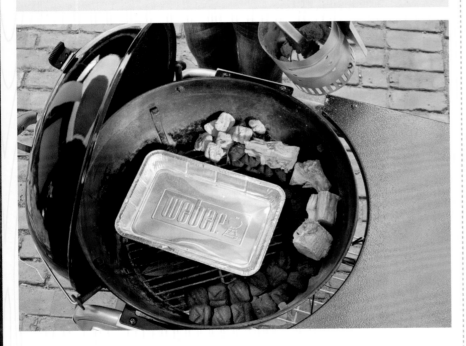

Start by forming two rows of briquettes around the perimeter on about half of the charcoal grate. The longer the snake, the longer the fire will last. The briquettes need to be neatly packed and touching. Stack another two rows on top of the first two so that now you have a charcoal configuration that is two briquettes wide and two briquettes high. Arrange the wood chunks in a row over one end (the end where you will start the fire burning).

In a chimney starter light 10–12 briquettes. Meanwhile, place a disposable foil tray on the charcoal grate beside the snake and fill the tray about three-quarters full with water. When the briquettes are ashed over, pile them carefully, using tongs, over one end of the snake. Make sure the bottom of the grill is swept clean of ash and the bottom vent is wide open so the fire gets plenty of air.

Set the cooking grate in place, close the lid and adjust the damper on the lid so the vent is about halfway open. Preheat the grill until the temperature falls between 130 and 150°C/250 and 300°F. Then lay your ribs over indirect heat, bone side down, so that no part of any rack is directly above the snake. Use the damper on the lid to control the airflow and temperature of the fire. Sit back and let the snake do its thing.

RUB
1 tablespoon light brown sugar
1 tablespoon smoked paprika
1 tablespoon onion flakes
1 tablespoon mild chilli powder
1 tablespoon sea salt
2 teaspoons freshly ground
    black pepper

2 racks baby back ribs, each
    1.1–1.4kg/2½–3lb
2 tablespoons extra-virgin olive oil

SAUCE
175ml/6fl oz tomato ketchup
125ml/4fl oz water
4 tablespoons light brown sugar
4 tablespoons black treacle
1 tablespoon Worcestershire sauce
1 tablespoon mild chilli powder
1 teaspoon sea salt
½ teaspoon freshly ground black pepper

1   Mix the rub ingredients. Using a blunt knife, slide the tip under the membrane in the middle of the back of each rack of ribs. Lift and pull off each membrane (see how-to, page 73). Brush the racks with the oil and season them all over with the rub, putting more of the rub on the meaty side of the racks. Allow the racks to stand at room temperature while you prepare the grill.

2   Prepare the charcoal grill for indirect cooking over low heat (130–150°C/ 250–300°F) using the snake method (see photo and set-up instructions, left).

3   Meanwhile, in a saucepan combine the sauce ingredients and bring to a gentle boil over a medium-high heat, stirring frequently. Reduce the heat to medium-low and simmer for 5–10 minutes until the sauce thickens slightly to a light syrupy consistency, stirring occasionally.

4   Lay the racks on the cooking grate, bone side down and positioned over the foil tray. Close the lid and grill the racks over **roasting/indirect low heat** for 1 hour, maintaining the temperature of the grill between 130 and 150°C/250 and 300°F by opening the vents wider to increase heat or partially closing the vents to decrease heat, checking the temperature frequently.

5   After the first hour of cooking time, lightly spray the racks with water and swap their positions for even cooking. Continue cooking over **roasting/indirect low heat** for another hour.

6   After the second hour of cooking, transfer the racks from the grill to a large rimmed baking tray. Close the grill lid to maintain the temperature. Brush the racks on both sides with some of the sauce, and then wrap each rack individually in heavy-duty aluminium foil. Return the racks to the grill, bone side down and positioned over the foil tray, and continue cooking over **roasting/indirect low heat** for 45 minutes.

7   After 45 minutes of cooking in the foil, remove the racks from the grill to check for doneness. Close the grill lid to maintain the temperature. Unwrap the racks and check to see if the meat has shrunk back from the ends of most of the bones by 5mm/¼ inch or more. If it has not, continue to cook the racks in the foil until it does, 10–15 minutes more. Remove the racks from the foil and lightly brush both sides with some of the sauce.

8   Return the racks to the grill, bone side down and positioned over the foil pan, and cook over **roasting/indirect low heat** for about 10 minutes until the sauce has set into the meat. Just before serving, lightly brush with another layer of sauce. Cut the racks into individual ribs and serve warm.

PB AND J RIBS

SERVES: 6–8 | **PREP TIME:** 30 MINUTES | **COOKING TIME:** ABOUT 3 HOURS
SPECIAL EQUIPMENT: WATER SMOKER, 4 LARGE HANDFULS APPLE/CHERRY WOOD CHUNKS

The ideas behind my recipes sometimes come from scattered experiences in my past. Here is one example. Long before I was a cookbook author, I was a young schoolteacher in San Francisco with so many classes to manage and papers to grade that I often missed lunch. I kept a loaf of bread along with jars of peanut butter and jelly in my desk to make sandwiches I could wolf down while covering recess. As unsophisticated as those sandwiches were, they sustained me through unpredictable days trying to steer a rowdy group of adolescents. Later I taught at a school in Jakarta, Indonesia, where I was amazed by myriad ways of making peanut dipping sauces for skewered meats and seafood called satay. Maybe peanut butter doesn't have to be so childish after all, I thought.

Those taste memories have stayed with me through my career in barbecue. As I was working on this book, I was searching for ways of presenting familiar foods in unexpected ways. I hit on this: synthesising pieces of my childhood and early adulthood with my relatively new fascination with barbecue. Does it work? I think so. The raspberry glaze is reminiscent of the fruity sweetness in some barbecue sauces today, taking the edge off the spiciness in the dry rub, and the salty, creamy qualities of the peanut sauce add however much nutty richness you feel like spreading on top. At the very least the recipe is a good example of how barbecue continues to evolve. Sometimes as cooks we look to the past for something new.

RUB
2 tablespoons mild chilli powder
2 tablespoons paprika
2 tablespoons light brown sugar
1 tablespoon onion flakes
1 tablespoon sea salt
1 tablespoon freshly ground
    black pepper

4 racks baby back ribs, each
    1.1–1.4kg/2½–3lb

GLAZE
250ml/8fl oz raspberry jam
125ml/4fl oz unsweetened apple juice
2 tablespoons balsamic vinegar

SAUCE
250g/9oz creamy peanut butter
175–250ml/6–8fl oz unsweetened apple juice
2 tablespoons cider vinegar

1   Mix the rub ingredients. Using a blunt knife, slide the tip under the membrane in the middle of the back of each rack of ribs. Lift and pull off each membrane (see how-to, page 73). Season the racks evenly with the rub, putting more of the rub on the meaty side. Allow the racks to stand at room temperature while you prepare the smoker.

2   Prepare the smoker for indirect cooking with very low heat (130–150°C/ 250–300°F), filling the water pan half to three-quarters full with water.

3   Add the wood chunks to the charcoal and close the lid. When smoke appears, place the racks, bone side down, over ***roasting/ indirect very low heat***. Put the lid on the smoker, and then close the top vent about halfway. Cook the racks for 2½ hours, maintaining the temperature of the smoker between 130 and 150°C/250 and 300°F. Meanwhile, make the glaze and sauce.

4   In a saucepan, mix the glaze ingredients. Bring to a simmer over a medium heat and cook for 3–5 minutes, stirring occasionally. Remove from the heat.

5   In another saucepan, combine the peanut butter, 125ml/4fl oz of the apple juice and the vinegar. Heat slowly for about 2 minutes over a medium heat until the sauce is smooth, whisking constantly. Remove from the heat.

6   After 2½ hours, lightly brush the racks on both sides with the glaze. Continue to cook for 30 minutes more.

7   After 3 hours total cooking time, the meat will have shrunk back from most of the bones by 5mm/¼ inch or more. If it has not, continue cooking until it does. They are done when you lift a rack at one end with tongs, bone side up, and the rack bends so much in the middle that the meat tears easily. If the meat does not tear easily, continue to cook until it does. Another way to test for doneness is to push two adjacent rib bones in opposite directions. When the racks are fully cooked, the meat between the bones should tear easily (but should not be mushy either).

8   Return the saucepan with the peanut sauce to a medium heat. Add 60–125ml/2–4fl oz of the remaining apple juice and warm for a few minutes, stirring occasionally. Lightly brush the racks with more glaze, and then cut the racks into individual ribs. Serve warm with the peanut sauce.

NOUVEAU 'CUE
RIBS

12 BONES

The folks at 12 Bones Smokehouse (Asheville, NC) are famous for their wild ways with ribs. The flavour combinations change daily and are posted on a chalkboard next to the counter, and they always include a few conservative preparations like plain brown sugar or Memphis-style dry rub. The real draws, though, are the edgier offerings like sweet butterscotch or extra-hot pineapple habanero. 12 Bones has earned the most notoriety for their blueberry-chipotle ribs, which have a sweet, fruity hit upon first bite and a mellow, smoky heat that shines through underneath – a totally unexpected but delightful combination.

SOUTHERN STYLE

DEEP IN THE SOUTH, WHERE TRADITIONS RUN WIDE AND DEEP, BARBECUED RIBS HAVE BEEN COOKED THE SAME WAY FOR GENERATIONS. MANY PIT MASTERS SEASON THEIRS WITH NOTHING MORE THAN SALT AND PEPPER, ALLOWING THE SMOKE OF THE PIT TO PLAY A LEADING ROLE. OTHERS START WITH A PAPRIKA- AND SPICE-LACED RUB OR FINISH THEIR RACKS WITH A SWEET, TANGY BARBECUE SAUCE. DINERS CAN CHOOSE BETWEEN 'DRY' (NO SAUCE) OR 'WET' (PLENTY OF SAUCE) RIBS, BUT THE TASTE OF THE MEAT IS FAMILIAR TO ANYONE WHO HAS EATEN SOUTHERN-STYLE BARBECUE.

THESE DAYS, THOUGH, MORE AND MORE COOKS ARE STARTING TO LOOK AT THESE BIG SLABS OF BONE AND MEAT AS PLATFORMS FOR EXPERIMENTATION. THESE SO-CALLED 'NOUVEAU 'CUE' PIT MASTERS – COOKS WHO TAKE THEIR CRAFT SERIOUSLY BUT DON'T FEEL PARTICULARLY CONSTRAINED BY TRADITIONAL RECIPES AND STYLES – ARE BRINGING A NEW BOLD SET OF IDEAS.

HEIRLOOM MARKET BBQ
ATLANTA, GA

At Heirloom Market BBq (Atlanta, GA), Southern barbecue classics get fused with spicy Korean flavours, reflecting the backgrounds of co-owners Cody Taylor, a self-described 'hillbilly chef,' and Jiyeon Lee, a former South Korean pop star who moved to the United States to pursue a culinary career. They smear their ribs with gochujang hot pepper paste, and then coat them with a sweet Georgia-style dry rub that's laced with paprika, garlic, onion and – for a little kick – Korean chilli flakes. If you like, you can even top those ribs with a Korean 'sweet heat' barbecue sauce, which has a base of gochujang paste blended with lemon-lime soda.

SOUTHERN SOUL BARBEQUE
St Simons Island, Georgia

Sweet heat is also the order of the day at Southern Soul Barbeque (St Simons Island, GA), and co-owner and pit master Harrison Sapp doesn't feel hemmed in by old Georgia standards. A self-taught cook, he sprinkles his St Louis-cut ribs with a sugar-laced rub. Midway through, he takes them off the pit, drizzles them with tupelo honey and rubs on a generous layer of brown sugar.

After a few more hours in the smoke, the ribs are finished on a hot grill with a little more honey, resulting in beautiful, mahogany-hued slabs with an almost candy-like crust. That sweetness is complemented nicely by the restaurant's Hot Georgia Soul Sauce laced with Sriracha. Who knew that one of Thailand's trendiest sauces would find a welcome home on the coast of Georgia.

PORK RIBS AREN'T THE ONLY RIBS GETTING A TWIST. BEEF IS THE STAR OF THE SHOW IN TEXAS, AND AT THE GRANARY 'CUE & BREW (SAN ANTONIO, TX), THE BEEF RIBS GET A TREATMENT MORE OFTEN ASSOCIATED WITH NEW YORK DELIS THAN TEXAS BARBECUE JOINTS. TO START, A FULL SHORT RIB PLATE IS BRINED WITH PASTRAMI SPICES, AND THEN SMOKED AND TRIMMED DOWN TO INDIVIDUAL RIBS. BY DAY, THE SHORT RIB PASTRAMI IS SERVED ON PAPER-LINED TRAYS WITH PICKLES AND A DRAMATIC SMEAR OF YELLOW BEER MUSTARD. AT NIGHT IT GETS THE WHITE-PLATE TREATMENT COMPLETE WITH SAUERKRAUT AIOLI AND MICRO-GREEN GARNISH. IT'S A DARING BLEND OF TRADITIONAL BARBECUE AND CONTEMPORARY FLAVOURS AND A SHINING EXAMPLE OF HOW RIBS CAN BE A SPRINGBOARD FOR BARBECUE INNOVATION.

LESSONS FROM THE LEGENDS
SPARERIBS

If Webster published a dictionary of American barbecue, you would find Mike Mills listed first under the definition of legend. In the early 1990s his Apple City Barbecue team won a jaw-dropping 32 Grand Championships. The team retired in 1994 after their fourth World Championship and third Grand World Championship at Memphis in May. They also won the Grand Championship at the Jack Daniel's World Invitational Barbecue Cooking Contest in 1992.

Today Mills oversees 17th Street Barbecue, with two locations in southern Illinois, and two versions of the restaurant in Las Vegas. He is a partner in Blue Smoke, a pioneer of upscale urban barbecue in New York City, and, with his daughter, Amy, he has a bestselling cookbook and a consulting company for the barbecue industry.

I asked Mike for his long perspective about the barbecue world today. 'I've seen it evolve from a hole in the ground or a shack in the back to fancy restaurants with today's motorised stainless-steel pits. I've watched many regional styles merge and evolve into something else entirely. . . I think that overall the quality of barbecue today is better than it has ever been, but some places have lost their way. Trying to be so different, they lost some of that old-time flavour. I think barbecue should be about the meat. Nowadays, seasonings and sauces get too much of the attention. I don't care for all those thick, sweet sauces that sit on top of meat like toothpaste.'

THE HOLLYWOOD CUT

In barbecue competitions, one way to impress the judges is to give them as much meat as possible on each rib. To do this at home, sacrifice and discard every other bone so that each bone you serve has twice as much meat as usual.

TRIMMING

A full rack of spareribs has 13 ribs holding together meat that is tougher and fattier than what you get on baby back ribs. Weighing 2.3–2.7kg/ 5–6lb, the rack includes a flap of meat (called the 'skirt') hanging off the middle of the bone side and also a triangular section (called the 'point') at one end. To make the St Louis-style cut, trim off both of those chewy sections, and then remove the cartilaginous section of meat (the 'rib tips') that extends below the bones. Find the joint just below the longest rib at one end. Cut through that joint with a sharp, heavy knife and a lot of pressure, and run your knife under the bottom of the bones, creating a straight-sided rectangle weighing 1.4–1.8kg/3–4lb. Now peel off the membrane clinging to the bones and trim off the obvious areas of silver skin and excess fat.

ALOHA SPARERIBS
WITH COCONUT-GINGER GLAZE

SERVES: 4-6 | **PREP TIME:** 20 MINUTES | **GRILLING TIME:** 2¼-2½ HOURS | **SPECIAL EQUIPMENT:** 3 LARGE HANDFULS APPLE, CHERRY OR HICKORY WOOD CHIPS; GAS GRILL WITH AT LEAST 3 BURNERS; METAL SMOKER BOX

Easy does it. That's the right mantra some days. It doesn't get much easier than barbecuing ribs on a gas grill that can hold temperatures steady for as long as you like.

If you have a smoker box, great. Before you fire up the grill, fill the box with soaked and drained wood chips, and then set the box under the cooking grate, right over a burner or two, so the chips will smoke easily.

RUB
2 tablespoons curry powder
2 teaspoons garlic granules
2 teaspoons onion flakes
2 teaspoons paprika
2 teaspoons sea salt
2 teaspoons freshly ground
   black pepper

2 racks St Louis-style spareribs (see page 83), each 1.1–1.4kg/2½–3lb

GLAZE
1 tablespoon toasted sesame oil
1 tablespoon peeled, grated
   fresh ginger
1 teaspoon crushed chilli flakes
250ml/8fl oz unsweetened coconut
   milk, stirred
4 tablespoons soy sauce
2 tablespoons light brown sugar
Grated zest and juice of 1 lime

1. Soak the wood chips in water for at least 30 minutes.

2. Combine the rub ingredients. Season the racks all over with the rub, putting more on the meaty side. Refrigerate the racks until ready to grill.

3. In a saucepan, combine the oil, ginger and chilli flakes. Warm over a medium heat just until the ginger sizzles, about 30 seconds, stirring once or twice (do not burn the oil or it will be bitter). Add the remaining glaze ingredients, mix well and bring to a simmer. Simmer for about 3 minutes. Remove the saucepan from the heat.

For this recipe, don't even bother with peeling the membrane off the ribs. The membrane on spareribs is not as tough as it is on baby back ribs. Just season the ribs with a mellow mix of spices and let them cook in the aromatic smoke. After about an hour, baste them with a coconut-ginger glaze that keeps them moist and evokes a Hawaiian holiday.

4   Before lighting the gas grill, drain and add
the wood chips to a metal smoker box. Set
the smoker box under the cooking grate
and over a burner on one side of the grill.
Prepare the grill for indirect cooking over
high heat (230–290°C/450–550°F), heating
the wood chips in the smoker box. When the
wood begins to smoke, lower the temperature
of the grill to low heat, as close to 150°C/300°F
as possible.

5   Lay the racks, bone side down and flat,
on the cooking grates over *roasting/indirect
low heat*. Close the lid and cook for 1 hour,
maintaining the temperature of the grill as close
to 150°C/300°F as possible. You may need
to turn off one of the burners temporarily,
especially on hot days. The wood chips should
smoke for about 30 minutes. If they catch
fire, spray a little water over the smoker box.

6   After the first hour of cooking, baste the
racks on both sides with glaze and swap
their positions for even cooking. Continue
cooking, bone side down, over *roasting/
indirect low heat* for 1 hour more, basting
the racks on both sides every 30 minutes.

7   Now that the racks have cooked for 2 hours
at 150°C/300°F they should be close to
done. They are completely done when you lift
a rack at one end with tongs, bone side up,
and the rack bends so much in the middle
that the meat begins to tear easily. This
may take 15–30 minutes more.

8   Remove the racks from the grill, allow to rest
for 5–10 minutes and then cut between the
bones into individual ribs. Serve warm.

ROTISSERIE SPARERIBS
WITH ROOT BEER-BOURBON GLAZE

SERVES: 4–6 | **PREP TIME:** 30 MINUTES | **GRILLING TIME:** 2–2½ HOURS
SPECIAL EQUIPMENT: 2 LARGE HANDFULS PECAN, APPLE OR HICKORY WOOD CHIPS;
ROTISSERIE; LARGE DISPOSABLE FOIL TRAY

Ribs on the rotisserie? You bet! The rotisserie works wonders when you are cooking just one or two racks. The even heat and slow rotation of the ribs allow for a nice crust on the outside and tender, moist meat within. The key is to skewer the ribs in an 'S' shape that exposes as much meat as possible to the circulating heat. Use a ring of aluminium foil in the centre to keep a space between the racks so they develop as much crust as possible and so it is easier to brush on the sticky glaze.

RUB
2 tablespoons light brown sugar
1 tablespoon sea salt
1 tablespoon mild chilli powder
2 teaspoons paprika
1 teaspoon garlic powder
1 teaspoon ground cumin
1 teaspoon freshly ground black pepper
½ teaspoon ground allspice
½ teaspoon mustard powder

2 racks St Louis-style spareribs (see page 83), each each 1.4–1.5kg/ 3–3½lb

GLAZE
500ml/18fl oz root beer (not diet)
250ml/8fl oz bourbon
75g/3oz packed light brown sugar
1 cinnamon stick
1 bay leaf
4 tablespoons cider vinegar
1 teaspoon vanilla extract
½ teaspoon sea salt
1 tablespoon grated orange zest
½ teaspoon hot pepper sauce

1 large orange, cut into wedges

1   Soak the wood chips in water for at least 30 minutes.

2   Combine the rub ingredients. Using a blunt knife, slide the tip under the membrane covering the back of each rack of ribs. Lift and loosen the membrane until you can prise it up, then grab a corner of it with kitchen paper and pull it off. Season the racks all over with the rub, putting more of it on the meaty side. Allow the racks to stand at room temperature for 1 hour before grilling.

3   Prepare the grill for indirect cooking over medium-low heat (about 150°C/300°F). Place a large disposable foil tray in the centre of the charcoal grate between the two piles of charcoal or in the middle of the cooking grates of a gas grill.

4   In a saucepan over a medium-high heat, bring the root beer, bourbon, brown sugar, cinnamon stick, bay leaf, vinegar, vanilla extract and salt to the boil. Cook for 20–25 minutes until the mixture is reduced to about 125ml/4fl oz, stirring occasionally. Remove from the heat, discard the cinnamon stick and bay leaf, and stir in the orange zest and hot sauce.

5   Place one pronged fork on to the rotisserie spit with the tines facing inward, about 25cm/10 inches from the end of the spit. Secure the fork, but do not tighten it yet. Thread one rack of ribs on to the spit in an 'S' shape by pushing the pointed end through the meat every three or four ribs and making sure that one end is secured by the tines of the fork. Form a thin snake out of foil and wrap it into a ring around the spit where the two racks will come together to prevent them from leaning against each other as they cook. Thread the second rack onto the spit in an 'S' shape like the first one, and then slide the second pronged fork on to the spit with the tines facing inward. Push the fork through the rack and secure it, but don't tighten it yet. Wearing insulated barbecue mitts or oven gloves, place the pointed end of the spit into the rotisserie motor. If necessary, adjust the racks so that they are centred on the spit over the foil tray. Tighten the forks.

6   Drain and add half of the wood chips to the charcoal or to the smoker box of a gas grill, following the manufacturer's instructions, and close the lid. Turn on the rotisserie motor and cook the racks over *roasting/indirect medium-low heat* for

1 hour, maintaining the temperature of the grill as close to 150°C/300°F as possible. Drain and add the remaining handful of wood chips to the charcoal or smoker box, and continue cooking until the meat starts to shrink away from the ends of the bones, about 45 minutes. Brush the racks with half of the glaze and continue to cook and glaze until the meat has shrunk back from the ends of most of the bones by 1cm/½ inch or more, about 15 minutes. At this point, check to see if the ribs are done. If the ribs are not done, glaze them and continue cooking for another 15–30 minutes.

7   Turn off the rotisserie motor and, wearing insulated barbecue mitts or oven gloves, carefully remove the spit from the grill. Gently loosen the forks and slide the ribs off the spit. Transfer to a chopping board, brush the remaining glaze on both sides, cover loosely with foil, and allow to rest for 10 minutes. Cut the racks between the bones into individual ribs, and squeeze the orange wedges over the ribs. Serve immediately.

CHERRY-SMOKED SPARERIBS
WITH CRANBERRY-GINGER BARBECUE SAUCE

SERVES: 6–8 | **PREP TIME:** 30 MINUTES | **COOKING TIME:** ABOUT 3½ HOURS | **SPECIAL EQUIPMENT:** WATER SMOKER, 2 LARGE HANDFULS CHERRY WOOD CHUNKS, 2 LARGE HANDFULS PECAN WOOD CHUNKS, SPRAY BOTTLE, HEAVY-DUTY ALUMINIUM FOIL

Awesome spareribs call for a series of coordinated and interdependent steps that add up to more than the sum of their parts. First you buy thick meaty ribs and slather them with a thin coat of mustard to help the spice rub hold on. The rub in this case is based on demerara sugar, which I like because it is sweet but not easily burnt. You then smoke the racks with pecan and cherry wood for two hours. The pecan is used mostly for its nutty flavour, and the cherry is used mostly for the dark colour it creates in the ribs. Next you spray the ribs with apple juice, re-season them with the rub and wrap them in foil to cook in their juices during the final 1½ hours on the smoker. When they are fully cooked, you brush them with a glistening sauce – in this case, something a bit unusual that initially tastes sweet and then finishes with a tinge of ginger. It may not be as unusual as the blueberry-chipotle sauce that pit masters serve at the wildly popular 12 Bones Smokehouse in Asheville, North Carolina, but it is a sure sign of new and evolving American barbecue sauces.

RUB
4 tablespoons demerara sugar
2 tablespoons paprika
2 tablespoons mild chilli powder
4 teaspoons onion flakes
4 teaspoons sea salt
2 teaspoons ground ginger
2 teaspoons freshly ground black pepper

125ml/4fl oz prepared mustard
4 racks meaty spareribs, each
    about 1.4kg/3lb, membrane removed

SAUCE
250ml/8fl oz tomato ketchup
250ml/8fl oz cranberry jelly
125ml/4fl oz unsweetened apple juice
75ml/3fl oz cider vinegar
115g/4oz honey
2 tablespoons black treacle
1 tablespoon Worcestershire sauce
1 teaspoon mild chilli powder
1 teaspoon ground ginger
¼ teaspoon freshly ground black pepper

125ml/4fl oz unsweetened apple juice
Sea salt (optional)

1   In a small bowl, mix the rub ingredients. Reserve 3 tablespoons of the rub for seasoning the racks later. Spread the mustard evenly over both sides of the racks. Use the rub in the small bowl to season the racks on both sides, especially the meaty side. Allow the racks to stand at room temperature while you prepare the smoker.

2   Prepare the smoker for indirect cooking with very low heat (130–140°C/250–275°F). Fill the water pan half to three-quarters full with water.

3   Add half of the wood chunks to the charcoal. When smoke appears, place two racks on the bottom cooking grate and two racks on the top cooking grate, bone side down. Cook over *roasting/indirect very low heat*, with the lid closed, for 1 hour. After 1 hour, add the remaining wood chunks to the charcoal. Cook for 1 hour more. Meanwhile, prepare the sauce.

4   In a small saucepan, whisk the sauce ingredients. Bring to a simmer over a medium heat and cook for about 5 minutes until slightly thickened, stirring occasionally. Remove from the heat.

5   Pour the apple juice into a spray bottle. Cut four long sheets of heavy-duty aluminium foil, each about 120cm/4ft long.

6   After 2 hours of cooking (when the colour of the racks is dark brown), remove the racks from the smoker. Lay each rack on one end of a sheet of foil, spray both sides with apple juice, and season with the reserved rub. Fold over the other end of each sheet of foil to enclose the rack and seal the ends on all sides to trap the steam.

7   Return the wrapped racks to the smoker and cook, bone side up, over *roasting/indirect very low heat*, with the lid closed, for about 1 hour.

8   Remove the racks from the smoker and take them out of the foil. Discard the foil. Brush the racks evenly on both sides with some of the sauce, return to the smoker, and cook bone side down, over *roasting/indirect very low heat* for 15–30 minutes until the sauce has cooked into the meat a bit. To check for doneness, slide a cocktail stick into the meat between the bones. It should slip in and out with little resistance.

9   Just before serving, lightly brush the racks with sauce. Cut the racks into individual ribs (Hollywood style, if you wish, see page 82) and serve warm with any extra sauce on the side. If liked, as a final step, season the meaty side of the ribs with a little bit of salt to boost the flavours.

DONENESS

With spareribs, get them tender but not too tender. When you slide a sharp cocktail stick through the meat between the bones, it should move in and out easily; however, if you pull the bones apart, some meat should still cling to the bones. If all the meat slips off the bones, the ribs are overcooked.

BARBECUED CHAR SIU

SERVES: 6 | **PREP TIME:** 15 MINUTES | **MARINATING TIME:** 24–48 HOURS | **GRILLING TIME:** 45 MINUTES–1 HOUR
SPECIAL EQUIPMENT: CHARCOAL GRILL, 2 LARGE HANDFULS APPLE OR CHERRY WOOD CHIPS, INSTANT-READ THERMOMETER

MARINADE
125ml/4fl oz hoisin sauce
125ml/4fl oz bourbon
4 tablespoons soy sauce
4 tablespoons honey
2 tablespoons toasted sesame oil
2 tablespoons peeled, grated
   fresh ginger
1 tablespoon crushed garlic
2 teaspoons Chinese five spice
½ teaspoon ground white pepper

1 boneless pork loin joint, about
   1.4kg/3lb
Ramen (optional)
Sliced spring onions (optional)

In Chinatown neighbourhoods all over America, the enticing aroma of char siu – or Cantonese roasted pork – wafts down the narrow streets from the old-school restaurants, some of them still using charcoal for the way the wood aromas mingle with the flavours of a sweet and salty marinade. Thin slices of char siu are wonderful in a bowl of ramen.

1   In a large bowl, whisk the marinade ingredients. Pour off and reserve 125ml/ 4fl oz of the marinade for basting the roast. Place the meat in a large, resealable plastic bag and pour in the remaining marinade. Press the air out of the bag and seal tightly. Turn the bag to distribute the marinade, place in a bowl and refrigerate for at least 24 hours or up to 48 hours, turning occasionally.

2   Remove the meat from the bag and discard the marinade in the bag. Allow the joint to stand at room temperature for 30 minutes before grilling.

3   Soak the wood chips in water for at least 30 minutes.

4   Prepare the charcoal grill for indirect cooking over medium heat (180–230°C/ 350–450°F).

5   Drain and add the wood chips to the charcoal. Grill the pork over **roasting/ indirect medium heat** for 45 minutes–1 hour, with the lid closed, until an instant-read thermometer inserted into the centre of the meat registers 65°C/150°F, basting occasionally with the reserved marinade. Do not baste during the final 15 minutes of cooking time. Remove from the grill and allow to rest for 10 minutes (the internal temperature will rise 5–10 degrees during this time). Cut into 5-mm/¼-inch-thick slices. Serve warm with ramen and sliced spring onions, if liked.

The outside of the meat will develop a lovely, savoury crust thanks to the marinade of hoisin sauce, bourbon, soy sauce and honey. In restaurants, char siu is often much redder in colour, not from smoke but from red food colouring. Let the meat rest properly before you slice into it. If you see steam coming off the slices, let the meat rest longer; the steam is moisture you are losing.

PORK LOIN SPIEDIES

SERVES: 6 | **PREP TIME:** 10 MINUTES | **MARINATING TIME:** 2 HOURS | **GRILLING TIME:** 9–11 MINUTES
SPECIAL EQUIPMENT: 6 LONG BAMBOO SKEWERS, 1 LARGE HANDFUL HICKORY WOOD CHIPS, INSTANT-READ THERMOMETER

MARINADE

250ml/8fl oz extra-virgin olive oil
4 tablespoons red wine vinegar
4 tablespoons fresh lemon juice
4 tablespoons finely chopped mint
4 tablespoons finely chopped flat-leaf
　　parsley
2 tablespoons finely chopped dill
2 teaspoons crushed garlic
2 teaspoons sea salt
1½ teaspoons fennel seeds
½ teaspoon freshly ground black
　　pepper

675g/1½lb trimmed pork loin, cut into
　　4-cm/1½-inch chunks
6 Italian or French sandwich rolls,
　　cut lengthways in half but not all
　　the way through

A spiedie is a type of submarine sandwich hailing from Binghamton, New York, and now enjoyed across the central part of the state. Cubes of meat are marinated with a combination of Italian seasonings and mint, and then cooked and arranged, skewer and all, in a long roll or slice of Italian bread without much more fuss or fandango. Have a big bag of potato crisps on hand!

1　In a large bowl, whisk the marinade ingredients. Reserve 6 tablespoons of the marinade to drizzle over the cooked pork. Place the pork chunks in the large bowl with the remaining marinade, cover and refrigerate for 2 hours, stirring once.

2　Soak the skewers and wood chips (separately) in water for at least 30 minutes.

3　Prepare the grill for direct cooking over medium heat (180–230°C/350–450°F).

4　Thread the pork cubes on to the skewers. Discard the marinade. Drain and add the wood chips to the charcoal or to the smoker box of a gas grill, following manufacturer's instructions, and close the lid. When smoke appears, grill the skewers over **grilling/direct medium heat** for 9–11 minutes, with the lid closed, until the meat is evenly seared and cooked to an internal temperature of 63°C/145°F, turning occasionally. During the last minute of grilling time, toast the rolls, cut side down, over **grilling/direct heat**.

5　To serve this dish in its authentic style, place a skewer on each roll and, using the roll to grasp the meat, twist and pull out the skewer, leaving the pork cubes in a neat line right down the middle of the roll. Drizzle each spiedie with 1 tablespoon of the reserved marinade and serve straightaway.

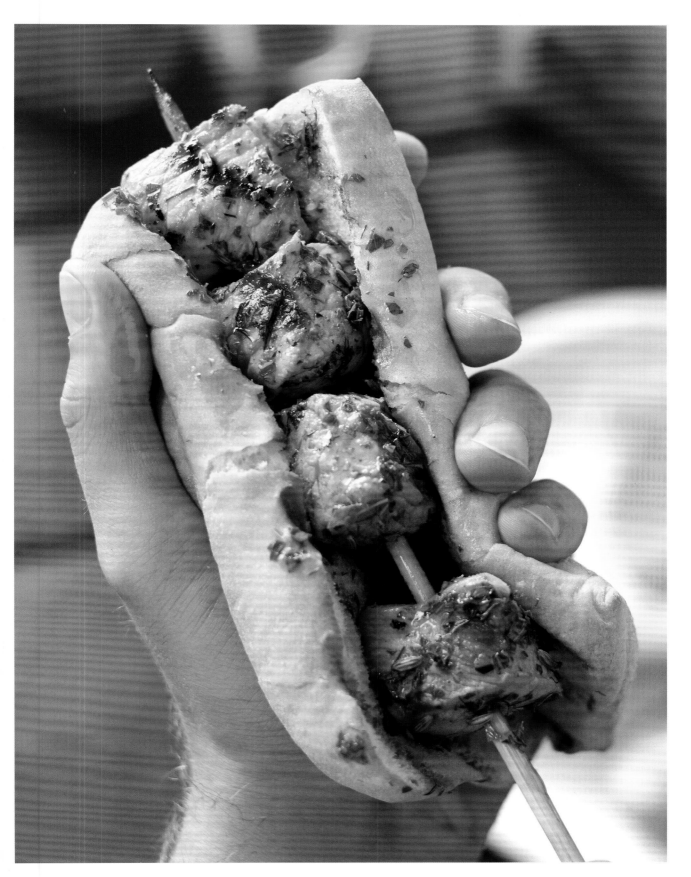

PORK LOIN SANDWICHES
WITH GREEN CHILLIES, GRUYÈRE AND GRILLED ONIONS

SERVES: 4 | **PREP TIME:** 20 MINUTES | **MARINATING TIME:** 30–45 MINUTES | **GRILLING TIME:** 10–12 MINUTES
SPECIAL EQUIPMENT: 1 LARGE HANDFUL CHERRY WOOD CHIPS, CAST-IRON FRYING PAN OR GRILL PRESS

MARINADE

4 tablespoons extra-virgin olive oil
2 tablespoons cider vinegar
1 teaspoon mild chilli powder
¾ teaspoon sea salt
¼ teaspoon freshly ground black
   pepper
¼ teaspoon garlic powder

4 boneless pork loin chops, each
   115–140g/4–5oz and about 1cm/
   ½ inch thick
125ml/4fl oz mayonnaise
3 tablespoons shop-bought
   barbecue sauce
1 red onion, about 225g/8oz, cut into
   4 slices, each about 8mm/
   ⅓ inch thick
4 crusty rolls, split
8 thin slices Gruyère cheese
200-g/7-oz can whole mild green
   chillies, drained, opened flat and
   seeds removed

There seems to be no end to the growing popularity of pressed sandwiches, including Cubans and panini. Here is a new version that stacks smoked pork with grilled onions, cheese and chillies. If you like, you could add some whole coriander leaves in there. You could also use pickled jalapeño slices instead of the milder green chillies. I like ciabatta rolls for this recipe; they have a nice crust and enough density to stand up to all the meaty juices.

1 Soak the wood chips in water for at least 30 minutes.

2 In a bow, combine the marinade ingredients. Place the pork chops in the marinade, turn to coat evenly and allow to stand at room temperature for 30–45 minutes.

3 Prepare the grill for direct and indirect cooking over medium heat (180–230°C/350–450°F).

4 Mix the mayonnaise and barbecue sauce. Set aside until ready to use.

5 Drain and add the wood chips to the charcoal or to the smoker box of a gas grill, following the manufacturer's instructions, and close the lid. When smoke appears, grill the chops and onion slices over **grilling/direct medium heat** for 6–8 minutes, with the lid closed, until the chops are almost fully cooked and the onions are charred, turning once or twice. Remove from the grill.

6 Spread the cut side of the rolls with the mayonnaise mixture. Place the bottom halves of the rolls on a baking sheet and top each with 1 cheese slice, 1 pork chop, 1 onion slice that has been separated into rings, 1 green chilli, another slice of cheese and the top half of the roll. Press the top of the roll firmly with your hand to compress the sandwich (try not to break the bread).

7 Place the sandwiches over **roasting/indirect medium heat** and, using a spatula, cast-iron frying pan or grill press, press them down, one at a time. Close the lid and grill for 2 minutes. Turn the sandwiches over, press them down again, close the lid and grill until the bread is toasted and the cheese is melted, about 2 minutes more. Remove the sandwiches from the grill, wrap each in baking parchment, cut in half and skewer with cocktail sticks, if liked. Serve immediately.

Use your hand to press the sandwiches before they go on the grill, and then press them again into the hot cooking grate using a spatula, cast-iron frying pan or a heavy grill press like the one shown here.

ROSEMARY-LEMON PORK CHOPS
WITH EMBER-SMOKED BUTTER

SERVES: 4 | **PREP TIME:** 25 MINUTES | **MARINATING TIME:** 2–4 HOURS | **GRILLING TIME:** 6–8 MINUTES
CHILLING TIME: ABOUT 1 HOUR | **SPECIAL EQUIPMENT:** CHARCOAL GRILL, ALL-NATURAL LUMP CHARCOAL

MARINADE

4 tablespoons extra-virgin olive oil
Grated zest and juice of 1 lemon
2 tablespoons finely chopped
    rosemary leaves
1 tablespoon Dijon mustard
1 tablespoon crushed garlic

Sea salt
Freshly ground black pepper
4 boneless or bone-in pork chops,
    each about 225g/8oz and 2.5cm/
    1 inch thick

BUTTER

75g/3oz unsalted butter, softened
Grated zest of 1 lemon
2 teaspoons finely chopped rosemary
    leaves
1 teaspoon Dijon mustard
1 teaspoon crushed garlic

It's time to play with fire. The idea of setting a charcoal ember on a slice of seasoned butter right before serving the marinated pork chops is much more than a show-stopping scene. Yes, the butter will smoke viciously and melt over the sides of the chops. Yes, your guests will gasp with delight. But the real excitement is in the flavour that the infused butter adds to the chops. Of course, you should only use 100% natural lump charcoal for this technique.

1   Mix the marinade ingredients, including 1¼ teaspoons salt and ½ teaspoon pepper. Coat the pork chops on all sides with the marinade, place in a bowl, cover and refrigerate for 2–4 hours. Meanwhile, make the butter.

2   In a bowl, mash the butter ingredients, including ½ teaspoon salt and ¼ teaspoon pepper, with the back of a fork. Form the mixture into a log, 7.5–10cm/3–4 inches long. Set the log in the bowl, cover and refrigerate for at least 1 hour.

3   Prepare the charcoal grill with all-natural lump charcoal for direct cooking over medium-high heat (200–230°C/ 400–450°F).

4   Lift the pork chops from the bowl, allowing the excess marinade to drip off, and discard the marinade. Grill the chops over **grilling/ direct medium-high heat** for 6–8 minutes, with the lid closed, until still slightly pink in the centre, turning once. Transfer to a metal tray and allow to rest for 3–5 minutes. Cut the butter lengthways into four long pieces and set each one on top of a pork chop. Using long-handled tongs, lift a large ember, about the size of an orange, from the bed of charcoal and very carefully set the burning ember on top of each piece of butter for 1–2 seconds. The butter will smoke and melt. Return the burning ember to the grill. Serve the pork chops straightaway.

PORK CHOPS
WITH SWEET SOY GLAZE AND SPRING ONION-SESAME RICE

SERVES: 6 | **PREP TIME:** 15 MINUTES
MARINATING TIME: 30 MINUTES | **GRILLING TIME:** ABOUT 8 MINUTES

MARINADE

2 tablespoons soy sauce
2 tablespoons rice wine, dry sherry or
    lemon juice
2 tablespoons water
½ teaspoon hot chilli-garlic sauce,
    such as Sriracha

6 boneless pork loin chops, each about
    140g/5oz and 2cm/¾ inch thick

GLAZE

2 tablespoons soy sauce
1 tablespoon honey
1 tablespoon tomato ketchup
1 tablespoon rice wine, dry sherry or
    lemon juice
2 teaspoons hoisin sauce
½ teaspoon hot chilli-garlic sauce,
    such as Sriracha
¼ teaspoon Chinese five spice
⅛ teaspoon garlic granules
⅛ teaspoon onion powder

2 teaspoons sesame seeds
500ml/18fl oz water
200g/7oz long-grain rice
Sea salt
Vegetable oil
½ teaspoon freshly ground black
    pepper
2 spring onions, white and light green
    parts finely chopped, dark green
    tops thinly sliced

This recipe emerges from ancient traditions of Korean barbecue, where marinades and glazes are often used together for flavours that are big, bold and complex, yet so quick and simple to execute. Grilled over charcoal, this is Asian-American barbecue in minutes.

1   Prepare the grill for direct cooking over medium heat (180–230°C/350–450°F).

2   Whisk the marinade ingredients. Place the pork chops in a large, resealable plastic bag and pour in the marinade. Press the air out of the bag and seal tightly. Turn the bag to distribute the marinade, and set aside at room temperature for 30 minutes, turning the bag once or twice.

3   Combine the glaze ingredients. Reserve half of the glaze to use on the grilled chops.

4   Meanwhile, heat a saucepan over a medium heat on the hob. Add the sesame seeds and toast for 2–3 minutes until light golden, stirring often. Transfer the seeds to a plate. Add the water, rice and ½ teaspoon salt to the same saucepan and bring to the boil over a high heat. Reduce the heat to low, cover tightly and cook for 15–18 minutes until the rice is tender and the liquid is absorbed.

Remove from the heat and set the covered saucepan aside. The rice will stay warm for 15 minutes.

5   Remove the chops from the bag, shaking off the excess marinade. Discard the marinade. Generously brush the chops on both sides with oil, season evenly with ¾ teaspoon salt and the pepper, and then grill over *grilling/direct medium heat* for about 6 minutes, with the lid closed, until browned on both sides, turning once. Brush the tops of the chops with the glaze and continue grilling, with the lid closed, until the meat is still slightly pink in the centre, about 2 minutes more. Remove from the grill.

6   Stir the white and light green parts of the spring onions and the sesame seeds into the rice, fluffing with a fork. Spoon the reserved glaze over the pork chops and top with the dark green spring onion tops. Serve warm.

SMOKED PORK FILLET
WITH BLACKBERRY-SAGE SAUCE

SERVES: 6 | PREP TIME: 30 MINUTES | GRILLING TIME: 15–20 MINUTES
SPECIAL EQUIPMENT: 1 SMALL HANDFUL APPLE OR PECAN WOOD CHIPS, INSTANT-READ THERMOMETER

SAUCE

15g/½oz unsalted butter
2 tablespoons finely chopped shallot
340g/12oz blackberries
4 tablespoons honey
2 tablespoons tomato ketchup
2 tablespoons balsamic vinegar
2 teaspoons finely chopped sage
  leaves
1 teaspoon Worcestershire sauce
½ teaspoon freshly ground black
  pepper
⅛ teaspoon sea salt

RUB

2 teaspoons brown sugar
1 teaspoon sea salt
1 teaspoon mustard powder
1 teaspoon paprika
½ teaspoon onion flakes
½ teaspoon garlic granules
½ teaspoon freshly ground black
  pepper

2 pork fillets, each about
  565g/1¼lb trimmed of excess
  fat and silver skin
2 teaspoons rapeseed oil

Vaguely familiar and different at the same time, this recipe works because of the way that smoked pork plays so well with sweet, fruity sauces. What a sauce this one is! I think it's one of the best in the book. You might want to strain out the blackberry seeds from the purée before you mix in the whole blackberries. Don't worry about eating pork that looks a little pink in the middle. Official guidelines consider it safe at 63°C/145°F, when it is still nice and juicy.

1 Soak the wood chips in water for at least 30 minutes.

2 In a small saucepan over a medium heat, melt the butter. Add the shallot and cook for about 2 minutes until lightly browned, stirring often. Add 250g/9oz of the berries, the honey, ketchup, vinegar, sage, Worcestershire sauce, pepper and salt. Bring to the boil, and then reduce the heat to medium-low. Cook the sauce at a steady simmer until the juices have thickened slightly, about 10 minutes, stirring often and mashing some of the berries to release their juice. Remove from the heat. Purée the sauce in a blender (in batches) with a small opening in the lid to let the steam escape, and return to the saucepan. You should have about 250ml/8fl oz of sauce. Stir in the remaining berries. Allow the sauce to cool until tepid and slightly thickened.

3 Combine the rub ingredients, mashing well with a fork to mix thoroughly. Brush the pork fillets with the oil and season evenly with the rub. Allow the meat to stand at room temperature for 15–30 minutes before grilling.

4 Prepare the grill for direct cooking over medium heat (180–230°C/350–450°F).

5 Drain and add the wood chips to the charcoal or to the smoker box of a gas grill, following the manufacturer's instructions, and close the lid. When smoke appears, grill the pork over *grilling/direct medium heat* for 15–20 minutes, with the lid closed, until the outsides are evenly seared and the internal temperature reaches 63°C/145°F, turning every 5 minutes. Remove from the grill and allow to rest for 5 minutes (the internal temperature will rise 5–10 degrees during this time). Cut the fillets crossways into 1-cm/½-inch slices. Serve warm with the sauce.

BACON-WRAPPED PORK FILLET
WITH CIDER-BALSAMIC REDUCTION

SERVES: 8 | **PREP TIME:** 20 MINUTES, PLUS ABOUT 30 MINUTES FOR THE REDUCTION | **GRILLING TIME:** 40–45 MINUTES
SPECIAL EQUIPMENT: 2 LARGE HANDFULS APPLE WOOD CHIPS, LARGE DISPOSABLE FOIL TRAY, INSTANT-READ THERMOMETER

RUB
1 tablespoon brown sugar
1 teaspoon smoked paprika
½ teaspoon mild chilli powder
1 teaspoon sea salt
½ teaspoon freshly ground black
　　pepper

2 pork fillets, each about 565g/
　　1¼lb, trimmed of excess fat
　　and silver skin
450g/1lb streaky bacon

REDUCTION
700ml/1¼ pints apple cider
125ml/4fl oz balsamic vinegar
6 tablespoons black treacle
1 cinnamon stick
⅛ teaspoon ground allspice
175ml/6fl oz heavy whipping cream
Sea salt
Freshly ground black pepper

This recipe is my ode to the pork farmers of Iowa, who produce some exceptionally flavourful meat. I'd like to sit all of them down at one long table that stretches across Iowa pastures and feed them spice-rubbed pork fillet wrapped in blankets of bacon, smoked over apple wood, and served with a sweet and creamy cider reduction. For the easiest wrapping, be sure to use streaky bacon rather than thick-cut.

1　Soak the wood chips in water for at least 30 minutes.

2　Combine the rub ingredients, and then season the meat evenly with the rub.

3　On a work surface, lay out half of the bacon in one layer, with each slice slightly overlapping the next (just barely overlap the bacon so it cooks evenly. You may not need the full quantity of bacon). Place one of the fillets on top of the bacon. The length of the fillet should be perpendicular to the strips of bacon. Roll it up Swiss roll style and when the bacon just overlaps itself going round the pork, use a sharp knife to cut off any extra. Repeat with the remaining bacon and pork fillet. Allow the meat to stand at room temperature for 30 minutes before grilling.

4　Place a large disposable foil tray underneath the cooking grate to catch the bacon drippings. You may have to crumple the foil tray a bit, but that's okay. Or, if you are using a charcoal grill, place the foil tray on the charcoal grate between the two piles of charcoal. Then prepare the grill for indirect cooking over medium heat (180–230°C/350–450°F).

5　Drain and add half of the wood chips to the charcoal or to the smoker box of a gas grill, following the manufacturer's instructions, and close the lid. When smoke appears, cook the fillets, bacon seam side down, over **roasting/indirect medium heat** for 20 minutes, centred over the drip pan, with the lid closed. Turn the fillets over, drain and add the remaining wood chips to the charcoal or smoker box, close the lid and cook for 15 minutes. Turn the meat over again and continue grilling for 5–10 minutes more until an instant-read thermometer inserted into the centre of the meat registers 63°C/145°F. Remove the pork from the grill, tent with foil and allow to rest for 5 minutes (the internal temperature will rise 5–10 degrees during this time).

6　While the pork cooks, prepare the reduction. In a saucepan over a high heat, combine the cider, vinegar, treacle, cinnamon stick and allspice. Bring to the boil and cook for 25–30 minutes until thick enough to coat the back of a spoon. Remove and discard the cinnamon stick. Stir in the cream, season with salt and pepper, and cook for 1 minute more.

7　Cut the pork crossways into slices and serve warm with the reduction.

Cook the cider-balsamic reduction until it is thick enough to coat the back of a spoon. If you swipe a fingertip through the sauce and you see a clean line over the spoon, the sauce is ready. Then it's time to stir in the cream.

DOUBLE-SMOKED HAM
WITH STRAWBERRY-MANGO SALSA

SERVES: 8-10 | PREP TIME: 30 MINUTES | GRILLING TIME: 1¼-2 HOURS
SPECIAL EQUIPMENT: 4 LARGE HANDFULS APPLE, CHERRY OR HICKORY WOOD CHIPS,
2 LARGE DISPOSABLE FOIL TRAYS, INSTANT-READ THERMOMETER

1 bone-in smoked gammon joint, about 3.5kg/7½lb

SALSA

2 mangoes, each about 340g/12oz, peeled and cut into 1-cm/½-inch dice
340g/12oz strawberries, hulled and cut into 1-cm/½-inch dice
2 tablespoons finely chopped spring onion (white and light green parts only)
2 tablespoons fresh lime juice
2 tablespoons finely chopped mint
1½ tablespoons agave nectar or honey
1 tablespoon rice vinegar
1 tablespoon finely chopped jalapeño chilli
1½ teaspoons peeled, finely grated fresh ginger

GLAZE

75ml/3fl oz strawberry jam
2 tablespoons wholegrain mustard

Here is a fairly easy ham recipe that feeds a crowd with juicy, smoked meat and a colourful strawberry and mango salsa with accents of mint, ginger and jalapeño. Try it as a festive main course for an Easter dinner. The quality of gammon is crucial. Avoid any that have been pumped with solutions; the label should make no mention of 'natural juices' or other additives. The knuckle end is fattier (better) than the fillet end and is easier to carve because it has just one straight bone, as opposed to the convoluted pelvic bone of the fillet end.

1   Allow the gammon to stand at room temperature for 30-40 minutes before grilling.

2   Soak the wood chips in water for at least 30 minutes.

3   Prepare the grill for indirect cooking over medium-low heat (about 180°C/350°F).

4   Place one large disposable foil tray inside the other to create a single tray of double thickness. Score the ham in a large criss-cross pattern about 1cm/½ inch deep on all sides, except the cut side, and place it, cut side down, in the foil trays.

5   Drain and add half of the wood chips to the charcoal or to the smoker box of a gas grill, following the manufacturer's instructions, and close the lid. When smoke appears, place the tray with the gammon over *roasting/indirect medium-low heat*, close the lid and cook for 1¼-1½ hours until an instant-read thermometer inserted into the thickest part of the meat (not touching the bone) registers 49°C/120°F, checking periodically to be sure the meat is not browning too quickly. If it is

getting too dark, tent lightly with foil. After the first 30 minutes of cooking time, drain and add the remaining wood chips to the charcoal or smoker box.

6   Meanwhile, in a bowl combine the salsa ingredients. Allow to stand at room temperature until ready to serve.

7   In a small bowl, whisk the glaze ingredients, breaking up the jam. Remove the foil tent, if using, and brush half of the glaze on the top and sides of the joint; cook for 15 minutes. Then brush the meat with the remaining glaze and continue cooking for 10-15 minutes more until an instant-read thermometer inserted in the thickest part of the meat (not touching the bone) registers 57-60°C/135-140°F. If the glaze gets too dark, cover the joint loosely with aluminium foil for the remainder of the cooking time. Remove from the grill, tent loosely with foil and allow to rest for 15-45 minutes (the internal temperature will rise 5-10 degrees during this time).

8   Carve the ham and serve warm with the salsa.

By scoring a gammon joint, you expose more of the rind to the heat and smoke in your grill. This simple step is how you develop gloriously sweet, crispy edges where the glaze seeps into the creases. Run the tip of a sharp knife about 1cm/½ inch deep into the rind, making long cross-hatch slits about 2.5cm/1 inch apart.

BARBECUING
without boundaries
IN NEW YORK CITY

╫ ╫ ╫ ╫ ╫ ╫ ╫ ╫ ╫ ╫ ╫ ╫ ╫ ╫ ╫ ╫ ╫ ╫ ╫

Barbecue is a food and preparation method that has long been identified with the American South, but that doesn't keep Northerners from trying. Honest attempts at barbecue can now be found all over the country. Many are still in the copycat phase – find a style or styles and make an attempt at replication – but in New York City there's a shift towards a flavour all their own.

Twenty years ago, barbecue was just getting its legs in New York. Virgil's Real Barbecue opened in Times Square and the Brother Jimmy's BBQ chain began their expansion across the city with menus that read like a culinary lucky dip – Carolina pork, Texas brisket and Memphis ribs. A little later, Blue Smoke upped the game in quality, but it was still working from a borrowed menu. Pearson's Texas Barbecue was the only game in town with a real focus, but the final version was gone in 2005 before their brisket ever really got its time in the spotlight. The barbecue cupboard was looking bare in New York City. That void was soon filled by Fette Sau, in the Williamsburg neighbourhood of Brooklyn, and Hill Country Barbecue Market, in Lower Manhattan. These were the first of the meat market-style barbecue joints, where smoked meats are chosen individually and served on paper. With their connection to Kreuz Market, Hill Country is all Texas style, and, while Fette Sau branded itself as uniquely Brooklyn, it feels more like a mash-up of Kansas City and Texas. Now, a new breed of joints is taking their New York barbecue to another level.

At Hometown Bar-B-Que in Brooklyn, pit master Billy Durney sports a Texas tattoo on his calf, homage to where he did some barbecue training at Louie Mueller Barbecue in Taylor, Texas. As expected from such tutelage, his brisket and beef ribs are on point, but the menu ranges far beyond those two Texas classics. You'll also find sweet Korean sticky ribs, a Vietnamese-style lamb belly banh mi with the added crunch of mooli, and spicy/sweet jerk baby back ribs. 'All of these are using southern techniques of smoking, then I'm manipulating the flavours after they come off the smoker,' says Durney. It's like a barbecue world tour under one roof, but it's not just a facsimile of other traditions.

It would be remiss not to mention the groundbreaking but now defunct Fatty 'Cue that came to Brooklyn in 2010. It may have been the first barbecue joint in New York to bring flavours unique to the city. Beef brisket was served with kimchi and bao buns, lamb ribs were marinated with fermented shrimp before being smoked, and big pork spareribs – fragrant with fish sauce and sweet from a palm sugar glaze – got their spice from Indonesian long peppers. It may have been a restaurant ahead of its time (it closed in 2014), but those dishes laid a foundation that allowed others in the city to be more creative with barbecue than just a salt-and-pepper rub.

Similar Asian flavours can be found at Fletcher's Brooklyn Barbecue, where a menu mainstay is pork char siu; pork shoulder steaks marinated in a Chinese-style sauce and then smoked. Instead of cooking the pork to the point where it can be pulled, at Fletcher's they slice it thinly, like a brisket. The result is smoky, tangy, salty and sweet – more interesting than most versions of simple pulled pork.

In discussing contemporary versus traditional barbecue, we shouldn't forget pastrami. It's New York's original indigenous barbecue. To make it, beef belly or brisket is cured, rubbed with black pepper and coriander, and then smoked and steamed until tender. It's usually found between two slices of rye, but Danny Bowien of Mission Chinese Food in Manhattan slams it into a completely unfamiliar context. His house-made pastrami is cubed and fried with celery, peanuts, potatoes and Tianjin chillies in his now famous Kung Pao pastrami dish. Even with all the strong flavours competing on your tongue, the smoke of the pastrami comes through full force. That bold smokiness can also be found elsewhere on the adventurous menu – in a whole smoked pork jowl, and in smoked prime rib served in New York fashion with a king crab leg garnish. As Billy Durney puts it so well, 'The beauty of cooking barbecue in New York is that we don't have any of our grandfathers' stipulations of what we can and cannot do.'

COUNTRY-STYLE PORK RIBS
WITH LOUISIANA HOT SAUCE

SERVES: 6–8 | **PREP TIME:** 30 MINUTES | **GRILLING TIME:** ABOUT 1 HOUR
SPECIAL EQUIPMENT: 2 LARGE HANDFULS PEACH OR HICKORY WOOD CHIPS

RUB

1 tablespoon paprika
1 tablespoon brown sugar
1 teaspoon garlic powder
1 teaspoon sea salt
½ teaspoon dried thyme
½ teaspoon dried oregano
½ teaspoon celery salt
½ teaspoon onion powder
½ teaspoon mustard powder

1.6–1.8kg/3½–4lb boneless country-
  style pork ribs (shoulder blade
  steaks)
2 tablespoons Worcestershire sauce

SAUCE

75g/3oz unsalted butter
1 large onion, about 250g/9oz, finely
  chopped
4 tablespoons finely chopped green
  pepper
75ml/6fl oz Louisiana-style or other
  hot chilli sauce
3 tablespoons brown sugar
1½ tablespoons fresh lemon juice
1½ tablespoons paprika
1½ teaspoons hot pepper sauce
1½ teaspoons onion powder
1½ teaspoons garlic powder
½ teaspoon freshly ground black pepper

4 tablespoons tomato ketchup
2 tablespoons fresh orange juice

Country-style pork ribs aren't really ribs at all. They are normally cut from the shoulder (fairly close to baby back ribs) and sometimes they don't even contain bones. Really, they are more like pork chops than anything else. That's why they are sometimes called blade chops or blade steaks. Whatever the name, they are meaty and delicious when you smoke them gently over indirect heat and then char them for five minutes or so right before serving them with a lip-smacking barbecue sauce.

1 Soak the wood chips in water for at least 30 minutes.

2 Combine the rub ingredients. Brush the meat with the Worcestershire sauce and season evenly with the rub. Allow to stand at room temperature for 15–30 minutes before grilling.

3 Prepare the grill for indirect cooking over medium-low heat (150–180°C/300–350°F).

4 In a saucepan over a medium heat, melt 20g/¾oz of the butter. Add the onion and green pepper and cook for about 4 minutes until slightly softened, stirring occasionally. Add the Louisiana-style hot sauce, brown sugar, lemon juice, paprika, hot pepper sauce, onion powder, garlic powder and pepper. Bring to a simmer and cook for 3 minutes more, stirring occasionally. Remove from the heat and whisk in the remaining butter, whisking until melted. Reserve 175ml/6fl oz of the sauce to serve with the ribs.

5 Drain and add half of the wood chips to the charcoal or to the smoker box of a gas grill, following the manufacturer's instructions, and close the lid. When smoke appears, place the ribs over *roasting/indirect medium-low heat*, close the lid and cook for 30 minutes. Turn the ribs over, brush generously with some of the sauce, drain and add the remaining wood chips to the charcoal or smoker box, close the lid and continue cooking for 15 minutes. Turn the ribs over, brush generously with more of the sauce and grill until the ribs are fully cooked and nicely glazed, about 10 minutes more.

6 Raise the temperature of the grill to medium-high heat (220–230°C/425–450°F). Grill the glazed ribs over *grilling/direct medium-high heat* for 5–7 minutes, with the lid closed, until nicely browned and marked by the grill, turning once or twice.

7 In a saucepan over a medium-low heat, warm the reserved sauce with the ketchup and orange juice. Serve the ribs warm with the sauce on the side.

GARLIC- AND LEMON-BRINED BACON

SERVES: 12 | **PREP TIME:** 15 MINUTES | **COOLING TIME:** 4–6 HOURS FOR THE BRINE AND 1–2 HOURS FOR THE BACON
BRINING TIME: 48 HOURS | **DRYING TIME:** 12 HOURS | **COOKING TIME:** 2–3 HOURS | **SPECIAL EQUIPMENT:** WATER SMOKER,
3 LARGE HANDFULS PECAN OR APPLE WOOD CHUNKS, INSTANT-READ THERMOMETER

BRINE
3.5 litres/6 pints water
400g/14oz granulated sugar
250g/9oz sea salt
Zest of 4 lemons, zest removed with a
    vegetable peeler in long, wide strips
2 heads of garlic, smashed and peeled
2 tablespoons black peppercorns
1½ teaspoons pink curing salt
2 bay leaves

2 pieces boneless pork belly, each
    about 900g/2lb, rind removed
2 tablespoons dried sage
1 teaspoon crushed chilli flakes

Bacon continues to be all the rage with chefs and backyard smokers. Making your own takes 2 days of brining, half a day of drying the meat in the refrigerator, and about 3 hours of smoking, but the DIY approach allows you to customise the flavours. Here I've blurred the lines of tradition by packing the brine with garlic and lemon, and I've coated the meat with sage and chilli flakes, so the bacon has an Italian-American character that I think you will love.

1   In a large, non-reactive saucepan, combine the brine ingredients. Bring just to a simmer over a medium-high heat, stirring a few times at first until the sugar dissolves and all the salt dissolves. Cool for 4–6 hours to room temperature.

2   Submerge the pork belly in the brine, cover and refrigerate for 48 hours, turning the meat occasionally.

3   Remove the pork belly from the pan and blot dry with kitchen paper. Discard the brine. Season the meat side of the pork belly with the sage and chilli flakes. Place on a wire rack set inside a large, rimmed roasting tray and refrigerate, uncovered, for 12 hours.

4   Prepare the smoker for indirect cooking with very low heat (110–130°C/225–250°F). Fill the water pan three-quarters full with water.

5   Add the wood chunks to the charcoal. Transfer the pork belly from the wire rack to the smoker and cook over **roasting/indirect very low heat** for 2–3 hours, with the lid closed, until an instant-read thermometer inserted into the thickest part of the meat registers 65°C/150°F.

6   Remove the bacon pieces from the smoker and cool for 1–2 hours to room temperature. Wrap tightly in clingfilm and store in the refrigerator for up to 1 week; or store in the freezer for up to 3 months. To serve, slice crossways into strips about 3mm/⅛ inch thick and grill on a rack set inside a baking tray or fry in a frying pan.

You will need a couple of pieces of pork belly, preferably from the centre of the belly where the meat is relatively even in thickness. After the bellies are brined and dried to firm up the texture of that fatty meat, coat them with spices and smoke them at very low temperatures.

BOSTON BACON FATTIES

SERVES: 8 | PREP TIME: 30 MINUTES | GRILLING TIME: 1½–2 HOURS
SPECIAL EQUIPMENT: 1 LARGE HANDFUL HICKORY WOOD CHIPS, INSTANT-READ THERMOMETER

900g/2lb sweet Italian sausage, casings removed
25g/1oz Parmesan cheese, finely grated
32 thick-cut bacon rashers, about 1.4kg/3lb
50g/2oz drained marinated artichoke hearts, chopped
25g/1oz drained marinated sun-dried tomatoes, chopped
1½ roasted red peppers (from a jar), chopped

In the BBQ world, a basic (or naked) fatty is a roll of sausage that is smoked and sliced like meat loaf, but barbecuers don't always leave well alone, so there are versions filled with sautéed onions, cheese and even hot dogs. Many cooks like to make even more extravagant fatties by wrapping them in a bacon weave, which I think is an excellent idea. To give this version a touch of Boston's North End, I stuffed it with ingredients you would find on an Italian antipasto plate. Keep the fire low so the bacon gets crisp without burning.

1   Soak the wood chips in water for at least 30 minutes.

2   Prepare the grill for indirect cooking over low heat (130–180°C/250–350°F).

3   Mix the sausage and cheese thoroughly but gently. Divide the meat into two equal portions.

4   Lay a large sheet of greaseproof paper on a work surface. On the paper, using half of the bacon rashers (eight going in one direction and eight in the other), weave a tight square, as if you are making a lattice pie. The finished size should be about 28 x 28cm/11 x 11 inches (don't be afraid to stretch the bacon strips a little to fit).

5   Lay a large sheet of greaseproof paper on another work surface. Press one of the meat portions into a 20-cm/8-inch square. About 5cm/2 inches from the side nearest you, arrange half of the artichokes, half of the sun-dried tomatoes and half of the peppers in parallel, horizontal lines, leaving about 2.5cm/1 inch at each end. Roll up the sausage tightly around the fillings, and then pinch the ends to seal everything in. This should look like a small meat loaf. Place this meat loaf at the edge of the bacon weave closest to you. Using the greaseproof paper underneath the bacon to help, roll the bacon blanket around the sausage, tucking the ends in as you go. Set aside, seam side down. Repeat with the remaining ingredients, making a second wrapped fatty.

6   Drain and add the wood chips to the charcoal or to the smoker box of a gas grill, following the manufacturer's instructions, and close the lid. When smoke appears, grill the fatties over *roasting/indirect low heat* for 1½–2 hours, with the lid closed, until an instant-read thermometer inserted into the thickest part of the meat registers 68°C/155°F. Remove from the grill and allow to rest for 10 minutes (the internal temperature will rise 5–10 degrees during this time). Cut into 2.5-cm/1-inch-thick slices and serve straightaway.

1   *Working on a piece of greaseproof paper, create a bacon weave. Keep the bacon rashers tight. The finished size should be about 28 x 28cm/11 x 11 inches.*

2   *Arrange the artichokes, tomatoes and peppers in a horizontal line on the sausage square. Leave room, about 2.5cm/1 inch, on either side.*

3   *Roll up the sausage around the filling, and pinch the edges to seal everything in.*

4   *Place the sausage roll on the bacon weave, and roll it up.*

PORK

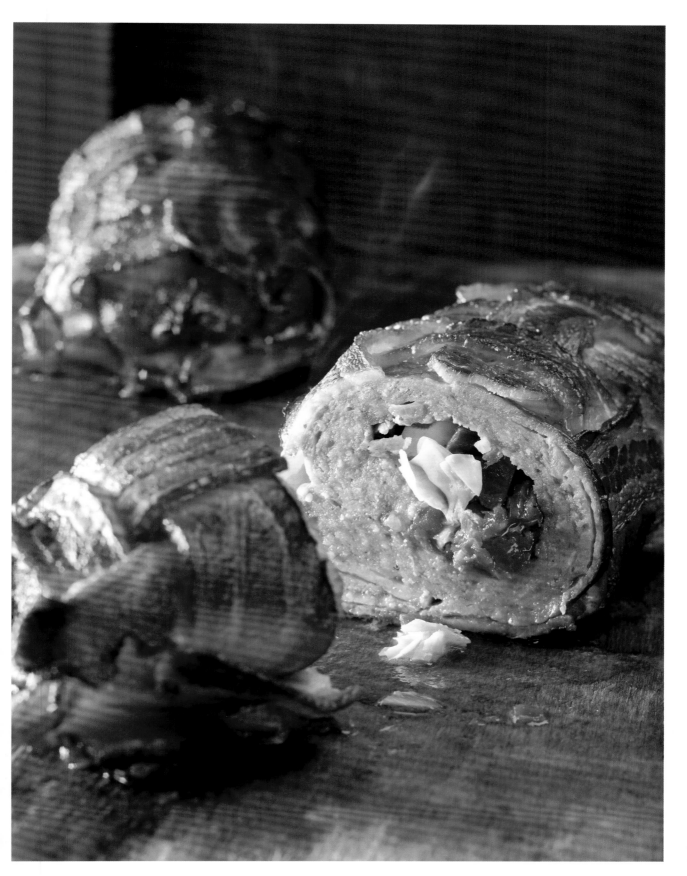

PIZZAS
WITH PROSCIUTTO, PARMESAN AND PROVOLONE

SERVES: 6–8 (MAKES TWO 30-CM/12-INCH PIZZAS) | **PREP TIME:** 25 MINUTES | **RISING TIME:** 1¼–1½ HOURS
GRILLING TIME: 6–9 MINUTES PER PIZZA | **SPECIAL EQUIPMENT:** NONSTICK ALUMINIUM FOIL

DOUGH
250ml/8fl oz warm water
    (40–46°C/105–115°F)
1 tablespoon extra-virgin olive oil
1¾ teaspoons sea salt
1½ teaspoons fast-action dried yeast
375g/13oz plain flour, plus more as
    needed
Extra-virgin olive oil
1 garlic clove, finely chopped
115g/4oz aged provolone cheese,
    coarsely grated
1 large red onion, 175–200g/6–7oz,
    thinly sliced
115g/4oz Parma ham, thinly sliced
115g/4oz Parmesan cheese, finely
    grated
50g/2oz fresh baby rocket

When I was a young chef fresh out of cooking school, I ate one of the most memorable meals of my life at a restaurant in Providence, Rhode Island. At Al Forno, pioneering chefs Johanne Killeen and George Germon elevated humble pizzas to remarkable expressions of art, jostling them over hardwood charcoal fires so the smoke drifted into the blistered crust and bubbling toppings. When you do this at home, have all your supplies within reach, because the thin crust cooks quickly over a live fire.

1   In a large bowl, combine the water, oil, salt and yeast. Mix in about 350g/12oz flour to make a stiff dough that cannot be stirred. Turn the dough out on to a floured work surface and knead by hand for about 6 minutes, working in the rest of the flour, or more as needed, until the dough is smooth, supple and slightly tacky.

2   Coat a bowl with oil. Shape the dough into a ball, place in the bowl and turn to coat with the oil. Cover the bowl tightly with clingfilm. Allow to stand in a warm, draught-free area until the dough is doubled in volume, 1¼–1½ hours; or refrigerate the dough for 6–8 hours. Return to room temperature before using.

3   Prepare the grill for direct cooking over medium heat (180–230°C/350–450°F).

4   In a small bowl, whisk 4 tablespoons oil and the garlic.

5   Divide the dough into two equal balls. On an oiled square of nonstick aluminium foil, using your hands, stretch out one ball of dough to a 30-cm/12-inch round. Brush the top side of the dough with olive oil.

6   Lay the dough on the cooking grate with the foil side facing up. Grab one corner of the foil with tongs and peel it off. Cook the dough over *grilling/direct medium heat* for 2–3 minutes, with the lid closed, until the underside is golden. Transfer to the back of a baking sheet with the grilled side facing up. Brush with 1 tablespoon of the garlic oil, leaving a 1-cm/½-inch border. Top with half of the provolone and half of the onion. Drape half of the Parma ham over and around the onion, and top with 4 tablespoons of the Parmesan, half of the rocket and another 4 tablespoons cheese. Return the pizza to the grill, close the lid and continue grilling for 4–6 minutes more until the rocket wilts, the cheese melts and the crust is crisp and golden brown. Transfer to a chopping board, drizzle with 1 tablespoon of the garlic oil, cut into wedges and serve warm. Make another pizza with the remaining ingredients.

THREE-CHEESE PIZZAS
WITH SAUSAGE, MUSHROOMS AND PEPPERS

SERVES: 6–8 (MAKES TWO 30-CM/12-INCH PIZZAS) | **PREP TIME:** 40 MINUTES | **RISING TIME:** 1¼–1½ HOURS
GRILLING TIME: 13–16 MINUTES, PLUS 12–15 MINUTES PER PIZZA | **SPECIAL EQUIPMENT:** PIZZA STONE,
PIZZA PEEL (OPTIONAL), PERFORATED GRILL PAN, SILICONE PASTRY BRUSH

DOUGH
250ml/8fl oz warm water
    (40–46°C/105–115°F)
1 tablespoon extra-virgin olive oil
1¾ teaspoons sea salt
1½ teaspoons fast-action dried yeast
375g/13oz plain flour, plus more as
    needed

Extra-virgin olive oil
1 red pepper, about 225g/8oz
225g/8oz chestnut mushrooms, cut
    into quarters
Sea salt
Freshly ground black pepper
340g/12oz crumbled Italian sausage
115g/4oz pecorino cheese, finely
    grated
115g/4oz fontina cheese, coarsely
    grated
½ small onion, thinly sliced crossways
225g/8oz fresh mozzarella cheese,
    well drained, thinly sliced
4 teaspoons thyme leaves
Crushed chilli flakes

There is something both ancient and modern about baking a freshly made pizza in a wood-burning oven. You can replicate this on your grill by preheating a pizza stone for a full 10 minutes right on the cooking grate. A really hot stone will expand the air bubbles inside the dough, giving you a soft, cloud-like interior above a crisp, toasted exterior.

1   In a large bowl, combine the water, oil, salt and yeast. Mix in about 350g/12oz flour to make a stiff dough that cannot be stirred. Turn the dough out on to a floured work surface and knead by hand for about 6 minutes, working in the rest of the flour, or more as needed, until the dough is smooth, supple and slightly tacky.

2   Coat a bowl with oil. Shape the dough into a ball, place in the bowl and turn to coat with the oil. Cover the bowl tightly with clingfilm. Allow to stand in a warm, draught-free area until the dough is doubled in volume, 1¼–1½ hours; or refrigerate the dough for 6–8 hours. Return to room temperature before using.

3   Prepare the grill for direct cooking over medium heat (180–230°C/350–450°F) and preheat a perforated grill pan for 10 minutes.

4   Grill the red pepper over *grilling/direct medium heat* for 10–12 minutes, with the lid closed, until blackened and blistered all over, turning occasionally. Place the pepper in a bowl and cover with clingfilm to trap the steam. Allow to stand for about 10 minutes. Remove and discard the charred skin, stalk and seeds, and cut the pepper into 5-mm/¼-inch strips.

5   Brush the mushrooms with oil, season with ¼ teaspoon salt and ¼ teaspoon pepper and then arrange in a single layer on the grill pan. Grill over *grilling/direct medium heat* for 3–4 minutes, with the lid closed, until golden brown, stirring once or twice. Transfer to a plate.

6   In a frying pan over a medium heat, warm 1 tablespoon oil. Add the sausage and sauté for 6–8 minutes until cooked through, stirring frequently. Using a slotted spoon, transfer the sausage to a plate lined with kitchen paper.

7   Prepare the grill for indirect cooking over high heat (260–290°C/500–550°F) and preheat the pizza stone for about 10 minutes, following the manufacturer's instructions.

8   Divide the dough into two equal balls. On a lightly floured work surface, using a rolling pin or your hands, roll or stretch out one ball of dough to a 30-cm/12-inch round. Liberally dust a pizza peel or a rimless baking sheet with flour. Transfer the dough round to the pizza peel. Top the dough with 4 tablespoons of the pecorino and 4 tablespoons of the fontina, leaving a 1-cm/½-inch border. Spread half of the onion, peppers, mushrooms and sausage over the cheese. Distribute half of the mozzarella over and between the toppings, and 4 tablespoons fontina and 4 tablespoons pecorino over the pizza. Season with 2 teaspoons of the thyme, a pinch of salt and a pinch of black pepper.

9   Carefully slide the pizza on to the preheated pizza stone. Grill over *roasting/indirect high heat* for 12–15 minutes, with the lid closed, until the crust is golden and crisp and the cheese is melted. Transfer to a chopping board, top with chilli flakes, cut into wedges and serve warm.

10   Use a silicone pastry brush to brush off any flour left on the pizza stone. Close the lid and reheat the pizza stone for 10 minutes. Make another pizza with the remaining ingredients.

PORK

3

RED MEAT

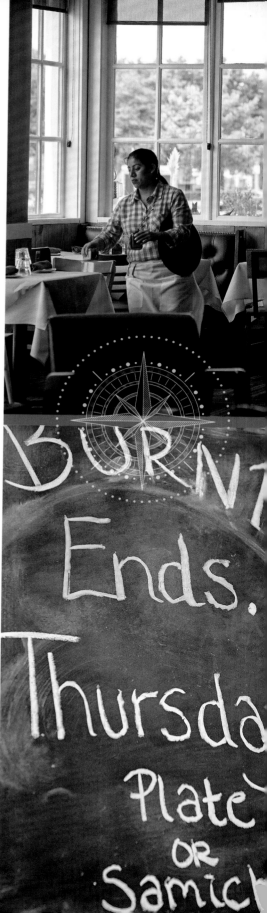

BACON CHEESEBURGERS
WITH KENTUCKY BOURBON SAUCE

SERVES: 4 | **PREP TIME:** 20 MINUTES, PLUS ABOUT 35 MINUTES FOR THE SAUCE | **GRILLING TIME:** 8–10 MINUTES
SPECIAL EQUIPMENT: 2 LARGE HANDFULS HICKORY OR MESQUITE WOOD CHIPS

SAUCE

2 teaspoons vegetable oil
2 bacon rashers, cut into
 1-cm/½-inch wide strips
1 onion, finely chopped
1 garlic clove, minced
4 tablespoons bourbon
250ml/8fl oz tomato ketchup
4 tablespoons water
3 tablespoons cider vinegar
3 tablespoons black treacle
2 tablespoons brown sauce
1 tablespoon spicy brown mustard
1 teaspoon liquid smoke
½ teaspoon hot pepper sauce

8 bacon rashers
675g/1½lb minced beef (80% lean)
1 teaspoon sea salt
½ teaspoon freshly ground black
 pepper
115g/4oz smoked Cheddar
 cheese, grated
4 hamburger buns, split
4 leaves romaine lettuce, shredded
8 slices ripe tomato

Like all of America's iconic foods, cheeseburgers can be either inspired or insipid depending on how they are made. For me, the surest way to elevate an ordinary cheeseburger to greatness is to grill it with wood. Anyone with a quarter of a taste bud will notice the difference when the comforting smells of smouldering wood chips have seeped into these burgers. Since they don't spend a lot of time on the grill, be sure to use a stronger-flavoured wood like hickory or mesquite, and let it build up a good head of smoke before you add the patties.

1 Soak the wood chips in water for at least 30 minutes.

2 In a heavy saucepan over a medium heat, warm the oil. Add the bacon strips and fry for 3–5 minutes until browned and crisp. Using a slotted spoon, transfer the bacon to kitchen paper to drain and cool, leaving the drippings in the saucepan.

3 Add the onion to the saucepan, reduce the heat to medium-low and cook for for 8–10 minutes until soft and golden brown, stirring occasionally. Stir in the garlic and cook until fragrant, about 1 minute. Add the bourbon, increase the heat to medium-high and boil to reduce slightly, about 1 minute. Add the remaining sauce ingredients and bring to the boil over medium-high heat. Reduce the heat to low and simmer for about 20 minutes, uncovered, until the mixture thickens and is reduced to about 500ml/18fl oz, stirring occasionally. Turn off the heat and stir in the fried and cooled bacon. Cover and keep warm.

4 Meanwhile, in a frying pan over a medium heat, fry the eight bacon rashers for 8–10 minutes until browned and crisp, turning occasionally. Transfer the bacon to kitchen paper to drain.

5 Mix the minced beef, salt and pepper, then gently form four burgers of equal size, each about 2cm/¾ inch thick. With your thumb or the back of a spoon, make a shallow indentation about 2.5cm/1 inch wide in the centre of the burgers to prevent them from forming a dome as they cook. Refrigerate until ready to grill.

6 Prepare the grill for direct cooking over medium-high heat (about 200°C/400°F).

7 Drain and add the wood chips to the charcoal or to the smoker box of a gas grill, following the manufacturer's instructions, and close the lid. When smoke appears, grill the burgers over **grilling/direct medium-high heat** for 8–10 minutes, with the lid closed, until cooked to medium doneness (70°C/160°F), turning once. During the last minute of grilling time, place one-quarter of the cheese on each burger to melt, and toast the buns, cut side down, over direct heat.

8 Build each cheeseburger on a bun with lettuce, tomato slices, a burger, bacon rashers and sauce. Serve warm.

Don't do this! Smashing burgers with a spatula may make them flatter, but it also pushes juices and fat out, triggering flare-ups. If you like flat burgers, use your thumb or the back of a spoon to make a shallow well in the centre of the raw patties before you put them on the cooking grate. As they cook, that well will fill in and flatten out nicely.

TRIPLE BEER BURGERS

SERVES: 4 | **PREP TIME:** 20 MINUTES, PLUS ABOUT 20 MINUTES FOR THE SAUCE
GRILLING TIME: 24-31 MINUTES | **SPECIAL EQUIPMENT:** LARGE DISPOSABLE FOIL TRAY

One of the secrets of making especially juicy burgers is adding a little beer to the raw meat. If you use too much, the patties get too wet to develop a good crust and they tend to fall apart, but just a little full-bodied beer helps in a big way.

1 garlic clove, finely chopped
Extra-virgin olive oil
250ml/8fl oz tomato ketchup
275ml/9fl oz IPA or dark ale
2 tablespoons cider vinegar
1 tablespoon brown sugar
3 teaspoons Worcestershire
    sauce
Sea salt
1 onion, cut crossways into 8-mm/⅓-
    inch slices
1 tablespoon Dijon mustard
675g/1½lb minced beef (80% lean)
1 teaspoon smoked paprika
¼ teaspoon freshly ground black
    pepper
4 pretzel rolls or hamburger buns, split
4 leaves round lettuce

1. In a saucepan over a medium heat, sauté the garlic for about 1 minute in 1 tablespoon oil until fragrant. Add the ketchup, 125ml/4fl oz of the beer, the vinegar, brown sugar, 2 teaspoons of the Worcestershire sauce and ½ teaspoon salt and bring to a gentle boil. Reduce the heat to low and simmer for 15–20 minutes until the sauce is the consistency of ketchup, stirring often. Allow to cool.

2. Prepare the grill for direct cooking over medium-high heat (200–260°C/400–500°F).

3. Brush the onion with oil, and then grill over *grilling/direct medium-high heat* for about 6 minutes, with the lid closed, until lightly charred, turning once. In a large disposable foil tray, mix 125ml/4fl oz beer, the mustard and 1 teaspoon salt. Add the onions to the beer mixture. Grill over *grilling/direct medium-high heat* for 10–15 minutes, with

the lid closed, until most of the liquid is evaporated and the onion is soft, stirring occasionally. Remove from the grill.

4. Mix the minced beef, paprika, pepper, 1½ teaspoons salt, the remaining beer and 1 teaspoon Worcestershire sauce, and then gently form four patties of equal size, each about 2cm/¾ inch thick. With your thumb or the back of a spoon, make a shallow indentation about 2.5cm/1 inch wide in the centre of the patties to prevent them from forming a dome as they cook.

5. Grill the burgers over *grilling/direct medium-high heat* for 8–10 minutes, with the lid closed, until cooked to medium doneness (70°C/160°F), turning once. During the last 30 seconds to 1 minute of grilling time, toast the rolls, cut side down, over direct heat.

6. Build each beer burger on a roll with lettuce, a burger, onions and sauce. Serve warm.

GASTROPUB LAMB BURGERS

SERVES: 4 | PREP TIME: 20 MINUTES
GRILLING TIME: 7-9 MINUTES

These burgers strut with a little upscale swagger on account of minced lamb, a mixed olive tapenade with gourmet oomph and big slabs of summer's best tomatoes. The brioche bun adds another elegant element, but any rich bread would be great.

565g/1¼lb minced lamb, preferably from the shoulder
3 garlic cloves, crushed
2 tablespoons finely chopped flat-leaf parsley
½ teaspoon dried oregano
Sea salt
Freshly ground black pepper

TAPENADE
75g/3oz pitted mild green olives, such as Picholine, drained
75g/3oz pitted brine-cured black olives, such as Kalamata, drained
2 tablespoons extra-virgin olive oil
1 tablespoon red or white wine vinegar
Finely grated zest of 1 orange
2 garlic cloves, thinly sliced

4 brioche buns, split
8 slices ripe tomato, each about 5mm/¼ inch thick

1 Combine the lamb, garlic, parsley, oregano, ¼ teaspoon salt and ¼ teaspoon pepper. Mix well, and then gently form four patties of equal size, each about 2cm/¾ inch thick. With your thumb or the back of a spoon, make a shallow indentation about 2.5cm/1 inch wide in the centre of the patties to prevent them from forming a dome as they cook. Refrigerate the patties until ready to grill.

2 In a food processor combine the tapenade ingredients. Pulse on and off until finely chopped and well blended, scraping down the inside of the bowl several times.

3 Prepare the grill for direct cooking over medium-high heat (200–260°C/400–500°F).

4 Lightly season the patties on both sides with salt and pepper, and then grill over **grilling/direct medium-high heat** for 7–9 minutes, with the lid closed, until cooked to medium doneness (70°C/160°F), turning once. During the last 30 seconds to 1 minute of grilling time, toast the buns, cut side down, over direct heat. Remove from the grill and let the burgers rest for 2–3 minutes.

5 Build each lamb burger on a bun with a burger, tapenade and tomato slices. Serve warm.

MINCED RIB EYE STEAK SLIDERS
WITH CARAMELISED ONIONS AND TOMATO-BACON JAM

SERVES: 6 (MAKES 12 SLIDERS | PREP TIME: 20 MINUTES, PLUS ABOUT 55 MINUTES FOR THE JAM
AND 25–35 MINUTES FOR THE ONIONS | GRILLING TIME: ABOUT 4 MINUTES

JAM
225g/8oz smoked bacon, cut into
    5-mm/¼-inch strips
1 Spanish onion, 225–285g/
    8–10oz, chopped
675g/1½lb plum tomatoes, chopped
3 tablespoons light brown sugar
2 tablespoons cider vinegar
1 tablespoon hot pepper sauce
    or Sriracha

Sea salt
Freshly ground black pepper
2 tablespoons extra-virgin olive oil
2 large Spanish onions, about
    675g/1½lb total, each cut in half
    and thinly sliced
900g/2lb ground rib eye steak
1 tablespoon Worcestershire sauce
12 slider buns, split

Grinding up rib eye steaks might sound like a crazy splurge, and I'll admit that it is not essential for an everyday burger, but it sure does improve the rich, meaty flavours in these little sliders. If you don't have a meat grinder, ask your butcher to grind the meat for you. This business of using freshly minced beef from one or more special cuts of meat is a burgeoning trend in the world of gourmet burgers.

1   In a large frying pan over a medium heat, fry the bacon for 5–7 minutes until browned and crisp, turning occasionally. Using a slotted spoon, transfer the bacon to a large, heavy saucepan. Set aside. Drain off all but 1 tablespoon fat from the pan. Add the chopped onion and sauté for 3–4 minutes until softened but not coloured, stirring occasionally. Transfer the onion and the remaining jam ingredients, including 1 teaspoon salt and ½ teaspoon pepper, to the saucepan with the bacon. Bring to the boil over a medium-high heat and cook until the sugar dissolves, stirring frequently. Reduce the heat to medium-low and simmer for 40–45 minutes, partially covered, until most of the juices are absorbed and the mixture is thickened to a moist, jam-like consistency, stirring frequently.

2   In another large frying pan over a medium heat, warm the oil. Add the onions and 1 teaspoon salt and cook for 10–15 minutes until the onions begin to turn light golden, stirring occasionally. Reduce the heat to medium-low and cook for 15–20

minutes more until the onions are deep golden brown and caramelised, stirring frequently. Remove from the heat and stir in ¼ teaspoon pepper.

3   Prepare the grill for direct and indirect cooking over high heat (200–260°C/450–550°F).

4   Mix the minced steak, Worcestershire sauce, 1 teaspoon salt and ¾ teaspoon pepper, and then gently form 12 patties of equal size, each about 5cm/2 inches in diameter and 1cm/½ inch thick.

5   Grill the burgers over **grilling/direct high heat** for about 4 minutes, with the lid closed, until cooked to medium doneness (70°C/160°F), turning once when the burgers release easily from the cooking grate without sticking (if flare-ups occur, move the burgers temporarily over indirect heat). During the last 30 seconds to 1 minute of grilling time, toast the buns, cut side down, over direct heat.

6   Build each slider on a bun with a burger, onions and jam. Serve warm.

These decadent sliders benefit from caramel-lacquered onions and this sweet, smoky condiment that simmers down to a moist, jam-like consistency. The recipe may make more jam than you need for the sliders, but that's a good thing – it's also delicious served with cheese or spread on crostini. The jam may be refrigerated for up to 1 week.

COWBOY STEAKS
WITH SMOKED SHALLOT BUTTER

SERVES: 4–6 | **PREP TIME:** 15 MINUTES | **GRILLING TIME:** ABOUT 1 HOUR
SPECIAL EQUIPMENT: 2 LARGE HANDFULS MESQUITE WOOD CHIPS, SMALL DISPOSABLE FOIL TRAY

BUTTER
1 large shallot, peeled and cut
  lengthways into quarters
1 teaspoon extra-virgin olive oil
¼ teaspoon smoked paprika
50g/2oz unsalted butter, softened
1 tablespoon finely chopped flat-leaf
  parsley
2 teaspoons dry sherry (optional)
1 teaspoon freshly grated lemon zest

Sea salt
Freshly ground black pepper
2 bone-in rib eye steaks, each about
  900g/2lb and 5cm/2 inches thick
Extra-virgin olive oil
½ teaspoon garlic powder

To make manly carnivores sing for joy like Maria prancing through the Alps in The Sound of Music, *serve them marbled bone-in rib eye steaks (aka cowboy steaks) that come with their own handles. The handles are not really for picking up the steaks, but the bones do protect and flavour the meat alongside it, making those parts often the juiciest and tastiest of all. Season these thick steaks well and let them stand at room temperature long enough so that the salt can draw out moisture and the meat can reabsorb those juices with the seasonings. That usually takes 30–40 minutes.*

1 Soak the wood chips in water for at least
   30 minutes.

2 Prepare the grill for direct and indirect
   cooking over medium-high heat (about
   230°C/450°F).

3 In a small disposable foil tray, combine the
   shallot quarters, oil and paprika. Drain and
   add one handful of the wood chips to the
   charcoal or to the smoker box of a gas grill,
   following manufacturer's instructions, and
   close the lid. When smoke appears, place
   the foil tray with the shallot over ***roasting/
   indirect medium-high heat***, close the lid
   and cook until the shallot is tender, about
   40 minutes. Transfer to a chopping board
   and allow to cool for 10 minutes. Chop the
   shallot, transfer to a small bowl, and add the
   remaining butter ingredients, including ½
   teaspoon salt and ¼ teaspoon pepper, mixing

thoroughly. Refrigerate, covered, until firm.
Remove from the refrigerator about
10 minutes before serving.

4 Lightly brush both sides of the steaks with
   oil and season evenly with 2 teaspoons salt,
   ½ teaspoon pepper and the garlic powder. Allow
   the steaks to stand at room temperature
   for 30–40 minutes before grilling.

5 Drain and add the remaining wood chips to
   the charcoal or smoker box. When smoke
   appears, sear the steaks over ***grilling/direct
   medium-high heat*** for 6–8 minutes, with
   the lid closed, turning once. Then move the
   steaks over ***roasting/indirect medium-high
   heat***, close the lid and continue cooking to
   your desired doneness, 12–14 minutes more
   for medium rare. Remove from the grill and
   allow to rest for 3–5 minutes. Serve warm,
   topped with the butter.

For a great steak to reach the level of a feast, it needs something special like the sweet succulence of this smoky shallot butter. Cook a quartered shallot in mesquite smoke until tender and golden. Chop the shallot and blend with softened butter, parsley, lemon zest and maybe a little sherry.

MESQUITE T-BONES
WITH SMOKED TOMATO SALSA

SERVES: 4–6 | **PREP TIME:** 15 MINUTES
GRILLING TIME: 36–55 MINUTES | **SPECIAL EQUIPMENT:** 2 LARGE HANDFULS MESQUITE WOOD CHIPS

6 plum tomatoes

RUB
2 teaspoons freshly ground black pepper
½ teaspoon ground cumin
½ teaspoon paprika
¼ teaspoon onion powder
¼ teaspoon garlic powder

Sea salt
2 T-bone steaks, each 675–900g/
    1½–2lb and about 4cm/1½ inches
    thick
1 large chopped shallot
1½ tablespoons fresh lemon juice
1 tablespoon extra-virgin olive oil
1½ teaspoons chopped thyme leaves
1 teaspoon crushed garlic
¼ teaspoon ancho chilli powder, or
    to taste

These thick T-bones call for a more interactive method of grilling than just turning them once over the flames, especially if you are cooking over charcoal, where the fire is inherently uneven. Turning the steaks every minute (or even more often) helps to cook them more evenly and quickly. When you flip steaks often, both sides stay hot throughout the grilling time, meaning the meat reaches the desired doneness faster.

1 Soak the wood chips in water for at least 30 minutes.

2 Prepare the grill for indirect cooking over low heat (130–180°C/250–350°F).

3 Drain and add one handful of the wood chips to the charcoal or to the smoker box of a gas grill, following the manufacturer's instructions, and close the lid. When smoke appears, grill the tomatoes over **roasting/indirect low heat**, with the lid closed, until the skins are wrinkled, 20–35 minutes, depending on the size and ripeness of the tomatoes (do not turn). Don't worry if the skins split. Very carefully transfer them to a large chopping board. Increase the temperature of the grill and prepare it for direct cooking over medium heat (180–230°C/350–450°F).

4 Roughly chop the tomatoes, skin and all, and remove any tough cores. Scrape them into a sieve set over a bowl and drain well.

5 Mix the rub ingredients, including 1 teaspoon salt. Season the steaks all over with the rub, including the sides, and refrigerate until ready to grill.

6 Drain and add the remaining wood chips to the charcoal or smoker box. When smoke appears, grill the steaks over **grilling/direct medium heat**, with the lid closed, until cooked to your desired doneness, 16–20 minutes for medium rare, turning often. Transfer to a chopping board and allow to rest for 5 minutes.

7 Place the well-drained tomatoes in a serving bowl (discard their juice or save for another use). Stir in the shallot, lemon juice, oil, thyme, garlic, chilli powder and ½ teaspoon salt. Carve the steaks and serve warm with the smoked tomato salsa.

Juicy, spicy steaks filled with bold mesquite aromas get even better with a fire-roasted salsa that echoes the smoky flavours and adds moisture to the plate. Grill the tomatoes until they are very soft. Chop them and then drain them in a sieve before mixing them with the other salsa ingredients.

If your definition of barbecue is a limited one, a few hours talking with chef Tim Byres will have you questioning your beliefs. His menus at two Smoke restaurants in the Dallas area highlight the diversity of wood as a cooking fuel like few others. Byres' creativity in coaxing the flavours of smoke and fire into meats and vegetables is unmatched by most chefs, and he's not done yet.

A vast hearth kitchen is the focal point of the newest Smoke restaurant in Plano. Chops, steaks, fish and fowl cover the wood grill while whole chickens hang overhead gathering the smoke on its way up. Flames rise and flicker in a dance with the cast of grill cooks who flip meat and prepare sauces in pans set directly on to wood coals. Food runners bump into customers who stand gazing into the open kitchen with mouthwatering anticipation. It's not your normal fine dining experience, and it's not your 'normal' barbecue, especially in Dallas, and that's just what Byres was hoping for.

Byres reflects on his decision to create a unique vibe in Dallas along with a new way of honouring American foodways. 'To be a great restaurant it seemed like you needed to have expensive stemware, linen napkins in the bathroom and an elite squad of valet attendants. That's when I decided to step out of the box.' He had worked in the five-star kitchens of Stephan Pyles and John Tesar, but fine dining had left him unfulfilled. He hit the ceiling of haute cuisine and it hurt. He had wandered too far from the gratifying days of his youth cooking outside. The first Smoke restaurant was Byres' attempt at finding his culinary soul again. He committed to getting reacquainted with firewood cooking, which he calls 'the origin of American foodways'.

> 'I ENJOY BARBECUE AND I ENJOY THE IDEA OF IT, BUT I ENJOY THE COMMUNITY OF IT MOST.'

As you'd expect from the name, Smoke features barbecue in the strictest sense of that word. Smoked brisket, the signature of Texas, is on the menu along with spareribs and pulled pork, but there's a lot more. Byres smokes his own hams, homemade sausages and thick-sliced bacon. Pork cheek also gets the low smoke treatment before making it on to a platter with sweet chillies and half-sour pickles. Byres is no one-trick pony.

The signature at Smoke in Dallas has become The Big Rib. It's a gargantuan beef short rib barely clinging to a bone the size of an adult forearm. Most Texas barbecue joints would insist on leaving such

a cut unadorned, but Byres brings a multifaceted chef's mentality of layering flavours. That means a healthy spoonful of chimichurri sauce, raw sliced shallots and coriander. 'You balance the char with sweet, acidic, and raw,' he explains. The combination is stunning on the palate and, if you close your eyes, you can see its origins in the traditional Texas barbecue garnish of dill pickle chips and raw onion.

At festivals these days, Byres has moved on to meat swords. These are sticks of reinforcing steel mounted to the edges of his aptly named 'meat sword box'. Raw meats – goat meat and skirt steak work especially well – are affixed to the swords, which hang

at an angle over the fire. They cook slowly over the far away heat source, but are flavoured by the smoke in a way similar to an indirect smoker. It's hard to say which category the meat sword box fits in, but Byres says that's the beauty. 'It's really direct and indirect heat cooking, but how direct or indirect? That's the swing.' He says the more important thing about the meat swords is that they bring people together. 'I enjoy barbecue and I enjoy the idea of it, but I enjoy the community of it most.' In a festival setting, people gather around to gawk at the spectacle of meat on metal sticks, but they stick around to share the food with friends and strangers alike.

Back at Smoke in Plano, the restaurant is quickly becoming known for one item that is about as direct-heat as you can get. The enormous tomahawk rib eye is called the Eisenhower steak. It gets heavily seasoned, then grilled dirty, which means directly on the hot coals, just like the 34th president preferred it. The crust is stout, while the meat within remains ridiculously juicy. The plating and presenting at the table on a board the size of a small coffee table becomes a bit of performance art. It's just the latest in Byres' ever-expanding barbecue repertoire.

When pressed about what genre of barbecue he'll tackle next, Byres is unsure. 'I don't know what next year's plan will be, but we need to come up with something fun and different.' For him, that is the nature of barbecue. It has always been ripe for reinterpretation.

COAL-COOKED SIRLOIN STEAKS
WITH BALSAMIC GLAZE

SERVES: 4 | **PREP TIME:** 15 MINUTES | **GRILLING TIME:** 6–7 MINUTES
SPECIAL EQUIPMENT: CHARCOAL GRILL, ALL-NATURAL LUMP CHARCOAL

GLAZE
150ml/5fl oz balsamic vinegar
2 teaspoons light brown sugar
1 garlic clove, smashed and peeled

RUB
2 teaspoons sea salt
2 teaspoons freshly ground black pepper
1 teaspoon mustard powder
½ teaspoon crushed chilli flakes

4 sirloin steaks, each 285–340g/
   10–12oz and 2.5cm/1 inch thick,
   trimmed of nearly all fat around
   the perimeter
Sea salt

As if the pyrotechnics of traditional grilling aren't exciting enough, cooking right on live coals is a thrilling showstopper. This method requires a charcoal grill, and while it may seem daunting to cook without the cooking grate, it is actually quite fun.

1   In a small saucepan over a medium-high heat, bring the glaze ingredients to the boil. Reduce the heat and simmer for 3–5 minutes until the glaze is reduced by about half, watching carefully that it does not boil and burn. Remove from the heat and leave to cool and thicken slightly. Discard the garlic.

2   Combine the rub ingredients, and then season the steaks evenly with the rub. (Do not brush the steaks with oil; this will cause flare-ups.) Allow the steaks to stand at room temperature for 15–30 minutes before cooking.

3   Set the cooking grate aside; you will not be using it for this recipe. Make sure that the bottom vent on the grill is open. Place a chimney starter on the charcoal grate, and pack and fill it over the brim with all-natural lump charcoal (do not use briquettes). You need enough charcoal that, when ashed

over, it will fill two-thirds of the charcoal grate. Place newspaper or paraffin cubes underneath the chimney starter (do not use lighter fluid), ignite it and let the charcoal burn until lightly covered with white ash. Wearing insulated barbecue mitts or oven gloves, turn the coals out on to the charcoal grate. Break apart the larger pieces of charcoal to create a relatively even bed of coals. Using a metal baking sheet, fan any loose ashes from the coals.

4   Place the steaks directly on the coals. Put the lid on the grill, open the top vent on the lid and cook until the steaks are browned and have reached your desired doneness, 6–7 minutes for medium rare, turning once and using a spatula to knock off any coals that may cling to the meat. Remove from the grill and allow to rest for 5 minutes. Just before serving, season the steaks with salt and drizzle with the glaze. Serve straightaway.

Use boneless steaks at least 2.5cm/1 inch thick for this method, and trim off nearly all the fat around the perimeter, as the extra fat will cause serious flare-ups.

Lump charcoal is the only choice with direct coal cooking because it is completely natural.

Use long-handled tongs to smash very large chunks of charcoal into smaller pieces; you want the bed of coals to be as even as possible with a minimum of peaks and valleys.

Before adding the steaks, fan any loose ashes off the coals with a metal baking sheet.

Surprisingly, the meat does not always get a deep, dark char from direct coal cooking. With the meat right on the coals, there is not as much air to promote browning.

As you turn each steak or remove it from the grill, use a spatula to knock off any charcoal pieces clinging to the meat.

RED MEAT

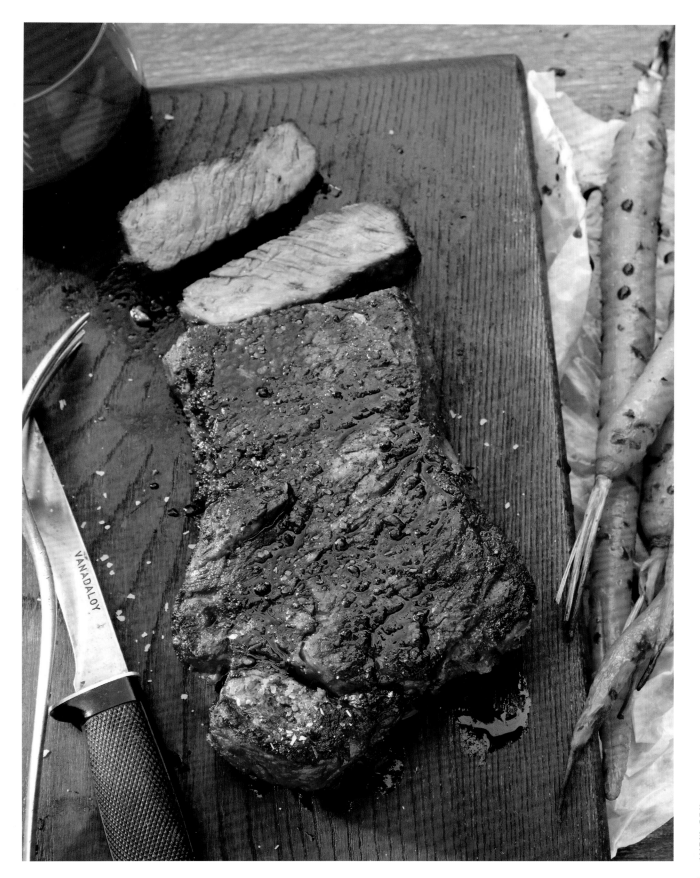

REVERSE-SEAR NEW YORK STEAKS
WITH RED WINE BUTTER

SERVES: 4 | PREP TIME: 15 MINUTES | STANDING TIME: 1 HOUR | GRILLING TIME: 29–39 MINUTES
SPECIAL EQUIPMENT: CHARCOAL GRILL, 2 LARGE HANDFULS HICKORY WOOD CHIPS, INSTANT-READ THERMOMETER

4 well-marbled sirloin strip steaks, each about 250g/8oz and 3–4cm/1¼–1½ inches thick
4 teaspoons extra-virgin olive oil
1½ teaspoons fine sea salt
2 teaspoons ground fennel seeds
350ml/12fl oz dry red wine, such as Cabernet
½ teaspoon red wine vinegar
1 shallot, finely chopped
Freshly ground black pepper
75g/3oz salted butter, cut into cubes, cold
1 tablespoon snipped chives

As an alternative to the traditional sear-n-slide method of grilling thick steaks, in which you sear them over direct heat and finish them over indirect heat, the reverse-sear method has recently captured the hopes and dreams of deeply devoted barbecue enthusiasts. Here, the steaks are first slow-roasted over low, indirect heat before they are finished over a ripping hot direct fire. The benefit is that the interior of the meat achieves an even pink colour from top to bottom (instead of the grey outer ring of overcooked meat in a sear-n-slide steak), and almost no precious juices are lost.

1 Brush the steaks on both sides with the oil. Combine the salt and fennel, and then rub evenly on to both sides of each steak. Allow the steaks to stand at room temperature for 1 hour before grilling.

2 Soak the wood chips in water for at least 30 minutes.

3 In a small, heavy saucepan, combine the wine, vinegar and shallot. Bring to a simmer over a medium-low heat and simmer until reduced to about 2 tablespoons. Remove from the heat and allow to stand at room temperature until 5 minutes before serving. (This may be done up to 2 hours in advance.)

4 Fill a chimney starter one-third full with charcoal (about 30 briquettes), and ignite. When covered with grey ash, dump the coals on one side of the charcoal grate, put the cooking grate in place and preheat for 10 minutes. The temperature of the grill should be about 150°C/300°F. Drain and add one handful of the wood chips to the charcoal. Grill the steaks over **roasting/indirect low heat**, for 25–35 minutes with the lid closed, until the interior temperature reaches 43–46°C/110–115°F.

5 While the steaks are cooking over indirect heat, light a full chimney starter filled with briquettes on a heatproof surface away from the grill. When the coals are very hot, transfer the steaks to a plate, remove the cooking grate and dump the hot coals over the remaining coals. Replace the cooking grate and lid and preheat the grate for 5 minutes. Drain and add the remaining wood chips to the charcoal. Grill the steaks over **grilling/direct high heat** for about 4 minutes, with the lid closed, until the interior temperature reaches about 55°C/130°F, turning once. Remove from the grill, season with pepper and allow to rest for 5 minutes.

6 Meanwhile, return the saucepan with the wine mixture over a medium-low heat on the hob or over direct heat on the cooking grate; cook until steaming. Remove from the heat and whisk in one cube of the cold butter. Whisk the butter constantly until the mixture is emulsified, and then begin to slowly add the remaining cubes of butter until the mixture is pale and smooth. Swirl in the chives. Serve the red wine butter over the warm steaks.

SANTA MARIA-STYLE RUMP ROAST
WITH GARLIC BREAD

SERVES: 4–6 | **PREP TIME:** 15 MINUTES | **CHILLING TIME:** 30 MINUTES–4 HOURS | **GRILLING TIME:** ABOUT 30 MINUTES
SPECIAL EQUIPMENT: CHARCOAL GRILL, 2 LARGE HANDFULS OAK OR PECAN WOOD CHUNKS, INSTANT-READ THERMOMETER

1 top rump, 1.1–1.4kg/2½–3lb and 3–4cm/1¼–1½ inches thick
1 tablespoon extra-virgin oil
1½ teaspoons sea salt
1 teaspoon garlic granules
Freshly ground black pepper
50g/2oz salted butter, melted
2 garlic cloves, finely chopped
12 slices sourdough bread, each about 1cm/½ inch thick
Shop-bought salsa

Santa Maria BBQ has quietly persevered in a swathe of central California since the mid-1800s, when the region was still part of Mexico. To this day cooks from Santa Barbara to San Luis Obispo continue to cook like the vaqueros (cowboys), who grilled rump roasts over a hot fire of coastal red oak, turning and flipping the meat occasionally to avoid scorching it. Another approach is to first roast the meat over indirect heat and then char it directly over the fire. Most Santa Maria locals still use top rump, but I've seen rib eyes and hefty sirloin steaks cooked there in a similar fashion – with just a simple rub and no sauce to speak of. The usual accompaniments are a mixed green salad, pinquito beans (small pink beans similar to kidney beans) and fresh salsa. Sometimes there is a cold macaroni salad and always there is excellent garlic bread.

1   Rub the joint all over with the oil. Combine the salt and garlic granules, and then rub evenly all over the meat, pushing it into the nooks and crannies. Place the meat on a rack set over a baking tray and refrigerate for at least 30 minutes or up to 4 hours.

2   Fill a chimney starter one-third full with charcoal (about 30 briquettes), and ignite. When covered with grey ash, dump the coals on one side of the charcoal grate, place half of the wood chunks on the charcoal, put the cooking grate in place and preheat the grill until the temperature is 93–130°C/200–250°F. Grill the meat over **roasting/indirect very low heat** for about 20 minutes, with the lid closed, until the interior temperature of the roast reaches 49–52°C/120–125°F.

3   Soon after the meat begins cooking, light a full chimney starter filled with briquettes on a heatproof surface away from the grill. When the coals are very hot, transfer the meat from the grill to a plate. Remove the cooking grate, dump the hot coals over the remaining coals and add the remaining wood chunks to the charcoal. Replace the cooking grate, close the lid and preheat the grill for direct cooking over high heat (230–290°C/450–550°F). Grill the beef over **grilling/direct high heat** for 10–12 minutes, with the lid closed, until the interior temperature reaches 55–57°C/130–135°F and the exterior is nicely charred, turning every 2–3 minutes or as necessary if flare-ups arise. Transfer to a carving board, season with pepper and allow to rest for 5 minutes.

4   Meanwhile, combine the melted butter and garlic, and then brush both sides of each piece of bread with the garlic butter. Grill the bread over **grilling/direct high heat** for about 1 minute until golden brown, turning once or twice. Cut the roast across the grain into 5-mm/¼-inch thick slices and serve warm with the garlic bread and salsa.

SANTA MARIA STYLE
— Barbecue —

Way out in the ranching country of Central California, there's a little known but proudly named barbecue style that bears as much resemblance to what they serve in Kansas City as a rattlesnake to a possum. It's called Santa Maria style – after the town of the same name – and here's the kicker: there's no sauce involved and, in its truest form, the beef is only cooked over a hardwood fire, specifically red (aka coastal live) oak. Sounds like what others call 'grilling.' Bite your tongue! 'We don't say "grill," we say "barbecue,"' explains Sandy Knotts, current custodian of Jocko's Steak House in nearby Nipomo. And, with all due respect to other styles of barbecue across this great land, without any sauce, you really taste the smoky-delicious meat.

Back in the 1900s, local ranchers and their vaqueros collaborated to create a way of turning local livestock into an outrageously great dinner. Almost as important as the meat are some classic sides: local pinquito beans (small pink beans indigenous to the area) are served with very mild salsa, and there's always plenty of butter-drenched garlic bread plus a simple green salad (this is California, after all).

In some spots, there's been no tampering with tradition. Santa Maria native Ike Simas, 87, has been cooking Santa Maria-style barbecue for most of his life. He's fed 4,500 people at the Cow Palace in San Francisco and President Reagan at the Western White House. He cooks for the Elks Lodge most weekends, and can feed 900 people for lunch, and then help a friend serve 300 that evening. He manhandles huge pieces of salt- and garlic salt-crusted sirloin with a long hook, and admits to disliking the cut that is – these days, anyway – most often associated with Santa Maria style: top rump. It is known in the US as tri tip, the cut was born back in the fifties, when a local grocer had the idea of barbecuing a funny-shaped piece of bottom sirloin that usually was just minced up into burger blend. But: 'We don't like that word,' Simas says of tri tip. 'That's not the meat that made us famous. In the old days, we always used rib eye, and I liked to poke holes in it and push in some pieces of garlic. But then it got too expensive, and we started using top rump.'

About an hour's drive north of Santa Barbara, a free-spirited chef and winemaker wearing a safari hat and Groucho Marx moustache is broadening the Santa Maria traditions with his own high-end sensibilities. At his roadside restaurant, Hitching Post II, Frank Ostini grills dry-aged fillet steak, bone-in Angus rib chops and other pricey proteins (like Texas quail and Gulf prawns) over red oak.

Forget the beans. He serves his steaks with thick, hand-cut French fries cooked twice in rendered beef fat, and somehow he still manages to call all that Santa Maria-style barbecue. Ostini is completely comfortable in his role as a culinary maverick, as long as the food is cooked over a live fire of red oak and tastes top notch. 'Tradition is a good excuse not to work at it,' he says. 'I like to take tradition into the future where it's even better than before.'

STEAK SANDWICHES ON TEXAS TOAST
WITH ESPRESSO BARBECUE SAUCE

SERVES: 4 | PREP TIME: 20 MINUTES, PLUS ABOUT 50 MINUTES FOR THE SAUCE
GRILLING TIME: 9–11 MINUTES | SPECIAL EQUIPMENT: 2 LARGE HANDFULS MESQUITE WOOD CHIPS

SAUCE
1 tablespoon extra-virgin olive oil
1 small onion, finely chopped
1 garlic clove, finely chopped
1 tablespoon mild chilli powder
1 teaspoon ground cumin
½ teaspoon paprika
125ml/4fl oz ketchup-style chilli sauce
125ml/4fl oz strong coffee
2 tablespoons light brown sugar
2 tablespoons balsamic vinegar

RUB
1½ teaspoons sea salt
1 teaspoon mild chilli powder
½ teaspoon ground cumin
½ teaspoon freshly ground black
    pepper

1 skirt steak, about 675g/1½lb and
    2cm/¾ inch thick
Extra-virgin olive oil
50g/2oz salted butter, softened
2 garlic cloves, finely chopped
4 slices white, French or Italian bread,
    each about 2.5cm/1 inch thick
75g/3oz baby rocket

Increasingly, coffee has broken out of its role as a beverage to become a cooking ingredient, too. In fact, it shows up in some old cowboy recipes as a slightly bitter flavour to complement spiciness and sweetness, as in this barbecue sauce. This sauce can be made with filter espresso or dark roast real coffee, so you don't have to run out to your local café. The sauce works beautifully with the full, meaty flavours of skirt steak. Texas toast is a speciality of that state, made from extra-thick slices of white bread, spread with butter and grilled until golden brown – a warm bed for the sliced steak and eye-opening sauce.

1. In a heavy saucepan over a medium-low heat, warm the oil. Add the onion and cook for about 30 minutes until super soft and very dark, stirring occasionally. Stir in the garlic and cook until fragrant, about 1 minute. Add the chilli powder, cumin and paprika and stir well. Add the remaining sauce ingredients and bring to the boil over a medium-high heat. Reduce the heat to low and simmer for 15–20 minutes, uncovered, until the sauce thickens and is reduced to about 250ml/ 8 fl oz, stirring occasionally.

2. Soak the wood chips in water for at least 30 minutes.

3. Mix the rub ingredients. Lightly brush the steak on both sides with oil and season evenly with the rub. Allow the steak to stand at room temperature for 15–30 minutes before grilling.

4. Combine the butter and garlic, and then spread on both sides of the bread slices. Stand the slices upright, cut sides together, on a plate until ready to grill.

5. Prepare the grill for direct cooking over medium heat (180–230°C/350–450°F).

6. Drain and add the wood chips to the charcoal or to the smoker box of a gas grill, following the manufacturer's instructions, and close the lid. When smoke appears, grill the steak over **grilling/direct medium heat**, with the lid closed, until cooked to your desired doneness, 8–10 minutes for medium rare, turning once. During the last minute of grilling time, brush the steak on both sides with some of the sauce, and turn once or twice to glaze the surface. Remove from the grill and allow to rest for 3–5 minutes.

7. Grill the bread slices over **grilling/direct medium heat** until lightly toasted, about 1 minute, turning once.

8. Cut the steak across the grain into thin slices. Build the sandwiches on the toasted bread with rocket, steak and sauce. Drizzle the sandwiches with the carving juices. Serve warm with additional sauce on the side. Any leftover sauce can be stored in the refrigerator in a covered container for up to 2 weeks.

The grain of a skirt steak looks a little like countless pieces of thread running in the same direction. If you make a cut in that same (parallel) direction, you get long stretches of thread that are hard to chew. But if you cut across (perpendicular to) the threads in very thin slices, you get short, little bits of thread that are easy to chew. Because skirt steak is so wide, make the slicing more manageable by cutting the steak in half lengthways before slicing each half across the grain.

HOMEMADE PASTRAMI
WITH CORIANDER-PEPPER RUB

SERVES: 6–8 | PREP TIME: 10 MINUTES | SOAKING TIME: 8–16 HOURS | COOKING TIME: 4½–5½ HOURS
STANDING TIME: 1 HOUR | CHILLING TIME: AT LEAST 8 HOURS | SPECIAL EQUIPMENT: SPICE MILL, WATER SMOKER, 2 LARGE HANDFULS
APPLE WOOD CHUNKS, HEAVY-DUTY ALUMINIUM FOIL, SPRAY BOTTLE FILLED WITH WATER, INSTANT-READ THERMOMETER

RUB
1½ tablespoons black peppercorns
1½ tablespoons coriander seeds
1½ teaspoons yellow mustard seeds
1½ teaspoons paprika
¾ teaspoon garlic granules
¾ teaspoon onion flakes
¾ teaspoon crushed chilli flakes

1 salt beef brisket, about
1.8kg/4lb, preferably the flat end
Vegetable oil

A butcher in a New York deli might take weeks to make cured, spice-crusted and smoked pastrami from raw beef brisket, but my streamlined version starts with shop-bought salt beef, greatly reducing the prep time.

1 In a spice mill, coarsely grind the peppercorns, coriander and mustard seeds (see tip No. 2 below). Put the ground spices in a bowl and add the remaining rub ingredients.

2 Drain the salt beef and rinse well under cold running water. If necessary, trim the fat cap so it is about 8mm/⅓ inch thick, but no less. Place the brisket in a deep roasting tin or other food-safe container and cover it completely with cold water. Refrigerate for at least 8 hours or up to 16 hours, changing the water every few hours.

3 Drain the meat and pat dry with kitchen paper. Very lightly brush the joint all over with oil and season evenly with the rub, pressing the rub firmly with your hands to make sure it adheres securely to the meat.

4 Prepare the smoker for indirect cooking with low heat (as close to 130°C/250°F as possible).

5 Add the wood chunks to the charcoal, then cook the brisket over *roasting/indirect low heat* for 2 hours, with the lid closed. Remove the meat from the smoker and place it on a large

sheet of heavy-duty aluminium foil. Spray the meat on both sides with water, and then tightly wrap in the foil. Return the brisket to the smoker and continue cooking over *roasting/indirect low heat* for 2½–3½ hours more, with the lid closed, until an instant-read thermometer inserted into the thickest part of the meat registers 88–90.5°C/190–195°F. Remove from the grill, open the foil, lift the brisket from the juices and place it on a clean piece of foil. Wrap it well and allow to stand for 1 hour. Refrigerate until completely chilled, at least 8 hours.

6 Unwrap the pastrami and cut it across the grain into very thin slices. Place a collapsible steamer inside a large saucepan. Add enough water to come up to 5mm/¼ inch from the bottom of the steamer and bring the water to the boil over a high heat. Add the sliced pastrami to the steamer and tightly cover the saucepan. Reduce the heat to very low. Steam for 15–20 minutes, occasionally moving the slices from top to bottom, until the pastrami is hot and the fat is translucent. Serve warm with bagels and scrambled eggs, if liked.

TIPS } HOMEMADE PASTRAMI

1
Purchase salt beef from the flat end of the brisket, not the thicker, fattier point end.

2
The peppercorns, coriander seeds and mustard seeds vary in size and hardness, so grind each spice separately to get the right coarseness. Use an electric spice mill.

3
Resist the temptation to tear into the pastrami right off the smoker, as it needs to be chilled overnight to facilitate thin slicing. Use a sharp, thin-bladed carving knife for slicing.

4
The classic way to reheat pastrami is over steam. If you prefer, reheat the slices in a microwave: spread the slices in a heatproof dish, sprinkle them with 2 tablespoons of water, cover the dish and microwave at medium until they are hot, 3–5 minutes.

5
Leftovers will keep for about 5 days in the refrigerator. Smoked meats do not freeze well.

BEEF DEBRIS PO'BOYS

SERVES: 6 | PREP TIME: 20 MINUTES | GRILLING TIME: 3¼–4¼ HOURS
SPECIAL EQUIPMENT: 3 LARGE HANDFULS PECAN OR OAK WOOD CHIPS, LARGE (6-LITRE/10-PINT) GRILLPROOF
CAST-IRON CASSEROLE

1 beef brisket, about 1.4kg/3lb and
    5cm/2 inches thick
Extra-virgin olive oil
Sea salt
Freshly ground black pepper
400ml/14fl oz beef stock
125ml/4 fl oz hearty red wine
3 tablespoons tomato purée
2 tablespoons Worcestershire sauce
675–900g/1½–2lb onions, cut into
    thin half-moons
8 large garlic cloves, coarsely chopped
2 teaspoons finely chopped thyme
2 bay leaves
6 crusty, oblong French rolls, split
Mayonnaise
Lettuce leaves
Tomato slices

Let's face it: debris is not a very appetising word, even if it does sound French. In New Orleans parlance, it refers to a beef pot roast that is cooked until it is fall-apart tender, making the scrap-like pieces that inspire its name. The added smoke makes a good thing even better. Tuck the succulent meat (and the onions cooked along with it), into a crusty roll, and you have a po'boy sandwich fit for the sandwich gods. The story of po'boy is another colourful, and questionable, bit of culinary lore that supposedly started with sandwiches being handed out to unemployed poor workers during a strike.

1 Soak the wood chips in water for at least 30 minutes.

2 Brush the beef all over with 1 tablespoon oil and season evenly with salt and pepper. Allow the roast to stand at room temperature for 30 minutes before grilling.

3 Prepare the grill for direct cooking over high heat (230–290°C/450–550°F).

4 Drain and add two handfuls of the wood chips to the charcoal or to the smoker box of a gas grill, following the manufacturer's instructions, and close the lid. When the wood begins to smoke, sear the meat over **grilling/direct high heat** for 8–10 minutes, with the lid closed, until lightly browned, turning once.

5 Reduce the temperature of the grill and prepare it for indirect cooking over medium heat (180–200°C/350–400°F). Slide the beef over **roasting/indirect medium heat** and continue cooking for 25–30 minutes, with the lid closed, until it is more deeply browned (do not turn).

6 Meanwhile, in a large bowl, whisk the stock, wine, tomato purée, Worcestershire sauce and 1 tablespoon oil until the tomato purée is dissolved. Add the onions, garlic, thyme, 1½ teaspoons salt and ½ teaspoon pepper

and mix well. Transfer half of the onion mixture, including about half of the liquid, to a large grillproof cast-iron casserole. When the meat is browned, place it on the onions, and then top with the remaining onion mixture and liquid. Tuck the bay leaves into the liquid. Do not cover the casserole at this point.

7 Drain and add the remaining wood chips to the charcoal or smoker box. Cook the beef in the casserole over **roasting/indirect medium heat** for 15–20 minutes, with the lid closed, until the onions begin to soften. Tightly cover the casserole with foil. Continue cooking for 2½–3¼ hours, with the lid closed, until the meat is so tender that there is no resistance at all when a fork is inserted, turning once.

8 Remove the casserole from the grill, transfer the beef to a carving board and allow to stand for 5 minutes. If you wish, toast the rolls, cut side down, on the grill over direct heat, about 1 minute. Spread the rolls with mayonnaise as liked. Cut the beef across the grain into thick slices. Stir any 'debris' that falls off back into the onions. Season the onion mixture and cooking juices with salt and pepper. Pile the beef, onion mixture, lettuce and tomato on the rolls. Serve warm.

ANCHO BEEF AND BEAN CHILLI

SERVES: 6–8 | **PREP TIME:** 40 MINUTES
GRILLING TIME: 2–2½ HOURS | **SPECIAL EQUIPMENT:** LARGE (6-LITRE/10-PINT) GRILLPROOF CAST-IRON CASSEROLE

3 ancho chillies, about 40g/1½oz
    total, stems removed and deseeded
3 guajillo chillies, about 20g/¾oz
    total, stems removed and deseeded
1–1.5 litres/1¾–2 pints beef stock
1 beef brisket, about 1.4kg/3lb,
    trimmed and cut into 2.5cm/
    1-inch pieces
Sea salt
Freshly ground black pepper
Extra-virgin olive oil
240g/8oz onions, finely chopped
4 garlic cloves, finely chopped
2 tablespoons hot chilli powder
1 tablespoon ground cumin
1 tablespoon paprika
2 teaspoons dried oregano
½ teaspoon ground allspice
3 tablespoons masa harina
2 cans (each 400g/14oz) fire-roasted
    chopped tomatoes in juice
2 cans (each 425g/15oz) red kidney
    beans, rinsed and drained
25g/1oz plain chocolate, chopped
Chopped spring onions
Grated Cheddar cheese
Your favourite hot sauce

The origin of chilli has long been debated, sometimes to a point of infuriation. Many legends point to the Inca, Aztec and Mayan people as the first to make it, but even more stories centre on cattle drivers and cowboys of the American West who popularised the dish. One thing that is fairly certain is that chilli is essentially a stewed mixture of meat, chillies, herbs, spices and sometimes, beans. We can argue for days about who makes the best chilli, or where it can be found, but the recipe right here is darn good, and you can make it right in your own backyard.

1   Bring a saucepan of water to the boil over a high heat. Add the chillies, remove from the heat and allow to stand until softened, about 30 minutes. Drain the chillies, transfer to a blender, and add 1 litre/1¾ pints of stock. Purée and set aside.

2   Prepare the grill for direct cooking over medium-low heat (150–170°C/300–325°F) and preheat a large grillproof cast-iron casserole, without its lid, for 10 minutes.

3   Season the meat with 1 teaspoon salt and ½ teaspoon pepper. Warm 1 tablespoon oil in the casserole and add half of the meat. Cook over **grilling/direct medium-low heat** for about 5 minutes, with the grill lid closed, until lightly browned, stirring twice. Transfer the meat to a plate. Repeat with the remaining meat, adding another tablespoon of oil, if necessary.

4   Return all of the meat to the casserole and stir in the onions and garlic. Close the grill lid and cook for 4–5 minutes until the onions are slightly softened. Stir in the chilli powder,

cumin, paprika, oregano and allspice and cook until fragrant, about 1 minute, stirring to coat the meat evenly with the spices. Add the puréed chilli mixture, masa harina, chopped tomatoes and their juice and ½ teaspoon salt. Put the lid on the casserole, leaving it slightly ajar, close the grill lid and adjust the temperature to direct low heat (130–150°C/250–300°F). Simmer the chilli for 1¾–2¼ hours until the meat is fork tender, stirring occasionally with a metal spatula and loosening the chilli from the bottom and sides of the casserole as needed. Add more stock if the chilli is becoming too thick, checking about every 20 minutes. Stir in the beans during the last 15 minutes of cooking time.

5   Wearing insulated barbecue mitts or oven gloves, carefully remove the lid of the casserole and add the chocolate, stirring until it is melted, about 1 minute. Remove the chilli from the grill and season with salt and pepper. Serve in bowls topped with spring onions, cheese and your favourite hot sauce.

It is no accident that three of the most significant, indigenous ingredients in Mexican food – corn, chillies and chocolate – are featured in this Mexican-American recipe. Dried corn is the basis for masa harina, the ground mixture we use to thicken chilli. Of course, the ancho and guajillo chillies give the chilli its deep, spicy character, and the chocolate takes the edge off the spiciness and rounds out the flavours.

HICKORY-SMOKED FORE RIB
WITH SHALLOT-CABERNET REDUCTION SAUCE

SERVES: 8–10 | **PREP TIME:** 30 MINUTES, PLUS ABOUT 1 HOUR FOR THE SAUCE | **GRILLING TIME:** 2–2½ HOURS
SPECIAL EQUIPMENT: 2 LARGE HANDFULS HICKORY WOOD CHIPS, KITCHEN STRING, INSTANT-READ THERMOMETER

RUB
1½ tablespoons sea salt
1 tablespoon ancho chilli powder
2 teaspoons dried basil
1½ teaspoons paprika
1½ teaspoons ground cumin
1½ teaspoons freshly ground black
    pepper

1 rib beef fore with 3 bones,
    about 3.2kg/7lb

SAUCE
75g/3oz unsalted butter
225g/8oz shallots, finely chopped
6 garlic cloves, finely chopped
1 large carrot, finely chopped
1 large celery stalk, finely chopped
2 bay leaves
1 tablespoon thyme leaves
1 bottle (750ml) Cabernet Sauvignon
    or other dry red wine
550ml/19fl oz beef stock
1½ tablespoons tomato purée
½ teaspoon sea salt
½ teaspoon freshly ground black
    pepper

Bring on the top-dollar barbecue and open your best bottle of wine or Scotch. The hardest part of making this dish is the shopping. After that, cut the bones off the meat so you can season more surface areas, make a decadent red wine sauce and cook the beast with smoke until the internal temperature is just under 49°C/120°F. It will continue to cook off the heat, producing utterly luscious, rosy slices and meaty ribs with gorgeously charred crusts.

1   Soak the wood chips in water for at least 30 minutes.

2   Combine the rub ingredients. Using a sharp knife, cut between the rib bones and the meat, keeping the three bones together as one unit, and leaving about 5cm/2 inches of the meat attached to the bottom of the bones. Season the meaty side of the rib bones and the joint all over with the rub. Using kitchen string, tie the rib bones back on to the joint in its original form (see photos below). Allow the meat to stand at room temperature for 1 hour before grilling.

3   In a large saucepan over a medium-high heat, melt 25g/1oz of the butter. Add the shallots, garlic, carrot, celery, bay leaves and thyme and cook for 4–5 minutes, until slightly softened, stirring occasionally. Add the wine, bring to the boil and cook for 15–17 minutes until the mixture resembles coarse, wet sand. Add the stock and tomato purée, return to the boil, reduce the heat to medium and simmer until reduced to 600ml/20fl oz, about 30 minutes. Remove the saucepan from the heat and pour the sauce through a sieve set over a medium bowl. Press on the solids with a spatula or large spoon to release the liquids. Discard the solids. Return the sauce to the saucepan and reserve.

4   Prepare the grill for indirect cooking over medium-low heat (as close to 180°C/350°F as possible).

5   Drain and add one handful of the wood chips to the smoker box of a gas grill, following the manufacturer's instructions, and close the lid. When smoke appears, grill the meat, bone side down, over *roasting/indirect medium-low heat* for 2–2½ hours, with the lid closed, until an instant-read thermometer inserted into the thickest part of the joint (not touching the bone) registers about 48°C/118°F for medium rare. Drain and add the remaining wood chips to the smoker box after the first hour of grilling. Remove the meat from the grill.

6   Separate the meat from the rib section, cover the ribs and meat with foil and allow to rest for 20 minutes (the internal temperature will rise 5–10 degrees during this time). Meanwhile, warm the sauce over a medium heat until just hot. Remove the sauce from the heat and whisk in the remaining butter until just melted. Season the sauce with the salt and pepper.

7   Cut the meat into thick slices and cut between the bones to make three individual ribs. Serve immediately with the warm sauce.

RACKS OF LAMB
WITH MUSTARD-CAPER BOARD DRESSING

SERVES: 4 | PREP TIME: 20 MINUTES | MARINATING TIME: 3-4 HOURS (OPTIONAL) | GRILLING TIME: 16-20 MINUTES
SPECIAL EQUIPMENT: 2 LARGE HANDFULS MESQUITE WOOD CHIPS, INSTANT-READ THERMOMETER

2 lamb racks, each
    about 675g/1½lb, frenched
Extra-virgin olive oil
Sea salt
Freshly ground black pepper
¾ teaspoon dried thyme, crumbled

BOARD DRESSING
4 tablespoons capers, drained
    and finely chopped
4 tablespoons finely chopped
    flat-leaf parsley
2 tablespoons Dijon mustard
40ml/1½fl oz brandy (optional)
40ml/1½fl oz extra-virgin olive oil
1 tablespoon finely chopped garlic
2 teaspoons red wine vinegar
1 teaspoon sea salt
1 teaspoon freshly ground black pepper

My friend Adam Perry Lang first coined the term 'board dressing' for the technique of assembling a handful of flavourful ingredients directly on a carving board and then carving meat directly on top. The juices from the meat mingle together with the flavourings to create a dressing or sauce, and ingredients are almost infinitely variable. The technique, if not the name, has been surging in popularity among grill aficionados lately, so with this recipe I'll show you how it's done.

1   Soak the wood chips in water for at least 30 minutes.

2   Trim off most of the fat from the meaty side of the lamb racks, exposing the meat in a few places. Lightly coat both sides of the racks with oil and season generously with salt, pepper and the thyme. If possible, refrigerate the racks, uncovered, for 3–4 hours. Allow the racks to stand at room temperature for 15–30 minutes before grilling.

3   Prepare the grill for direct cooking over medium-high heat (200–230°C/400–450°F).

4   Mound the board dressing ingredients in the centre of a large carving board and place it near the grill (place the carving board inside a baking tray, if liked).

5   Drain and add the wood chips to the charcoal or to the smoker box of a gas grill, following the manufacturer's instructions, and close the lid. When smoke appears, grill the racks, meaty side down, over **grilling/direct medium-high heat** for 8 minutes, with the lid closed, moving them around if flare-ups occur. Turn the racks over, bone side down, and then place a rectangle of foil underneath the bones to prevent them from burning. Continue grilling for 8–12 minutes more until the internal temperature reaches about 57°C/135°F and the meat is springy to the touch. To crisp the 'eye' of the meat at either end, use tongs to hold the racks with the ends directly on the cooking grate for a few seconds.

6   Using a fork, blend the board dressing ingredients together and gather into an oval shape. Transfer the racks directly to the carving board, meaty side down, right on top of the dressing. Allow the meat to rest for 3 minutes, and then cut into individual chops. Drag both sides of the chops through the board dressing. Serve warm.

When the lamb racks are cooked, immediately transfer them to the carving board and let them rest for a few minutes so that the meat juices can meld with the board dressing ingredients. Then cut the racks into individual chops and dredge them through the dressing on both sides.

LAMB CHOPS
WITH MOROCCAN RUB AND TOMATO-CHICKPEA SALAD

SERVES: 4 | **PREP TIME:** 25 MINUTES
GRILLING TIME: 8–10 MINUTES

RUB
2 teaspoons hot chilli powder
1 teaspoon sea salt
½ teaspoon freshly ground black
   pepper
½ teaspoon ground coriander
½ teaspoon ground cumin
½ teaspoon caraway seeds
¼ teaspoon garlic powder

2 lamb racks, each 675–900g/
   1½–2lb chine bones removed,
   frenched and trimmed of excess
   fat and silver skin
Extra-virgin olive oil
Sea salt

SALAD
1½ tablespoons fresh lemon juice
¼ teaspoon freshly ground black
   pepper
1 can (400g/14oz) chickpeas, rinsed
   and drained
225g/8oz multicoloured cherry
   tomatoes, each cut in half
4 tablespoons roughly chopped basil
75g/3oz thinly sliced hearts of
   romaine

Lemon wedges

Most lamb chops are just too thin and tiny for high heat. In the time it takes to char the outsides, the insides become overcooked. My recommendation is to scale back on the heat, buy whole racks of lamb and cut them into double chops, each about 4cm/1½ inches thick. This method does require some work with a knife to remove the layer of fat covering the meaty side and the bones. You also need to methodically cut away the meat and fat between the bones.

1   Mix the rub ingredients.

2   For each rack of lamb, remove the thick cap of fat covering the chops by slipping a thin-bladed knife into the seam below it and pulling away the fat with your hands. Make one long crossways cut over the top of the bones about 5cm/2 inches above the meaty centre of each chop. Slip your knife under the thin layer of meat and fat clinging to the bones and pull off that layer with your hands. Cut out the individual strips of meat between the bones. Scrape the bones clean with the blade of your knife. Then cut each rack into four chops, each about 4cm/1½ inches thick and including two rib bones (see photos below).

3   Lightly brush the chops on both sides with oil and season evenly with the rub. Allow the chops to stand at room temperature for 15–30 minutes before grilling.

4   Prepare the grill for direct cooking over medium heat (180–230°C/350–450°F).

5   In a serving bowl, whisk 3 tablespoons oil, the lemon juice, ½ teaspoon sea salt and the pepper. Add the chickpeas, tomatoes and basil and mix well.

6   Grill the chops over **grilling/direct medium heat**, with the lid closed, until cooked to your desired doneness, 8–10 minutes for medium rare, turning four times to grill all sides (if flare-ups occur, move the chops temporarily over indirect heat). Remove the chops from the grill, season with sea salt and allow to rest for 3–5 minutes.

7   Add the lettuce to the salad and mix well. Serve the chops warm with the salad and lemon wedges.

LAMB AND RED PEPPER KEBABS
WITH PICKLE JAR MARINADE

SERVES: 4-6 | **PREP TIME:** 25 MINUTES | **MARINATING TIME:** 4-8 HOURS
GRILLING TIME: 8-10 MINUTES | **SPECIAL EQUIPMENT:** 12 METAL OR BAMBOO SKEWERS

Don't let that brine in the pickle jar go to waste! It can make a terrific marinade that gives a boost to lamb. The amount of salt in brines tends to vary a lot from brand to brand, so taste the meat after cooking. If it needs a little more oomph, sprinkle some salt over the kebabs.

MARINADE
250ml/8fl oz brine from a jar of
  pickled dill cucumbers
1 large red onion, finely chopped
1 teaspoon caraway seeds
½ teaspoon crushed chilli flakes

900g/2lb boneless leg of lamb, cut
  into 2.5-4-cm/1-1½-inch pieces
4 medium dill cucumber halves, cut
  into 2.5-cm/1-inch chunks
1 red pepper, cut into 2.5-cm/1-inch
  pieces
Sea salt

1 Whisk the marinade ingredients. Place the lamb pieces in a large, resealable plastic bag and pour in the marinade. Press the air out of the bag and seal tightly. Turn the bag to distribute the marinade, place the bag in a bowl and refrigerate for 4-8 hours, turning the bag occasionally.

2 If using bamboo skewers, soak them in water for at least 30 minutes.

3 Prepare the grill for direct cooking over medium-high heat (200-230°C/400-450°F).

4 Remove the lamb pieces from the bag, leaving any spices on the meat. Discard the marinade. Thread the lamb pieces, dill cucumbers chunks and red pepper pieces alternately on to skewers, and then grill over **grilling/direct medium-high heat**, with the lid closed, until cooked to your desired doneness, 8-10 minutes for medium, turning occasionally. Remove from the grill and season with salt, if liked. Serve warm.

RED MEAT

154

MESQUITE-SMOKED BEEF RIBS
WITH BEER MOP

SERVES: 4–5 | **PREP TIME:** 15 MINUTES, PLUS ABOUT 20 MINUTES FOR THE MOP | **COOKING TIME:** 6–7 HOURS
SPECIAL EQUIPMENT: WATER SMOKER, 4 LARGE HANDFULS MESQUITE WOOD CHUNKS

Beef back ribs are the unsung, underrated understudies of American barbecue. Butchers cut beef from fore rib joints, almost always leaving most of the meat on the joints and making the bones almost bare. If you ever meet an agreeable butcher, ask him to cut a couple racks of back ribs with meat at least 2.5cm/1 inch thick. Barbecue these until the meat between the ribs is tender enough that you can slide a fork in and out with very little resistance.

2 racks beef back ribs, each 7 bones
    and 2.3–2.7kg/5–6lb, preferably
    meaty bones
2 tablespoons sea salt
1 tablespoon freshly ground
    black pepper

MOP
500ml/18fl oz passata
350ml/12fl oz pale ale
4 tablespoons dark brown sugar
4 tablespoons American mustard
4 tablespoons cider vinegar
1 teaspoon ground cumin
½ teaspoon sea salt
½ teaspoon ground cloves

1   Prepare the smoker for indirect cooking with very low heat (93–130°C/200–250°F), filling the water pan about three-quarters full with water.

2   Peel off the thin membrane on the underside of each rack of ribs. Rub the salt and pepper into the meat on both sides of the racks.

3   When the smoker reaches 130°C/250°F, add the wood chunks to the charcoal. Set the beef racks on the cooking grate, bone side down, and cook over *roasting/indirect very low heat*, with the lid closed, for 3 hours.

4   Meanwhile, in a heavy saucepan over a medium-high heat, whisk the mop ingredients until the brown sugar is dissolved. Bring to the boil, reduce the

heat to low and simmer slowly for 15–20 minutes until reduced to about half the original volume, stirring occasionally with a wooden spoon.

5   After 3 hours, mop the ribs all over, and then continue cooking over *roasting/indirect very low heat* for 3–4 hours more, with the lid closed, until you can slide a fork in and out of the meat with very little resistance, mopping every hour. Maintain a steady, even temperature between 93 and 130°C/200 and 250°F for the duration of the cooking time.

6   Remove the racks from the smoker, tent with foil and allow to rest for 10–15 minutes. Cut the racks between the bones so there is plenty of meat on both sides of each rib. Serve warm.

KOREAN SHORT RIB TACOS
WITH KOGI SAUCE AND PICKLED CUCUMBERS

SERVES: 6 | **PREP TIME:** 30 MINUTES | **PICKLING TIME:** 1 HOUR
MARINATING TIME: 24 HOURS | **GRILLING TIME:** 4–6 MINUTES

MARINADE
6 garlic cloves
1 Granny Smith apple, cored and cut into quarters
1 large onion, about 175g/6oz, cut into quarters
1 piece fresh ginger, about 5cm/ 2 inches long, peeled and coarsely chopped
250ml/8fl oz soy sauce
115g/4oz light brown sugar
4 tablespoons Asian rice wine or sherry
2 tablespoons toasted sesame oil
1 teaspoon freshly ground black pepper
½ teaspoon ground cayenne pepper

1.4kg/3lb beef short ribs, cut across the bone

PICKLED CUCUMBERS
1 cucumber, very thinly sliced
1 red jalapeño chilli, finely chopped
2 tablespoons unseasoned rice vinegar
1 teaspoon sea salt
½ teaspoon granulated sugar

KOGI SAUCE (see headnote*)
4 tablespoons *gochujang* (Korean fermented chilli paste)
60ml/4 tablespoons soy sauce
3 tablespoons granulated sugar
1 tablespoon toasted sesame oil
2 teaspoons unseasoned rice vinegar

1 large head butter lettuce, leaves separated
12 flour tortillas
25g/1oz fresh coriander leaves

Korean-American chefs like Roy Choi (in Los Angeles), David Chang (in New York City) and Edward Lee (in Louisville) have made it cool and modern to reimagine tacos and introduce words like gochujang (ko-chew-jang) into barbecue conversations. A thick paste of red chillies, fermented soya beans and glutinous rice, gochujang (see photo, opposite, top left) is a key ingredient in kogi sauce, which we might as well call a Korean barbecue sauce because of its spicy-sweet-salty nature and its affinity for charred meat. If you are unable to find gochujang, squeeze a little Sriracha sauce just by itself on these tacos*.

1 In a food processor, combine the garlic, apple, onion and ginger and process until finely chopped. Add the remaining marinade ingredients and process until puréed and well blended. Place the short ribs in a large, resealable plastic bag and pour in the marinade. Press the air out of the bag and seal tightly. Turn the bag to distribute the marinade, place in a bowl, and refrigerate for 24 hours, turning the bag occasionally. Allow the ribs to stand at room temperature for 30 minutes before grilling.

2 In a bowl, combine the pickled cucumber ingredients and stir to combine. Allow to stand at room temperature for 1 hour.

3 If you are using *gochujang*, whisk the kogi sauce ingredients.

4 Prepare the grill for direct cooking over high heat (230–290°C/450–550°F).

5 Remove the ribs from the bag and discard the marinade. Grill the ribs over **grilling/direct high heat**, with the lid closed, until charred, caramelised and cooked to medium rare, 4–6 minutes (depending on the thickness of the ribs), turning once. Remove from the grill and allow to rest for 3–5 minutes. Remove the bones and cut the meat crossways into thin slices.

6 Arrange a lettuce leaf on a tortilla. Top with meat, pickled cucumbers and kogi sauce (or Sriracha). Roll up and eat.

NEW MEXICO SHORT RIBS

SERVES: 6 | **PREP TIME:** 30 MINUTES
GRILLING TIME: 3½–4 HOURS | **SPECIAL EQUIPMENT:** LARGE (6-LITRE/10-PINT) GRILLPROOF CAST-IRON CASSEROLE

1.8kg/4lb bone-in beef short ribs, cut
    into 7.5–10-cm/3–4-inch pieces
3 tablespoons extra-virgin olive oil

BRAISING SAUCE
5 thick-cut bacon rashers, chopped
2 large red onions, chopped
2 green peppers, chopped
1 tablespoon chopped canned chipotle
    chillies in adobo sauce
1 tablespoon adobo sauce (from
    the can)
2 teaspoons finely chopped garlic
2 tablespoons chilli powder, preferably
    New Mexico
1 tablespoon smoked paprika
2 teaspoons dried oregano
2 teaspoons ground cumin
1¼ teaspoons sea salt
½ teaspoon freshly ground black
    pepper
800g/28oz canned chopped tomatoes
    in juice
1 bottle (350ml/12fl oz) pale ale
150ml/5fl oz fresh orange juice

2 tablespoons finely grated orange
    zest

In Texas they barbecue whole racks of beef plate ribs with a peppery bark. In New Mexico you are more likely to see those racks cut into blocks that are slowly braised in moist heat. By browning the short ribs right over direct heat and then braising them in a pot to the side of the hot coals, you create a smoky supper full of the flavours of the American Southwest. Tortillas would be a nice, natural accompaniment. Rice and beans would also go well with this meat. Or you might want to set the ribs on a soft bed of mashed potatoes and let the braising juices trickle onto the plate.

1   Prepare the grill for direct and indirect cooking over medium heat (180–200°C/350–400°F).

2   Generously brush the short ribs all over with the oil, and then grill over *grilling/direct medium heat* for about 10 minutes, with the lid closed, until browned, turning occasionally. Move the short ribs over indirect heat and prepare the braising sauce.

3   Place a large grillproof cast-iron casserole over *grilling/direct medium heat*. Add the bacon to the casserole, close the grill lid and fry for 6–7 minutes until browned, stirring occasionally. Add the onions and peppers and cook for 8–9 minutes until softened, stirring often (don't allow the temperature of the grill to go over 200°C/400°F). Stir in the chipotle chillies, adobo sauce and garlic and cook for 1 minute. Add the chilli powder, paprika, oregano, cumin, salt and pepper,

stirring until aromatic, about 20 seconds. Pour in the tomatoes, beer and orange juice. Scrape up any browned bits on the bottom of the casserole.

4   Transfer the short ribs to the casserole, stir well and bring to a full boil over *grilling/direct medium heat*, raising the heat, if necessary, to bring the liquid to the boil. Cover the casserole and slide it over indirect heat. Reduce the temperature of the grill to low heat (about 150°C/300°F), and cook over *roasting/indirect low heat* for 3–3½ hours, with the lid closed, until the meat is very tender (if the ingredients seem to be getting dry, stir in 125ml/4fl oz water every hour). Remove the casserole from the grill and stir in the orange zest. Allow to rest for 10 minutes, and then skim off the fat from the top of the sauce. Serve warm with rice and beans, wrapped in tortillas, or over mashed potatoes, if liked.

CENTRAL TEXAS BEEF SHORT RIBS

SERVES: 6–8 | PREP TIME: 15 MINUTES | COOKING TIME: 6–7 HOURS | RESTING TIME: 1–2 HOURS
SPECIAL EQUIPMENT: WATER SMOKER, 4 LARGE HANDFULS MESQUITE OR OAK WOOD CHUNKS, SPRAY BOTTLE FILLED WITH WATER, INSTANT-READ THERMOMETER; DRY, INSULATED COOLER

RUB
5 teaspoons coarsely ground black pepper
1 tablespoon sea salt
2 teaspoons garlic granules

2 racks beef short ribs, 4 bones per rack, each 1.8–2kg/4–4½lb and meat about 5cm/2 inches thick, trimmed of excess fat

This recipe comes straight out of an epic day I spent with third-generation pit master Wayne Mueller at Louie Mueller Barbecue in Taylor, Texas. He makes the greatest beef ribs I've ever tasted. Period.

1   Mix the rub ingredients, and then season the racks with the rub, putting almost all of it on the meaty side.

2   Prepare the smoker for indirect cooking with low heat (140–150°C/275–300°F). Fill the water pan about halfway with water. When the temperature reaches 140°C/275°F, add the wood chunks to the charcoal.

3   Cook the racks, bone side down, using the upper and lower cooking grates of the smoker, if needed, over **roasting/indirect low heat** for 6–7 hours, with the lid closed. After the first 3 hours, spray each rack a few times with water and swap their positions, if using both grates, putting the rack that was on the top grate on the bottom grate and vice versa.

Continue cooking over **roasting/indirect low heat**, with the lid closed, until the racks are so tender that the probe of a thermometer slides through the meat between the bones with very little resistance. When you press the meat with your fingertips, it should feel as soft as a marshmallow. The internal temperature in the thickest part of the meat should be about 93°C/200°F, but the tenderness of the meat is much more important than the temperature. Spray each rack one more time with water. Wrap each rack individually in three layers of clingfilm, and transfer to a dry, insulated cooler for 1–2 hours.

4   Unwrap the racks and cut between the bones into individual ribs. Serve warm. (Texans serve them without sauce.)

LOUIE MUELLER BARBECUE ⊙

The keys to Mueller's jaw-dropping results are not so much in a recipe as they are in understanding fire and thermal dynamics. He doesn't teach his restaurant cooks how many tablespoons of this or that to use; he teaches them how to stoke a proper fire and how to retain temperatures and humidity for consistency day after day. He teaches them how green wood burns differently from seasoned or cured wood. As he said to me, 'The hardest thing I do is to train people to be human thermostats. Apparently small, innocuous changes in the pits with things like wind speed, wind direction, barometric pressure and humidity will affect the way meat cooks – and so will what a cook did last night for fun. Barbecue is a matter of controlling all those variables with an intuition that you can only acquire with experience.' Mueller did, nevertheless, share some words of wisdom that all of us can use right away:

1   *In the beef short rib world, we have two distinct choices: There's the chuck rib, which is close to the shoulder of a steer. Then there's the plate rib, a rack a little lower on the steer and about 50% larger than the chuck rib. Its meat-to-bone ratio is much higher than that of chuck ribs. That's why Mueller cooks plate ribs.*

2   *He seasons the ribs with salt and pepper only, but more coarse ground pepper than you would think. He uses a ratio of 9:1 (pepper:salt).*

3   *He leaves the membrane on the racks and cooks them bone side down for the entire time (6–7 hours). At his restaurant, a wood fire of post oak burns at one end of a long, horizontal pit made of bricks and metal. The hot smoke flows horizontally over the top of the meat, right where he wants it. Occasionally he turns a rack 90 degrees to face it into the stream of heat, giving a particular side a bit more of a thermal blast, although the overall temperature in his pit never gets above 150°C/300°F.*

STAGING A COMEBACK WITH
LAMB AND BISON

Colorado

Colorado newspapers from the late 1800s and early 1900s regaled their readers with tales of 'monster' – their way of saying 'awesome' – barbecues where up to 30,000 people gorged on an eclectic buffet of domesticated livestock and wild game. Of this bounty, the locals held a special place in their hearts and mouths for American bison (mistakenly called 'buffalo') and Colorado-raised lamb. Later pushed off barbecue restaurant menus by beef, pork and poultry, bison and lamb are now poised to recapture their glory.

'We feature bison because my tribe is a Plains tribe (the Osage Nation), and bison was our main protein,' explains Ben Jacobs, co-owner of Tocabe, an American Indian eatery in Denver. The ribs are seasoned with a dry rub, refrigerated for 24 hours and then seared on a hot grill, 6–7 minutes per side. Next, the meat is slotted upright in a rib rack, placed in a pan half-filled with a bison stock or beer, covered with foil, roasted for two hours in a 220°C/425°F oven and quickly seared again on a smoky grill for a couple of minutes before serving. As a nod to the traditional condiment used by Jacobs' ancestors, Tocabe pairs its bison ribs with a seasonal berry barbecue sauce of blackberries, blueberries or huckleberries.

Colorado's wildest barbecued bison ambassador was the late Sam'l P. Arnold (1926–2006), who meticulously researched historical sources before opening up The Fort Restaurant in Morrison, Colorado; this iconic restaurant, opened in 1963, served up traditional American West cuisine. Executive chef Randy Savala now tends The Fort's smoker and notes that the restaurant has served bison ribs consistently for the last 10 years. 'We use hickory for the wood and also a hickory-based liquid smoke to finish off the process,' says Savala. 'We smoke our ribs for 10 hours at 96°C/205°F, and then finish them off when ordered in a 220°C/425°F oven for eight minutes to get them hot. We also put our [whisky] barbecue sauce on them during the finishing process. It seals in the flavour and doesn't dry them out.' Savala advises home cooks to treat bison like beef and start by finding the right rub. In this case 'right' means black and white. 'We only use salt and pepper before the smoking process because bison is sweeter than beef. We want to stand behind the product and not overpower it with a rub.'

Chef Coy Webb had 'something different' in mind in 2014 when he opened Roaming Buffalo Bar-B-Que in Denver. 'I grew up raising sheep on a Texas farm, and I was introduced to Colorado lamb while cooking in New Mexico. When I moved to Denver and decided to open up a barbecue joint, I wanted a place that would reflect my rustic cowboy heritage and show a unique part of Colorado history.' Along with beef, pork and poultry, Webb settled on a barbecue menu that showcases bison short ribs, lamb shanks and lamb shoulder. Depending on the size of the cut of meat and how much meat is on the bone, Webb cooks the bison short ribs for 5–7 hours, the lamb shoulder for 14–16 hours and the lamb shanks for 4½ hours at a temperature between 105 and 125°C/215 and 240°F. Webb uses a pecan wood blend, and recommends the same (or some other mellow wood) to cooks who want to try bison and lamb at home.

BRISKET

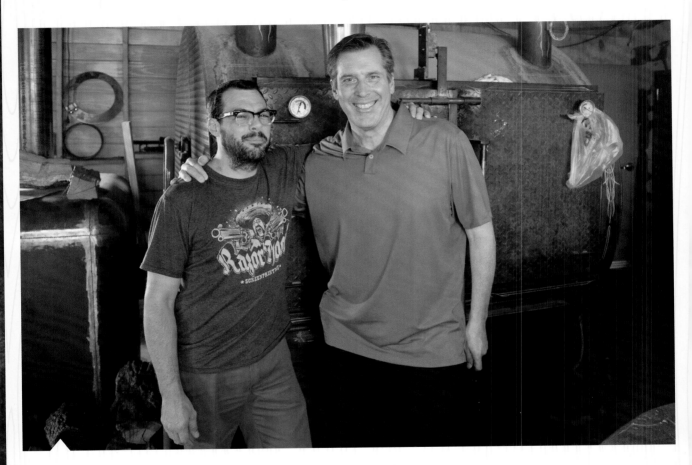

Aaron Franklin is the brightest star in the barbecue galaxy right now. Cooking at a joint that he opened in a trailer by Interstate 35 in Austin, Texas, he recently won the James Beard Award for Best Chef: Southwest (2015). Almost every day barbecue fanatics from all over the country (and the world) line up along a concrete pavement, through a carpark and up a residential street for several hours before the joint opens its doors. They eat with frenzied delight, sending selfies with Franklin's food all over the Internet and blogosphere, fuelling even more Franklin Barbecue mania.

When I sat down with Franklin, I asked him straight up: What is barbecue, anyway? His response was a little surprising: 'By definition, barbecue is anything cooked on live fire. Real simple. It could be grilling. It could be a hot dog. Hot dogs are cool. They take a few minutes. But to me barbecue is a soulful investment of time and love. It means something. On a personal level, I think of long-cooked meats and logs of wood. Here in Central Texas we have a pretty hard-core German-Czech scene going on, so I have tunnel vision about our style of barbecue....If other people want to think of barbecue as something else, that's cool.... People should make barbecue however they like.'

FUNDAMENTALS

A brisket is two muscles held together in one big hunk of meat that happens to be from the chest of the cow, so those muscles grow mighty tough while bearing a lot of weight and moving around the yard. The first muscle is the 'point' (sometimes called 'deckle'), which is a relative fatty section shown here between my hands.

Then there is the flat, a lean rectangular slab of beef that sits under the point and extends all the way to the opposite side of a brisket. A fundamental challenge in cooking brisket is getting two different cuts of meat to cook well in the same length of time. It's a little like getting the dark meat and light meat of a turkey to cook just right – only much more difficult.

One way of helping yourself is to buy brisket with a flat section that is nice and thick all the way to the skinny end. If the brisket tapers down to thinner than 2.5cm/1 inch, forget it. That thin meat will dry out long before the rest of the brisket is done. Another consideration is the overall size and weight. If you cook anything less than about 4.5kg/10lb, you are asking for trouble. You want something big enough that it can stay on the smoker long enough to melt a brisket's impressive amount of collagen to gelatine. Ideally, you will find a 'whole packer' in the range of 5.5–7kg/12–16lb.

TRIMMING

Franklin advises that as you trim your brisket you should try to imagine how smoke and heat will flow over it on your smoker. The meat should be aerodynamic, without any odd sections protruding into the airflow and potentially drying out or burning. For this reason, he cuts away more meat than most people. He cuts off long strips of meat, 2.5cm/1 inch or so wide, along the two longest sides of the brisket. At the end of the flat, he rounds off the corners like the bumpers of a sports car.

A thick layer of fat covers one entire side of a brisket. You need to trim that fat to an even thickness about 5mm/¼ inch, but no less. Otherwise the smoke can't penetrate very well.

Make sure you trim down any hard fat along the side of the brisket, and if you see any greyish meat in that area (a sign that area was sitting too long in its own juices), cut it off, too.

On the underside of the brisket, slip a thin-bladed knife under any thin sections of fat and silver skin clinging to the meat, and remove them.

With this side facing up, you should also see a big chunk of fat where the point and flat meet on one side. Cut that chunk off – it's too big and thick to render (melt).

SEASONINGS

A brisket will spend anywhere from 10–16 hours in a smoker, during which time ½ teaspoon of cumin or mustard powder or whatever spice you like would be overwhelmed (and essentially wasted) by all the smoke, so stick with two or three basic seasonings. In true Central Texas style, Franklin uses equal parts sea salt and coarsely ground black pepper sprinkled lightly over all sides of the meat.

BEGINNER BRISKET

SERVES: 10 | **PREP TIME:** 30 MINUTES
COOKING TIME: 6–7 HOURS | **RESTING TIME:** 2–3 HOURS
SPECIAL EQUIPMENT: WATER SMOKER, SPRAY BOTTLE FILLED WITH WATER, 6–8 LARGE
HANDFULS MESQUITE, OAK OR APPLE WOOD CHUNKS, INSTANT-READ THERMOMETER,
HEAVY-DUTY ALUMINIUM FOIL, DRY, INSULATED COOLER

To cook a brisket of 7kg/14lb or so, you are looking at about 16 hours from start to finish. Understanding that you may not always have that kind of time available, I wanted to give you a relatively easy recipe that you can start in the morning and enjoy by dinnertime. So here it is. It calls for a fairly small brisket (4.5–5.5kg/10–12lb) that is on the smoker for 6–7 hours and then in an insulated cooler for 2–3 hours. It may not produce the ultimate brisket, but it should be very satisfying. If you find that your slices in the flat are a little dry, that's not uncommon. Even the barbecue pros get dry slices occasionally. You can still enjoy the flat by chopping it up with some of the moist meat from the point and serving it on buns, maybe with some barbecue sauce for extra flavour and moisture.

After about 4 hours of cooking, the brisket should have a nice dark crust on the surface. This is when you should remove it from the smoker, spritz it with water on all sides and wrap it tightly in heavy-duty aluminium foil. Put it back on the smoker until it is as tender as a marshmallow. This usually happens when the internal temperature reaches 90–96°C/195–205°F, but not always. When the meat is soft, move your brisket to a dry, insulated cooler to rest for 2–3 hours. Do not skip this last step. It is crucial for helping the muscles relax.

1 whole, untrimmed beef brisket, including both the flat and point sections, 4.5–5.5kg/10–12lb
90g/3oz sea salt
4 tablespoons freshly ground black pepper
500ml/18fl oz your favourite barbecue sauce
10 hamburger buns, split

1   Using a very sharp knife, trim the fat on the fatty side of the brisket so that it is about 5mm/¼ inch, but no less. On the meatier side, remove the web-like membrane so that the coarsely grained meat underneath is visible. Be sure to remove any hard clumps of fat on either side of the joint.

2. Mix the salt and pepper, and then rub the meat evenly on all sides with the seasoning. Refrigerate the joint until ready to cook.

3. Prepare a smoker for indirect cooking with very low heat (about 110°C/225°F).

4. Spray the brisket on both sides with water to make the surface wet. Add half of the wood chunks to the charcoal. When smoke appears, place the joint, fat side down, on the top cooking grate, close the lid and cook over **roasting/indirect very low heat** until it has a nice dark crust on the surface, usually about 4 hours. After the first hour, add the remaining wood chunks to the charcoal. The surface colour of the meat is your indication that you have created a good 'bark' and the brisket will no longer absorb much smoke, so it is time to wrap it. Colour is the primary indication

of this, but you should also check the internal temperature of the meat now. It should be somewhere between 65 and 70°C/150 and 160°F in the thickest part of the meat.

5. Remove the meat from the smoker, spray it on both sides with water and double or triple wrap it tightly with heavy-duty aluminium foil.

6. Place the wrapped brisket, fat side down, on the top grate of the smoker and continue cooking over **roasting/ indirect very low heat** for 2–3 hours more, with the lid closed, until the meat is so tender that when you press it with your fingers through the foil it feels like a giant marshmallow and the internal temperature is 90–96°C/195–205°F (tenderness is a more important

indicator of doneness than temperature). The amount of time required will depend on the particular breed of cattle and other characteristics of the meat.

7. Transfer the brisket, still wrapped in foil, to a dry, insulated cooler. Close the cooler and let the meat rest for 2–3 hours.

8. Unwrap the joint and set it on a carving board, being careful to keep the precious meat juices in the foil.

9. Warm the barbecue sauce over a medium heat for about 5 minutes. Cut the brisket across the grain into thin slices and serve with as much or as little sauce as you like. If liked, add the meat juices to the sauce. If the meat from the flat is a little dry, coarsely chop it and mix with as much sauce as you like. Serve warm on buns.

BARBECUED BRISKET
WITH DALMATIAN RUB

SERVES: 10–12 | **PREP TIME:** 30 MINUTES | **COOKING TIME:** 8–10 HOURS | **RESTING TIME:** 2–3 HOURS
SPECIAL EQUIPMENT: 3 LARGE HANDFULS MESQUITE AND 3 APPLE/CHERRY WOOD CHUNKS, WATER SMOKER, SPRAY BOTTLE FILLED
WITH WATER, INSTANT-READ THERMOMETER; EXTRA-LARGE, HEAVY-DUTY ALUMINIUM FOIL ROASTING TRAY; DRY, INSULATED COOLER

*If you aspire to make a really good brisket, seek out a piece of meat you can
trust and season it simply with salt and pepper (aka Dalmatian rub). Rather
than taking your chances with a small brisket of questionable quality, look for a
larger one from a reputable brand like Certified Angus Beef, raised to meet higher
standards of taste and tenderness. You may need to go to a meat market or ask
your butcher to order the brisket for you, but a top-quality cut will improve your
chances of success more than any other single step.*

RUB
4 tablespoons sea salt
3 tablespoons freshly ground
    black pepper
3 tablespoons demerara
    sugar (optional)

1 whole, untrimmed beef brisket, including
    both the flat and point sections,
    5.5–7kg/12–14lb
125ml/4fl oz beef stock

After spending 12+ hours preparing your brisket, it's important to cut it properly, that is, against
the grain (as much as possible) so that it is tender. I follow the method that I learned at Franklin
Barbecue. Set the brisket on your board with the point facing up. Start making slices crossways
about 5mm/¼ inch thick on the flat end (see photo, top left). When you reach the part of the
flat where it meets the point, stop and set the slices aside, held firmly together so they do not
dry out. Now, rotate the remaining brisket 90 degrees so that the side you were just slicing is
facing away from you. Cut this piece in half (see photo, top right). You will know that you have
done a good job of cooking the brisket if the band of fat and collagen running between the flat
and point is nicely softened and the meat looks juicy (see photo, bottom left). Now you can
start slicing each half a little thicker than the slices from the flat (see photo, bottom right).
Remember not to cut the meat until you are ready to serve it. It stays warmer and juicier
when it is uncut.

1   Combine the rub ingredients.

2   Using a very sharp knife, trim the fat
on the fatty side of the brisket so that
it is about 5mm/¼ inch, but no less.
On the meatier side, remove the web-
like membrane so that the coarsely
grained meat underneath is visible. Be
sure to remove any hard clumps of fat
on either side of the joint. Try to round
off the corners of the brisket and make
them as aerodynamic as possible. Also,
if you notice any greyish corners or
areas, trim those off.

3   Season the meat evenly on all sides,
even the narrow sides, with the rub.
Cover and refrigerate the joint until
ready to cook, up to one day ahead.

4   Prepare the smoker for indirect
cooking with very low heat (about
110°C/225°F and no higher).

5   Add the wood chunks to the charcoal.
When smoke appears, spray the brisket
on the top and bottom with water to
make the surface damp (not wet).
Place the brisket, fat side down, on
the top cooking grate and close the
lid. Cook over ***roasting/indirect very
low heat***, with the lid closed, until the

surface looks like the photo below, usually 4–5 hours. The surface colour of the meat is your indication that you have created a good 'bark' and the brisket will no longer absorb much smoke, so it is time to cover it. Colour is the primary indication of this, but you should also check the internal temperature in the thickest part of the meat now. It should be somewhere between 65 and 70°C/150 and 160°F.

6 Remove the meat from the smoker and place it fat side down in an extra-large, heavy-duty aluminium foil roasting tray. Pour the stock over the brisket. Cover the tray tightly with foil and return the brisket in the covered tray to the smoker. Try to adjust the temperature of the smoker a bit lower, somewhere between 102 and 108°C/210 and 220°F, and continue cooking until the meat is so tender that when you press it with your fingers through the foil it feels like a giant marshmallow. This will probably take 4–5 hours more. Brisket is done when it is done, so it's a good rule of thumb to check the brisket hourly for both tenderness and temperature. The internal temperature should reach 90–96°C/195–205°F, although tenderness is a more important indicator of doneness than the temperature. The amount of time required will depend on

the particular breed of cattle and other characteristics of the meat.

7 Transfer the meat, still covered with foil in the roasting tray, to a dry, insulated cooler. Close the cooler and let the meat rest for 2–3 hours. Don't skip this step; it will really help loosen the muscles.

8 Uncover the brisket and transfer to a carving board, being careful to keep the precious meat juices in the pan. Then very carefully transfer the meat juices to a small bowl. If you notice that the colour of the brisket is not very dark, give it a couple of minutes out of the foil. The oxygen will help turn the outer colour nice and dark. Cut the brisket across the grain into thin slices. Dip each slice into the meat juices. Serve warm, with any extra juices drizzled on top.

AMERICAN KOBE BRISKET
WITH BURNT ENDS

SERVES: 10–12 | **PREP TIME:** 30 MINUTES | **COOKING TIME:** 10–12 HOURS | **RESTING TIME:** 2–3 HOURS
SPECIAL EQUIPMENT: EXTRA-LARGE, HEAVY-DUTY ALUMINIUM FOIL ROASTING TRAY; WATER SMOKER,
6 LARGE HANDFULS CHERRY WOOD CHUNKS, INSTANT-READ THERMOMETER; HEAVY-DUTY ALUMINIUM FOIL;
DRY, INSULATED COOLER; LARGE DISPOSABLE FOIL TRAY

The sport of barbecue has grown so intense and lucrative lately that some competitive barbecue teams are willing to shell out big bucks for super-premium meats like American-style Kobe. The name Kobe refers to a certain strain of Wagyu cattle raised in the Kobe region of Japan. In America some ranchers are crossbreeding Japanese Wagyu cattle with Angus cattle to produce an American-style Kobe beef with intensely marbled flesh and complex flavours. This quality of brisket (see photo below) is what competitors are buying from companies like Snake River Farms in the Pacific North-west.

1 whole, untrimmed Wagyu beef brisket, including both the flat and point sections, 5.5–7kg/12–14lb
4 tablespoons Worcestershire sauce

RUB
4 tablespoons sea salt
2 tablespoons paprika
1 tablespoon onion flakes
1 tablespoon ground cayenne pepper
1 tablespoon freshly ground black pepper

SAUCE (optional)
250ml/8fl oz your favourite barbecue sauce
250ml/8fl oz low-sodium beef stock

Years ago burnt ends were the crispy, fatty odds and ends of a brisket that pit masters in Kansas City would set aside on the carving board because they weren't worthy to sell. Nowadays customers pay more for mouthwatering burnt ends and competitors often try to impress judges with meticulously chosen cubes of meat dressed with sauce. The finest part of the brisket for burnt ends is the fatty point. Separate that first from the flat by cutting diagonally under the point and over the flat (see photo, left). Cut the point into long strips about 2.5cm/1 inch thick, and then cut the strips into 2.5-cm/1-inch cubes (see photo, right). Toss those in a small pan with a little sauce and barbecue them for an hour or so longer, until the sauce caramelises on the surface and the burnt ends look good enough to win a trophy.

1   Using a very sharp knife, trim the fat on the fatty side of the brisket so that it is about 5mm/¼ inch, but no less On the meatier side, remove the web-like membrane so that the coarsely grained meat underneath is visible. If the thin end (tip) of the flat section is thinner than 2.5cm/1 inch, trim that off so that the thin end is now at least 2.5cm/1 inch thick. Be sure to remove any hard clumps of fat on either side of the joint. Try to round off the corners of the brisket and make them as aerodynamic as possible. Also, if you notice any greyish corners or areas, trim those off.

2   Place the joint in an extra-large, heavy-duty aluminium foil roasting tray. Spread the Worcestershire sauce all over the meat. Mix the rub ingredients, and then season the brisket evenly on all sides with the rub. Cover and refrigerate the joint until ready to cook, up to one day before.

3   Prepare the smoker for indirect cooking with very low heat (about 130°C/250°F).

4   Add half of the wood chunks to the charcoal. When smoke appears, take the brisket out of the foil roasting tray, place it, fat side down, on the top grate and close the lid. Set aside the foil roasting tray. Cook the brisket over **roasting/ indirect very low heat**, with the lid closed, until the surface is very dark brown, usually about 6 hours. After the first hour, add the remaining wood chunks to the charcoal. The surface colour of the meat is your indication that you have created a good 'bark' and the brisket will no longer absorb much smoke.

5   Place the joint, fat side down, back in the foil roasting tray. Cover the tray tightly with foil and continue cooking until the meat is so tender that when you press it with your fingers through the foil it feels like a giant marshmallow. This will probably take 4–6 hours more.

Brisket is done when it is done, so it's a good rule of thumb to check the brisket hourly for both tenderness and temperature. Be patient! The internal temperature should reach 90–96°C/195–205°F, although tenderness is a more important indicator of doneness than the temperature.

6   Transfer the joint, still covered with foil in the roasting tray, to a dry, insulated cooler. Close the cooler and let the meat rest for 2–3 hours. Don't skip this step; it will really help loosen the muscles.

7   If you want to serve the brisket with a sauce, mix the barbecue sauce and stock in a saucepan and bring to a simmer over a medium heat, stirring often.

8   Transfer the brisket to a carving board, being careful to keep the precious meat juices in the pan (if liked, you can add the meat juices to the sauce, if using).

Remove the brisket flat from the point (see photo, previous page, bottom left). Return the flat to the roasting tray, cover the tray with foil, and place it back in the cooler to keep warm. Cut the point into 2.5- or 5-cm/1- or 2-inch cubes. Arrange them in a single layer in a large disposable foil tray. If liked, pour enough of the sauce over them to coat them lightly. Set the tray, uncovered, back on the smoker and cook for about 1 hour more.

9   When ready to serve, unwrap the flat and cut it across the grain into slices of about pencil thickness. Serve the meat slices and burnt ends warm with the sauce (if using) or with the meat juices.

SAN ANTONIO BRISKET ENCHILADAS

SERVES: 4–8 | **PREP TIME:** 1 HOUR | **GRILLING TIME:** ABOUT 40 MINUTES
SPECIAL EQUIPMENT: 33-X-23-CM/13-X-9-INCH GRILLPROOF BAKING TIN, NONSTICK ALUMINIUM FOIL

SAUCE

7 dried New Mexican chillies, stems
   removed and deseeded
4 dried mulato chillies, stems removed
   and deseeded (see caption and
   photo below)
675g/1½lb tomatoes, each cut in half
1 large onion, cut crossways into
   1-cm/½-inch slices
2 tablespoons extra-virgin olive oil
1 garlic clove
1 teaspoon oregano
1 teaspoon ground cumin
½ teaspoon ground cinnamon
½ teaspoon sea salt
½ teaspoon freshly ground black
   pepper

565g/1¼lb shredded smoked beef
   brisket
115g/4oz grated pepper jack or
   Cheddar cheese
8 flour tortillas (20cm/8 inches)
175g/6oz grated mild Cheddar cheese
4–8 large eggs
Soured cream (optional)
2 spring onions, thinly sliced

What are you going to do with leftover brisket? Do like they do in San Antonio, Texas, and make enchiladas, a combination of Tex-Mex cuisine and South-western barbecue that is a local point of pride. The key is that the brisket must be quite tender – in fact, shreddable with a fork. If you are using leftover brisket that's more suitable for slicing than shredding, spray the whole chunk with water, wrap it in aluminium foil and set the parcel on the grate over indirect medium heat until the meat shreds easily with a fork (1 hour or so).

1. Break up the dried chillies and put them in a large bowl. Cover with boiling water and set aside to soak for 20 minutes. Drain in a colander set over a bowl, catching and reserving the soaking liquid.

2. Prepare the grill for direct and indirect cooking over medium heat (180–230°C/350–450°F).

3. Brush the tomato halves and onion slices with the oil, and then grill over **grilling/direct medium heat** for 10–12 minutes, with the lid closed, until charred and softened, turning once or twice.

4. Place the tomatoes, half the onion slices, the drained chillies, garlic, oregano, cumin, cinnamon, salt and pepper in a blender. Cover and blend until smooth, adding just enough of the reserved soaking liquid to make a thick sauce. Strain the sauce through a sieve into a bowl.

5. Roughly chop the remaining onion slices and put in a large bowl. Add the shredded beef and pepper jack cheese and toss to combine.

6. Spread 125ml/4fl oz of the sauce on the bottom of a 33-x-23-cm/13-x-9-inch grill-proof baking tray. Lay out all the tortillas on a work surface and brush each with 2 tablespoons of the sauce. Then place about 70g/2½oz of the beef mixture in a line down the centre of each tortilla. Roll up the tortillas fairly tight and place them close together, seam side down, in the prepared baking tray so they are parallel to the short end of the tray. Pour the remaining sauce over the enchiladas and then distribute the Cheddar cheese evenly on top. Cover with a large sheet of nonstick aluminium foil and seal the edges tightly all around the tray.

7. Cook the enchiladas over **roasting/indirect medium heat**, with the lid closed, for 20 minutes. Remove the foil from the baking tray and continue cooking over **roasting/indirect medium heat** for 8–10 minutes more, with the lid closed, until the enchiladas are bubbling and the cheese is melted. Remove the pan from the grill and allow to rest for 5 minutes. While the enchiladas rest, fry the eggs. Serve the enchiladas warm with a fried egg on top and a dollop of soured cream on the side, if liked. Garnish with spring onions.

Dried mulato chillies give the sauce a subtle chocolate flavour. You can find these chillies at Mexican or Latin American stores or from online suppliers. Or substitute dried ancho chillies (actually, dried poblanos) for a milder flavour.

4

POULTRY

LEMON CHICKEN
WITH CHARRED CORN, TOMATOES AND FARRO

SERVES: 4 | **PREP TIME:** 45 MINUTES
MARINATING TIME: 1–4 HOURS | **GRILLING TIME:** 16–22 MINUTES

MARINADE

2 teaspoons finely grated lemon zest
4 tablespoons fresh lemon juice
1 tablespoon Dijon mustard
½ teaspoon dried oregano
2 garlic cloves, crushed

Extra-virgin olive oil
Freshly ground black pepper
Sea salt
4 boneless, skinless chicken breasts,
 each 175–225g/6–8oz
255g/9oz pearled farro
700ml/1¼ pints low-sodium chicken
 stock or water

CORIANDER PURÉE

30g/1oz fresh coriander
50g/2oz flat-leaf parsley
1 tablespoon fresh lemon juice
1 tablespoon red wine vinegar
2 garlic cloves, chopped
¼ teaspoon crushed chilli flakes

SALAD

2 corn on the cobs, husked
340g/12oz cherry tomatoes, each cut
 in half
2 spring onions (white and light green
 parts only), thinly sliced
10g/¼oz flat-leaf parsley, chopped
1 tablespoon fresh lemon juice

If you have a charcoal grill, fire it up for this dish, because the sweet smell of burning embers will imbue the chicken and corn with greater depth. Don't overcook either one. The breast meat should be moist and the corn kernels should be crisp-tender in the salad. Farro is an ancient grain that has attracted a lot of attention lately from chefs for its earthy nuttiness and pleasantly chewy texture. Be sure to buy the pearled variety, which has had the bran removed, so you don't have to soak the grain overnight. Feel free to substitute cooked rice or couscous, if you like.

1 Whisk the marinade ingredients, including 2 tablespoons oil, 1½ teaspoons pepper and 1 teaspoon salt. Place the chicken breasts in a large, resealable plastic bag and pour in the marinade. Press the air out of the bag and seal tightly. Turn the bag to distribute the marinade, place in a bowl and refrigerate for 1–4 hours, turning the bag occasionally.

2 In a saucepan, combine the farro, stock and 1½ teaspoons salt. Bring to the boil, reduce the heat to medium-low, cover and simmer for 15–20 minutes until the farro is tender. Drain off any remaining liquid and set aside.

3 In a food processor, combine the coriander purée ingredients, including 5 tablespoons oil, ½ teaspoon pepper and ½ teaspoon salt. Process until blended and almost smooth. Transfer to a bowl.

4 Prepare the grill for direct cooking over medium heat (180–230°C/350–450°F).

5 Lightly brush the corn with oil, and then grill over **grilling/direct medium heat** for 8–10 minutes, with the lid closed, until lightly charred and crisp-tender, turning as needed. Remove from the grill and, when cool enough to handle, cut the kernels from the cobs and transfer to a bowl. Add the remaining salad ingredients, including 2 tablespoons oil, 1 teaspoon salt and ½ teaspoon pepper, and stir to combine. Fold in the farro and coriander purée.

6 Grill the chicken, smooth side down first, over **grilling/direct medium heat** for 8–12 minutes, with the lid closed, until firm to the touch and opaque all the way to the centre, turning once. Remove from the grill and allow to rest for 3–5 minutes. Serve the chicken warm with the salad.

SMOKED CHICKEN BANH MI
WITH PICKLED JALAPEÑOS

SERVES: 4 | **MARINATING TIME:** 1 HOUR | **PREP TIME:** 40 MINUTES | **GRILLING TIME:** ABOUT 20 MINUTES
SPECIAL EQUIPMENT: 2 LARGE HANDFULS APPLE OR CHERRY WOOD CHIPS

MARINADE
4 tablespoons Vietnamese or Thai
    fish sauce
4 tablespoons fresh lime juice
2 tablespoons finely chopped shallot
2 tablespoons vegetable oil
1 tablespoon toasted sesame oil
2 garlic cloves, crushed

4 boneless, skinless chicken breasts,
    each about 175g/6oz
100ml/3½fl oz unseasoned rice
    vinegar
1 tablespoon granulated sugar
2 teaspoons sea salt
2 jalapeño chillies, cut crossways
    into 3-mm/⅛-inch rings
125ml/4fl oz mayonnaise
Finely grated zest of 1 lime
1 tablespoon fresh lime juice
¼ teaspoon hot chilli-garlic sauce,
    such as Sriracha
4 crusty, oblong rolls, split
140g/5oz shop-bought smooth
    chicken liver pâté, duck liver
    pâté or liverwurst, at room
    temperature
100g/3½oz cucumber, thinly sliced
½ small red onion, cut into thin rings
15g/½oz fresh coriander

For decades the banh mi sandwich lingered in obscurity as an unlikely love child of French and Vietnamese cooking. Recently, though, its unique layering of flavours, colours and textures has mainstream America taking notice. You can even find versions of it in barbecue restaurants. The fresh herbs and pickled vegetables represent authentic Vietnamese touches that now seem entirely natural mingled with the French elements of crusty bread and chicken liver pâté.

1   Soak the wood chips in water for at least 30 minutes.

2   Whisk the marinade ingredients. Place the chicken breasts in a large, resealable plastic bag and pour in the marinade. Press the air out of the bag and seal tightly. Turn the bag to distribute the marinade, place in a bowl and set aside at room temperature to marinate for 1 hour, turning the bag occasionally.

3   Meanwhile, combine the vinegar, sugar and salt and whisk to completely dissolve the sugar. Add the chilli rings, cover and refrigerate for 1 hour.

4   Mix the mayonnaise, lime zest and juice, and hot chilli-garlic sauce. Cover and refrigerate until ready to serve.

5   Prepare the grill for indirect cooking over medium-low heat (as close to 180°C/350°F as possible).

6   Remove the chicken from the bag and blot the excess marinade off the chicken with kitchen paper. Discard the marinade. Drain and add the wood chips to the charcoal or to the smoker box of a gas grill, following the manufacturer's instructions, and close the lid. When smoke appears, grill the chicken, smooth side up, over *roasting/indirect medium-low heat* for about 20 minutes, with the lid closed, until the meat is firm to the touch and opaque all the way to the centre, (the colour of the chicken will still be pale). Remove the chicken from the grill and allow to rest for 3 minutes. Cut the chicken diagonally and across the grain into 1-cm/½-inch slices.

7   Spread one side of each roll with the mayonnaise mixture. Spread the other half of each roll with chicken liver pâté. Divide the chicken, chilli rings, cucumber, onion and coriander evenly among the rolls. Serve immediately.

DUCK BREASTS
WITH SMOKY PEACH AND GINGER CHUTNEY

SERVES: 4 | PREP TIME: 20 MINUTES | GRILLING TIME: ABOUT 35 MINUTES
SPECIAL EQUIPMENT: 2 LARGE HANDFULS CHERRY WOOD CHIPS, GRILLPROOF FRYING PAN

CHUTNEY

4 firm but ripe peaches
25g/1oz unsalted butter, melted
115g/4oz dark brown sugar
1 shallot, finely chopped
4 tablespoons cider vinegar
2-cm/¾-inch piece of fresh ginger,
    finely chopped
½ teaspoon ground cinnamon

4 duck breasts, each 175–225g/6–8oz
1 teaspoon sea salt
¼ teaspoon freshly ground black
    pepper

No doubt, grilling duck breasts presents some challenges. There's so much fat in the skin that if the fire is too hot, the fat rushes out quickly and ignites in a blaze. If the fire is too low, the meat turns rubbery before the skin is barely brown. Recall the Goldilocks principle: the one in the middle (medium heat) is 'just right.' But don't get too comfortable. Even with medium heat, flare-ups occasionally happen, so you may need to move the duck over indirect heat temporarily. Forget it, you say? Please don't. Your diligence and responsiveness will be rewarded with one of my favourite recipes in the whole book.

1 Soak the wood chips in water for at least 30 minutes.

2 Prepare the grill for direct and indirect cooking over medium heat (180–230°C/350–450°F).

3 Cut each peach in half and save any juices. Brush the peach halves all over with the melted butter. Set aside any remaining butter.

4 Drain and add one handful of the wood chips to the charcoal or to the smoker box of a gas grill, following the manufacturer's instructions, and close the lid. When smoke appears, grill the peach halves, cut side up, over *grilling/direct medium heat* for 7–10 minutes, with the lid closed, until charred and beginning to soften. Remove from the grill, pull off and discard the skin and cut the peach halves into thin slices.

5 In a grillproof frying pan, combine the peach slices, brown sugar, shallots, vinegar, ginger, cinnamon and any reserved peach juices and remaining melted butter. Place the frying pan over *grilling/direct medium heat*, close

the lid and bring the mixture to a simmer, 7–9 minutes. Cook for about 10 minutes more, stirring occasionally, until the chutney has thickened. Remove from the heat and allow to cool.

6 While the chutney is cooking, use a very sharp knife to score the skin of each duck breast on the diagonal in a criss-cross pattern (do not cut through to the meat). Season the duck evenly on both sides with the salt and pepper.

7 Drain and add the remaining wood chips to the charcoal or smoker box and close the lid. When smoke appears, grill the duck breasts, skin side down first, over *grilling/direct medium heat*, with the lid closed, until the skin is browned and the meat is cooked to your desired doneness, 8–10 minutes for medium rare, turning once (as flare-ups occur, move the duck temporarily over indirect heat). Remove the duck from the grill, tent with foil and allow to rest for 3–5 minutes. Cut the duck crossways into slices and serve warm with the chutney.

One of the keys to rendering (melting) fat from duck breasts skilfully over medium heat is first cross-hatching the skin without cutting into the meat. Using a very sharp knife, score the skin on the diagonal in lines spaced about 1cm/½ inch apart. Then score criss-crossing lines, also about 1cm/½ inch apart, to create an even pattern.

DRUNKEN NOODLES
WITH CHICKEN AND BASIL

SERVES: 2–4 | **PREP TIME:** 25 MINUTES | **GRILLING TIME:** 6–8 MINUTES
SPECIAL EQUIPMENT: GRILLPROOF WOK OR VERY LARGE FRYING PAN

225g/8oz dried wide rice noodles

SAUCE
3 tablespoons oyster sauce
2 tablespoons Thai or Vietnamese
    fish sauce
2 tablespoons water
1 tablespoon soy sauce
1 tablespoon light brown sugar

2 tablespoons vegetable oil
4 boneless, skinless chicken thighs, each
    about 115g/4oz, cut into 2.5-cm/1-
    inch pieces
1 red pepper, cut into 1-cm/½-inch
    strips
175g/6oz fresh shiitake mushrooms,
    stalks removed, caps cut into
    1-cm/½-inch strips
4 spring onions, cut diagonally into
    thin slices
12 canned baby corn cobs, rinsed,
    drained and cut diagonally into
    2-cm/¾-inch pieces
3 garlic cloves, finely chopped
1 small red chilli, such as bird's-eye,
    chopped, including seeds
4 tablespoons water
40g/1½oz fresh Thai or holy basil,
    very coarsely chopped
1 lime, cut into wedges
Hot chilli-garlic sauce, such as Sriracha

Drunken noodles do not actually contain a drop of alcohol; the name is derived from their alleged power to cure a hangover. While this Thai stir-fry is not particularly smoky, the high heat from the grill gives the chicken a quick, deep sear that the average domestic hob cannot achieve. Experiment by adding other vegetables, such as thin asparagus or broccoli florets, or try peeled prawns instead of chicken. Standard basil will work well in this recipe, but Thai basil is worth looking for in Asian stores because even when the serrated leaves are cooked, they retain distinct liquorice and aniseed flavours.

1   In a large bowl, completely cover the noodles with very hot tap water. Allow to stand for 12–15 minutes until the noodles are softened but not fully tender, stirring occasionally (they will cook and soften a bit more during cooking, so do not oversoak). Drain the noodles, rinse under cold water and drain again.

2   Prepare the grill for direct cooking over high heat (230–290°C/450–550°F) and preheat a grillproof wok for 5–10 minutes.

3   Whisk the sauce ingredients until the sugar is dissolved.

4   Have all the ingredients prepped and ready to go before you begin cooking. Bring the noodles, sauce, oil, chicken thighs, red pepper, mushrooms, half the spring onions, baby corn, garlic, chilli, water and basil to the grill and keep close by.

5   When the wok is smoking hot, pour the oil into it, letting it run down the sides. Add the chicken and cook over **grilling/direct high heat** for about 1 minute, with the lid open, until seared on both sides, stirring occasionally. Add the red pepper, mushrooms, spring onions and baby corn and cook for 2–4 minutes, with the lid open, until the vegetables soften, stirring often. Stir in the garlic and chilli and cook until fragrant, about 30 seconds.

6   Add the noodles and water and cook until the water evaporates and the noodles are warm, about 1 minute, stirring and tossing constantly. Pour the sauce over the noodles and stir for about 1 minute more until the noodles are hot and coated with the sauce. Stir in the basil and cook until just wilted, about 30 seconds. Remove the wok from the grill. Transfer the noodles to plates or bowls and garnish with the remaining spring onions. Serve hot with lime wedges and hot chilli-garlic sauce.

For thousands of years, the focal point of a typical Chinese kitchen was a round hole over a firebox of burning wood and embers, with a wok fitted snugly inside the hole, making efficient use of a small amount of an expensive fuel. You can replicate the ancient art of stir-frying over a live fire by resting a wok in the hole of a special grate made for an outdoor grill.

CHICAGO:

THERE'S A NEW 'CUE IN TOWN

Chicago loves a good reinvention story. Whether it's the brutal, bone-stinging winters giving way to glorious summers, the habitually losing athletic teams emerging as champions or even the reversing current of its eponymous river, Chi-towners are accustomed to turning things around. With barbecue, it's no different.

'I think Chicago was a barbecue town waiting to happen,' said Barry Sorkin, a former IT executive and now owner of Smoque BBQ, an excellent upper-scale 'cue joint in the Irving Park neighbourhood. 'There were all these pent-up barbecue fanatics and there was no outlet for it, at least not for the generation of eaters weaned on cooking shows and food as a hobby.' And, if the queue of people usually extending out of the door at Smoque BBQ is any indication, he's right. Young Chicagoans craved the quality of 'cue proudly hailed in places like Kansas City and Austin. Chicago had its styles, true, but the people were ready for the next phase.

And boy, did that next phase come with a bang.

'We've seen a surge in fine-dining barbecue,' says Chicago-based food writer Kevin Pang of the flurry of restaurant openings since 2010. 'Barbecue has been elevated with sophisticated presentations and cooking techniques.' He is referring to places like Chicago q, in the ritzy Gold Coast neighbourhood, one of several places now barbecuing with fully automated, digitally controlled smokers that run on gas. Barbecue purists can argue about the authenticity of this approach, but with the benefit of wood logs, these smokers produce consistently great barbecue month after month.

Walking into Chicago q, you immediately feel a hip, urban vibe. This posh place pulses with energy, especially at night when crowds of young diners and drinkers pack the place for competition-worthy ribs, American-style Kobe brisket, and more than a few surprises, such as blackened alligator with Creole mustard aioli. The chef there is Lee Ann Whippen, a top-tier barbecue competitor who was approached by an investor to marry her cooking skills with country club class. The barbecue techniques are beyond reproach. The number of wines, craft beers and whiskeys is staggering. And the prices? Well, customers come prepared to pay.

'You ask people how they feel at the end of the meal, after they have shelled out a lot of money,' Whippen reflected. 'In most cases they say, "I feel wonderful, and I'll be back, and I'll bring more people."'

This is a starkly different scene from what Chicago barbecue was – and still is, but might not be much longer. Rarely ranked in the pantheon of originators, the Windy City's contribution to this cuisine reflects its gritty history of intermingling traditions. Essentially, up until very recently, it had been a tale of two 'cues, with north

and south sides finding themselves divided. To the north, Eastern Europeans seeking opportunity flooded the city from its inception, accompanied by sausages and rib racks boiled to the point of falling off the bone, and, as the style evolved, finished on a grill and drenched in sweet sauce. Restaurants such as Twin Anchors Restaurant & Tavern and Gale Street Inn Chicago built local empires on the practice. To the south, at stalwarts such as Lem's Bar-B-Q and Leon's BBQ, you will find techniques drawn from the migration of African Americans during the early 20th century. Popular rib tips and hot sausages are cooked in aquarium smokers – the fire-code-compliant cousins to open pits, which look exactly like you think they should – topped in house-made sauce, stuffed in a white plastic clamshell with a slice of white bread and often delivered through a bullet-proof turnstile.

South-side barbecue is in crisis now. Diners are now awash in nicer-looking options, and pit masters are ageing without apprentices training to take over. 'It's this history that is slowly dying off,' Pang said. 'I think the most shameful thing is that [this style of] barbecue is not a young person's game.'

But Chicago's next wave of barbecue is. While the city is not unique in offering gourmet 'cue, Chicago's stature as arguably America's foremost food city pits (ahem) it as a bit of a vanguard. Restaurateurs don't have to pledge allegiance to one style. Instead, history and creativity overlap. Old traditions and new technologies meet in the middle. Texas brisket and Carolina pulled pork coexist with a white tablecloth treatment. And so begins yet another chapter in Chicago's riveting food story – one where all barbecue finds a hospitable home, where IT execs and travelling competitors become restaurant stars, and where reinvention reigns.

LESSONS FROM THE LEGENDS
CHICKEN THIGHS

In 2015, while serving as a judge at the Memphis in May World Championship Barbecue Contest, I spent several hours with the Danish National BBQ team (pictured above), watching how they cook chicken and other meats. These intense Vikings had beaten out many wannabe contenders to make it on their country's elite team, and then they had trained for months to compete at this international spectacle on the banks of the Mississippi River. Considered one of the world's most prestigious competitions, with more than 250 teams working hard to qualify, it is a one-of-a-kind experience that includes two days of raucous parties with men dressed in drag and rubber pig masks followed by two days of serious business, that is, finessing luscious pieces of barbecue, including chicken, so they glisten like jewels for the judges.

BRINE TIME

If brining sounds like a chore to you, I understand. Sometimes I skip this step, too, but barbecue competitors will tell you that if you can drop some chicken thighs in a saltwater bath in the morning, here is what will happen by dinnertime:

1

Salt, being the good chemical that it is, will dissolve muscle proteins in the meat, loosening up the fibres in the chicken and making them more absorbent.

2

In will rush the flavours of the brine. I usually combine 125g/4½oz sea salt and 100g/3½oz sugar with 1 litre/1¾ pints water in a large saucepan. I bring that to the boil to dissolve the salt and sugar, and then I add about 2 litres/3½ pints of ice cubes to chill the mixture before adding the raw chicken.

3

After 6–8 hours, when the chicken is on the grill, much of that flavour and moisture will stay inside the meat. The relaxed muscle fibres will not constrict and drive out juices as much as they would without a brine. Your reward will be moist, succulent thighs.

PREPARING THIGHS FOR THE GRILL

To achieve crispy brown skins, you must start with dry chicken thighs. The skins naturally have a lot of water, fat and protein in them. They can be especially watery if you have brined them (as you should), so be sure to pat dry all surfaces with kitchen paper, and then season them on both sides. A little bit (not a lot) of oil will help the thighs to brown without sticking to the cooking grate.

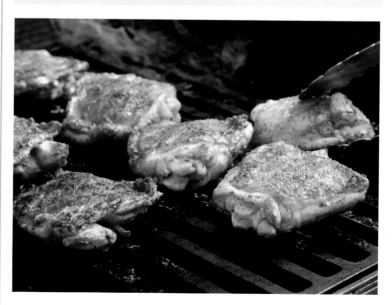

BROWNING BEFORE SAUCING

To achieve golden brown colours and crisp textures on the skins, direct heat helps a lot, as it quickly cooks out a lot of the remaining water and fat in the skins. After the step of browning over direct heat, you can move the thighs over indirect heat and brush them with the sauce of your choice. Sweet barbecue sauces could burn, so wait until the final 10–15 minutes of cooking time to apply those.

CHICKEN THIGHS
WITH SWEET APRICOT-HOISIN GLAZE

SERVES: 4 | PREP TIME: 20 MINUTES | GRILLING TIME: 31–36 MINUTES
SPECIAL EQUIPMENT: 2 LARGE HANDFULS CHERRY OR APPLE WOOD CHIPS,
LARGE DISPOSABLE FOIL TRAY

It used to be that I ate hoisin sauce only when I ordered Peking duck, moo shu pork or pho in Chinese and Vietnamese restaurants. But if you think about it, hoisin sauce's sweet, pungent flavours (sugar, vinegar, soya beans, spices, etc.) have all the elements of a worthy alternative to tomato-based barbecue sauces. When you simmer it with apricot jam, fresh lemon juice and ginger, you have a contemporary, Asian-style glaze for barbecued chicken.

For this recipe I have developed a sauce that would seem out of place in Memphis because it is so tropical in character, but I love the blend of pineapple and hoisin flavours. Feel free to use your own style of sauce, adding yet another twist to this on-going story of American barbecue.

RUB
1½ teaspoons sea salt
1½ teaspoons garlic powder
1 teaspoon ground cumin
¾ teaspoon freshly ground black pepper
½ teaspoon mild chilli powder
½ teaspoon ground ginger
⅛ teaspoon ground cinnamon

8 chicken thighs (with bone and skin), each 140–175g/5–6oz, trimmed of excess skin and fat, patted dry

GLAZE
150g/5oz apricot jam
4 tablespoons hoisin sauce
1 tablespoon fresh lemon juice
2 teaspoons peeled, finely chopped fresh ginger

1–2 tablespoons chopped fresh coriander

1 Soak the wood chips in water for at least 30 minutes.

2 Prepare the grill for direct and indirect cooking over medium-low heat (180–200°C/350–400°F).

3 Combine the rub ingredients, and then season the chicken thighs all over with the rub.

4 In a small saucepan over a medium heat, bring the glaze ingredients to a simmer. Cook until slightly thickened, about 3 minutes, stirring occasionally. Remove from the heat.

5 Drain and add the wood chips to the charcoal or to the smoker box of a gas grill, following the manufacturer's instructions, and close the lid. When smoke appears, grill the thighs, skin side down first, over *grilling/direct medium-low heat* for about 16 minutes, with the lid closed, until lightly browned, turning once. Place the thighs in a large disposable foil tray, place the tray over *roasting/indirect medium-low heat* and brush the thighs with some of the glaze. Close the lid, and cook for 15–20 minutes more until the juices run clear and the meat is no longer pink at the bone, brushing occasionally with the glaze. If the glaze becomes too thick as it cools, warm it briefly over a medium heat. Brush with any remaining glaze just before removing the thighs from the grill. Serve the thighs warm, garnished with the coriander.

BRINED CHICKEN THIGHS
WITH BLACK CHERRY BARBECUE SAUCE

SERVES: 6 | **PREP TIME:** 20 MINUTES | **BRINING TIME:** 6–8 HOURS OR OVERNIGHT | **GRILLING TIME:** ABOUT 2 HOURS
SPECIAL EQUIPMENT: 2 LARGE HANDFULS CHERRY WOOD CHIPS, 2 LARGE DISPOSABLE FOIL TRAYS

One of the surest ways to barbecue chicken so it's juicy is to brine it. Incorporating some black cherry juice into the brine will help with the overall flavour. If you use this kind of juice in the sauce, the brine and sauce will echo the same black cherry flavours.

In the barbecue competition world, one of the techniques that teams use to gain an edge is scraping the skin of each thigh so that when judges bite into it, their teeth cut easily through the skin. Scraping requires removing the skin from the meat, scoring the underside, and then, using a very sharp blade, scrape away most of the fat. The skins are then reattached, sometimes with cocktail sticks. It's a lot of tedious work, but 'bite-through skin' is now considered a must-have for earning top scores.

BRINE
1 litre/1¾ pints water
500ml/18fl oz tart black cherry juice
125g/4½oz sea salt
100g/3½oz brown sugar
2 litres/3½ pints ice cubes

12 large chicken thighs (with bone and skin), each about 200g/7oz, trimmed of excess skin and fat, patted dry

RUB
2 teaspoons paprika
1½ teaspoons sea salt
1½ teaspoons mild chilli powder
1½ teaspoons dried thyme
¾ teaspoon freshly ground black pepper

SAUCE
250ml/8fl oz tart black cherry juice
125ml/4fl oz tomato ketchup
4 tablespoons American mustard
2 tablespoons honey
1 teaspoon Worcestershire sauce

1   In a large saucepan, combine all the brine ingredients except the ice cubes. Bring to the boil, mixing well to dissolve the salt and sugar. Remove from the heat and add the ice cubes to cool down the brine. When the brine is cool, submerge the thighs in the brine and refrigerate for 6–8 hours or overnight.

2   Soak the wood chips in water for at least 30 minutes.

3   Mix the rub ingredients. Reserve ½ teaspoon of the rub to use in the sauce.

4   Prepare the grill for indirect cooking over low heat (about 150°C/300°F).

5   Remove the thighs from the saucepan and discard the brine. Season the thighs evenly with the rub, and then arrange them snugly, skin side down, in a single layer in two large disposable foil trays (six thighs in each tray).

6   Drain and add the wood chips to the charcoal or to the smoker box of a gas grill, following the manufacturer's instructions, and close the lid. When smoke appears, place the trays over *roasting/indirect low heat*, close the lid and cook for 1½ hours, turning the thighs once after 45 minutes.

7   In a saucepan, combine the sauce ingredients, including the ½ teaspoon reserved rub, and bring to a simmer over a medium heat. Cook for 3–5 minutes, stirring occasionally.

8   Take the thighs out of the trays and brush them all over with sauce. Grill the thighs on the cooking grates over *roasting/indirect low heat* for 20–30 minutes, with the lid closed, until the sauce is set. Remove from the grill and brush the thighs one more time with the sauce. Serve warm.

CHICKEN AND SAUSAGE GUMBO

SERVES: 8 | **PREP TIME:** 1 HOUR | **GRILLING TIME:** ABOUT 3½ HOURS | **SPECIAL EQUIPMENT:** 3 LARGE HANDFULS PECAN OR HICKORY WOOD CHIPS, GAS GRILL, LARGE (6-LITRE/10-PINT) GRILLPROOF CAST-IRON CASSEROLE

6 chicken thighs (with bone and skin), each 140–175g/5–6oz, trimmed of excess skin and fat, patted dry
Vegetable oil
Sea salt
Freshly ground black pepper
450g/1lb smoked sausage, such as andouille or spicy kielbasa
6 bacon rashers, cut crossways into 2.5-cm/1-inch pieces
125g/4oz plain flour
450g/1lb onions, finely chopped
5 celery stalks, finely chopped
1 green pepper, cut into 1-cm/½-inch dice
4 garlic cloves, finely chopped
2 litres/3½ pints low-sodium chicken stock
4 teaspoons Worcestershire sauce
Hot pepper sauce
1½ teaspoons dried thyme
2 bay leaves
225g/8oz okra, ends trimmed, cut crossways into 1-cm/½-inch slices
4 tablespoons roughly chopped flat-leaf parsley
900g/2lb long-grain rice, cooked

Gumbo is an epic Southern dish famous for its range of interpretations. Every Southern family comes at gumbo from a different path of ethnic and idiosyncratic distinctions. Consequently, the 'right' mix of meats and vegetables is debatable. Even the essential element of the roux has inspired fierce debate, with people arguing over the correct shade of browning in the roux before adding the vegetables. Gumbo comes from West African dialect for okra, so you would think this vegetable is mandatory – but if you aren't an okra fan, you can leave it out or substitute 225g/8oz green beans cut into bite-sized pieces. (Keep in mind, though, that the relatively long simmering time eliminates okra's gluey texture.)
Note: This recipe requires a lot of fluctuating temperatures, so it is best to use a gas grill.

1 Soak the wood chips in water for at least 30 minutes.

2 Brush the chicken thighs on both sides with oil and season evenly with 1 teaspoon salt and ½ teaspoon pepper. Set aside at room temperature while you prepare the grill.

3 Prepare the gas grill for indirect cooking over medium-low heat (about 180°C/350°F).

4 Drain and add half of the wood chips to the smoker box, following the manufacturer's instructions, and close the lid. When smoke appears, grill the chicken thighs, skin side up, over **roasting/indirect medium-low heat** for about 50 minutes, with the lid closed, until the meat is firm to the touch and the juices run clear. After 20 minutes, drain and add the remaining wood chips to the smoker box. Transfer the chicken to a bowl and set aside. Increase the temperature of the grill and the cooking method to direct medium heat (180–230°C/350–450°F).

5 Grill the sausages over **grilling/direct medium heat** for about 8 minutes, with the lid closed, until browned on all sides, turning occasionally. Remove from the grill, allow to rest for 5 minutes and then cut crossways into 5-mm/¼-inch thick slices.

6 In a large grillproof cast-iron casserole over **grilling/direct medium heat**, fry the bacon for 8–10 minutes, with the grill lid closed, until browned and crisp, stirring occasionally. Using a slotted spoon, transfer the bacon to kitchen paper to drain, and keep the bacon fat in the casserole.

7 Add 175ml/6fl oz oil to the bacon fat in the casserole. Whisk in the flour to make a thin roux. Cook over **grilling/direct medium heat** for 8–10 minutes until the roux is about the colour of a peanut, whisking almost constantly. You may stop cooking the

roux at this point, but longer cooking gives the best flavour. Reduce the temperature of the grill to direct medium-low heat (about 180°C/350°F) and continue cooking for 10–15 minutes more and whisking constantly until the roux smells toasted, smokes lightly and is just a shade lighter than milk chocolate, watching closely to prevent overbrowning.

8 Add the onions, celery and green pepper to the casserole. Cook over **grilling/direct medium heat** for 8–10 minutes, with the lid closed, until the onion is slightly softened and the mixture is quite sticky, stirring often. Stir in the garlic and cook for 1 minute. Gradually whisk in the stock. Stir in the Worcestershire sauce, 2 teaspoons hot sauce, the thyme, bay leaves, ¾ teaspoon salt and ½ teaspoon pepper. Increase the temperature of the grill to high heat (230–290°C/450–550°F) and bring the mixture to the boil. Then reduce the temperature of the grill to low heat (130–180°C/250–350°F) and simmer the gumbo over **grilling/direct low heat** for 1 hour, with the lid closed, stirring occasionally.

9 Add the chicken (and any accumulated juices) and sausage pieces to the gumbo and cook over **grilling/direct low heat**, with the lid closed, for 30 minutes. Add the okra and parsley and cook until the okra is very tender, 20–30 minutes more. Remove from the heat. Discard the bay leaves. Transfer the chicken to a chopping board to cool slightly. Cover the casserole to keep the gumbo hot.

10 Cut the chicken into bite-sized pieces, discarding the bones and skin, and chop the bacon. Add the chicken and bacon to the gumbo. Adjust the seasoning with more salt, pepper and hot sauce, if liked.

11 Heap cooked rice into each serving bowl and ladle gumbo over the rice. Serve hot, with hot sauce on the side.

JERK CHICKEN

MARINADE

1 Scotch bonnet or habanero chilli, deseeded and coarsely chopped (see caption and photo below)
6 large spring onions (white and light green parts only), coarsely chopped
4 tablespoons vegetable oil
2 tablespoons soy sauce
2 tablespoons fresh lime juice
2 tablespoons ground allspice, preferably freshly ground Jamaican allspice berries
2 tablespoons light brown sugar
1 tablespoon peeled, finely chopped fresh ginger
1 tablespoon coarsely chopped thyme leaves
1 teaspoon sea salt
½ teaspoon freshly grated nutmeg
½ teaspoon ground cinnamon
2 garlic cloves, coarsely chopped

1 whole chicken, 2–2.3kg/4½–5lb
1 lime, cut into wedges

Somewhere out in the sun-soaked West Indies lies American barbecue's point of origin (see page 5 for the real history), so I think it's fitting to feature a contemporary recipe in this cookbook from that part of the world, specifically Jamaica. With an intriguing blend of ingredients that includes chillies, spices, herbs and soy sauce, the thick marinade for this recipe uses the minimum amount of chillies; try to use the traditional Scotch bonnet type, and add a second chilli if you dare. The local trick from jerk aficionados is to let the chicken cook 'low and slow' to smoky tenderness over pimento wood. If the fire is too hot, the meat tends to scorch. If you would rather not shell out for pimento wood, which you'll need to buy online, use a more common fruitwood instead.

1 To avoid burning your skin, wear rubber gloves when you handle the chilli. In a blender, combine the marinade ingredients. Purée the marinade, stopping to scrape down the inside of the jug as needed, and add a little water if it is too thick. (A blender works best because it is easy to clean, and a plastic food processor bowl could pick up the marinade's strong flavour.)

2 Cut the chicken into six pieces: two breast halves, two leg quarters and two wings (cut off and discard the wing tips), and then place in a 33-x-23-cm/13-x-9-inch glass or ceramic baking dish. Pour the marinade over the chicken and use tongs to turn and coat the chicken. Cover with clingfilm and refrigerate for at least 4 hours or up to 18 hours, turning the chicken occasionally.

3 Soak the wood chips in water for at least 30 minutes.

4 Prepare the grill for direct and indirect cooking over medium-low heat (180–200°C/350–400°F).

5 Remove the chicken from the dish, letting any excess marinade drip back into the dish.

Transfer the marinade and juices in the dish to a small bowl, cover and refrigerate.

6 Drain and add half of the wood chips to the charcoal or to the smoker box of a gas grill, following the manufacturer's instructions, and close the lid. When smoke appears, grill the chicken, skin side up, over **roasting/indirect medium-low heat**, with the lid closed, for 45 minutes. Drain and add the remaining wood chips to the charcoal or smoker box before the old chips burn out. Turn the chicken over and baste with some of the reserved marinade. Continue grilling for 30–55 minutes more, with the lid closed, until the juices run clear and the meat is no longer pink at the bone, occasionally basting with the reserved marinade up until the last 20 minutes of grilling time. Discard any remaining marinade. If liked, to crisp and brown the skin, during the last 2–4 minutes, grill the chicken, skin side down, over **grilling/direct medium-low heat**, turning once. Remove from the grill and allow to rest for 3–5 minutes.

7 Using a heavy knife, cut the leg pieces in half at the joint and cut the breast pieces crossways in half. Serve warm with a squeeze of lime on top.

Scotch bonnet chillies (pictured here), and their look-alike cousin, habaneros, are two of the hottest chillies on the consumer market. Caribbean cooks have been cooking with these chillies for centuries and know to handle them with care. Learn from their experience! If you have sensitive skin, wear rubber gloves. Take care not to inhale the very strong fumes, especially when puréeing in a blender, and make the marinade in a well-ventilated kitchen.

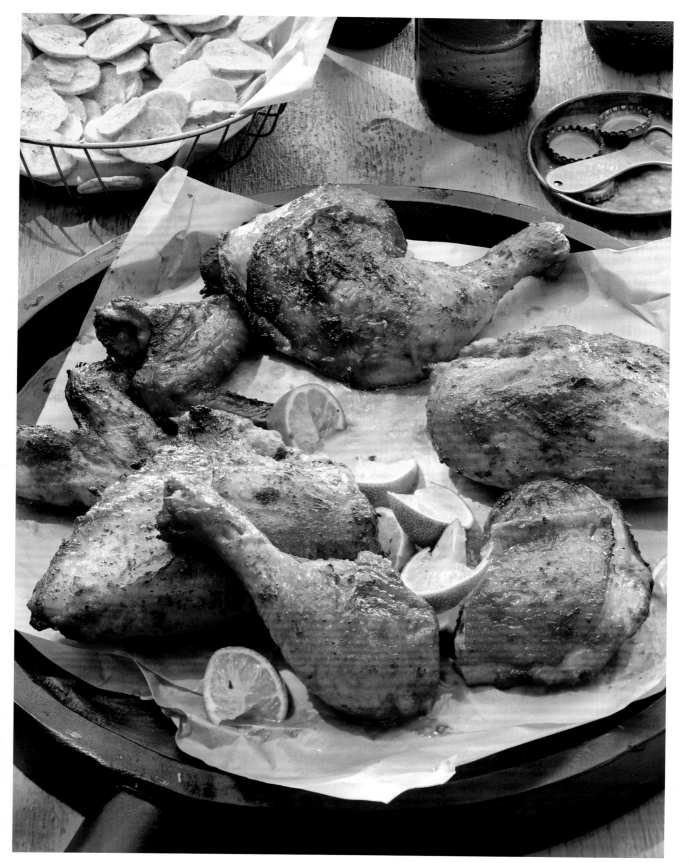

SPATCHCOCKED BBQ CHICKEN
WITH ALABAMA WHITE SAUCE

SERVES: 2–4 | PREP TIME: 15 MINUTES | GRILLING TIME: 25–30 MINUTES
SPECIAL EQUIPMENT: 1 LARGE HANDFUL HICKORY OR PECAN WOOD CHIPS, POULTRY SHEARS, INSTANT-READ THERMOMETER

PASTE
1 tablespoon extra-virgin olive oil
1 tablespoon fresh lime juice
1 tablespoon dark brown sugar
1 teaspoon ground cumin
1 teaspoon dried oregano
1 teaspoon dried thyme
1 teaspoon paprika
1 teaspoon sea salt
1 teaspoon freshly ground black pepper
½ teaspoon garlic powder

1 whole chicken, 1.8–2kg/4–4½lb,
   spatchcocked (see how-to below)

SAUCE
250ml/8fl oz mayonnaise
  4 tablespoons white wine vinegar
2 teaspoons freshly ground black pepper
¾ teaspoon granulated sugar
¼ teaspoon sea salt

In Alabama, white barbecue sauce is a special point of state pride. It is a vinegary, creamy sauce laced with lots of ground black pepper, and it has almost nothing in common with classic red barbecue sauce. A white colour is mandatory, but beyond that there are hundreds of variations. Some people make it sweeter. Some make it spicier by using cracked black peppercorns rather than ground pepper. The restaurant most famous for this kind of sauce is Big Bob Gibson's Bar-B-Q in Decatur. There, my friend Chris Lilly mixes his version in a big vat so he can dunk whole barbecued chickens into it. For this recipe I suggest spatchcocking (or butterflying) a chicken so you can get the most surface area right on the grate – and get the most flavour imaginable into the meat. Have a stack of napkins to hand! You'll want lots of sauce with every bite.

1   Soak the wood chips in water for at least 30 minutes.

2   Combine the paste ingredients. Massage the paste evenly all over the chicken. Set aside at room temperature while preparing the grill.

3   Prepare the grill for direct cooking over medium heat (180–230°C/350–450°F).

4   Drain and add the wood chips to the charcoal or to the smoker box of a gas grill, following the manufacturer's instructions, and close the lid. When smoke appears, grill the chicken, bone side down first, over **grilling/**

direct medium heat for 10 minutes, with the lid closed. Turn the chicken over and continue grilling for 15–20 minutes more until the juices run clear and an instant-read thermometer inserted into the thickest part of the thigh (not touching the bone) registers 70–74°C/160 –165°F. Remove from the grill and allow to rest for 10 minutes (the internal temperature will rise 5–10 degrees during this time).

5   Meanwhile, in a bowl, whisk the sauce ingredients until smooth. Cut the chicken lengthways in half or into pieces, and serve warm with the sauce for dipping.

1   *To spatchcock, place the chicken, breast side down, on a chopping board. Using poultry shears, cut from the neck to the tail end along either side of the backbone.*

2   *Once the backbone is out, you'll be able to see the interior of the chicken. Make a small slit in the cartilage at the bottom end of the breastbone. This will help the chicken to lie flat. Then, placing both your hands on the ribcage, crack the chicken open like a book.*

3   *Remove the breastbone by running your fingers along either side of the cartilage that lies between the breast halves to loosen it from the flesh. Grab the bone and pull up to remove it with the attached cartilage.*

4   *Turn the chicken over and press on the skin side to finish flattening the chicken. Cut off the wing tips because they would likely burn.*

ROSEMARY-LEMON BRICK CHICKEN
WITH BREAD SALAD

SERVES: 4–6 | PREP TIME: 30 MINUTES | MARINATING TIME: 4–24 HOURS | GRILLING TIME: ABOUT 1 HOUR
SPECIAL EQUIPMENT: POULTRY SHEARS, 3 LARGE HANDFULS PECAN WOOD CHIPS, CHARCOAL GRILL,
2 FOIL-WRAPPED BRICKS OR LARGE CAST-IRON FRYING PAN, INSTANT-READ THERMOMETER

MARINADE

Freshly grated zest and juice of
    2 lemons
2 tablespoons finely chopped
    rosemary leaves
4 garlic cloves, crushed
1 teaspoon smoked paprika

Extra-virgin olive oil
Sea salt
Freshly ground black pepper
1 whole chicken, about 2.3kg/5lb,
    spatchcocked (see how-to,
    page 196)
1 French baguette, trimmed to a length
    of 20cm/8 inches, cut lengthways
    in half

DRESSING

1 tablespoon fresh lemon juice
1 tablespoon red wine vinegar
1 garlic clove, crushed

340g/12oz cherry tomatoes, each
    cut in half
5 tablespoons roughly chopped
    flat-leaf parsley

Spatchcocking a chicken and barbecuing it under foil-wrapped bricks will score you points for style and a higher degree of difficulty than roasting it uncut; beyond style, however, this technique makes good culinary sense. The dark meat of the legs almost always takes longer to cook than the breast, but not in this case because here the legs are more exposed to the fire. Try as best you can to balance the bricks over the breast so they will protect the lean meat from too much heat. If you want a browner, crisper skin (and who doesn't?) towards the end of cooking, slide the whole bird carefully over direct heat.

1 Whisk the marinade ingredients, including 4 tablespoons oil, 2 teaspoons salt and 1 teaspoon pepper. Lay the chicken flat in a baking dish. Pour the marinade over the chicken and massage it into both sides. Cover with clingfilm and refrigerate for 4–24 hours.

2 Soak the wood chips in water for at least 30 minutes.

3 Prepare the charcoal grill for direct and indirect cooking over medium-high heat (about 200°C/400°F) creating a crescent moon fire, with the charcoal arranged around half of the perimeter of the charcoal grate.

4 Lightly brush the cut side of the baguette with oil, and then grill, cut side down, over *grilling/direct medium-high heat* for about 2 minutes, with the lid closed, until toasted, turning once. Remove from the grill and cut into bite-sized pieces.

5 In a large bowl, whisk the dressing ingredients, including 4 tablespoons oil, ½ teaspoon salt and ¼ teaspoon pepper. Add the bread and tomatoes and stir to coat. Allow the salad to stand at room temperature while you grill the chicken.

6 Drain and add the wood chips to the charcoal. Lay the chicken, bone side down and with the legs facing the fire, over *roasting/indirect medium heat*, and put two foil-wrapped bricks on top of the chicken. Close the lid and grill for 25 minutes. Remove the bricks. Using a large spatula, carefully turn the chicken over (keep the legs facing the fire), being careful not to tear the pieces apart. Replace the bricks and continue grilling over *roasting/indirect medium-high heat*, with the lid closed, for 25 minutes more. Remove the bricks. If the skin needs more browning, carefully slide the chicken over *grilling/direct medium-high heat* and grill for 5–10 minutes, with the lid off. The chicken is fully cooked when the juices run clear and an instant-read thermometer inserted into the thickest part of the thigh (not touching the bone) registers 70–74°C/160–165°F. Carefully remove the chicken from the grill and allow to rest for 10 minutes (the internal temperature will rise 5–10 degrees during this time). Cut the chicken into serving pieces.

7 Stir the parsley into the salad, and then spoon the salad on to a serving platter. Place the chicken pieces over the salad. Serve immediately.

BEER CAN CHICKEN
WITH CHIPOTLE SPICE RUB

SERVES: 4 | **PREP TIME:** 20 MINUTES | **GRILLING TIME:** 45 MINUTES–1 HOUR | **SPECIAL EQUIPMENT:** 3 LARGE HANDFULS MESQUITE WOOD CHIPS, WEBER STYLE™ POULTRY INFUSION ROASTER, INSTANT-READ THERMOMETER, FAT SEPARATOR

RUB

1 tablespoon extra-virgin olive oil
2 teaspoons sea salt
1 teaspoon brown sugar
1 teaspoon chipotle chilli powder
1 teaspoon ground cumin
1 teaspoon smoked paprika
½ teaspoon freshly ground black
    pepper
¼ teaspoon ground cayenne pepper

1 whole chicken, 1.8–2.3kg/4–5lb,
    neck, giblets and any excess fat
    removed
250ml/8fl oz beer, at room
    temperature

For all the fun and folklore surrounding a chicken standing with a beer can crammed inside it (oh, how undignified!) it's not the beer that matters. Almost any liquid will do, because what matters is steam. The key is that you use no more than a few spoonfuls of beer, wine, juice or water. Otherwise, the liquid will take ages to simmer, and simmering is what pays off. The evaporating liquid makes a juicy bird, restoring almost all of its dignity. If you want to skip the act of a chicken teetering on a can, get a poultry roaster – it will sit flat and sturdy on the cooking grate of your grill and hold whatever liquid floats your boat.

1   Soak the wood chips in water for at least 30 minutes.

2   Using a fork, mix the rub ingredients into a smooth paste.

3   Using your fingers, separate the chicken skin from the meat, starting at the neck cavity and moving along the breast, being careful not to tear the skin. Turn the chicken and, starting at the tail cavity, separate the skin from the thighs and legs. Carefully spread half of the rub under the skin, massaging it directly onto the meat. Massage the remaining rub all over the skin on both the front and back sides of the chicken. Fold the wing tips behind the chicken's back. Allow the chicken to stand at room temperature while you prepare the grill.

4   Prepare the grill for indirect cooking over medium heat (180–230°C/350–450°F).

5   Fill the cup of a Weber Style™ poultry roaster with beer. Lower the larger cavity of the chicken over the cup.

6   Drain and add two handfuls of the wood chips to the charcoal or to the smoker box of a gas grill, following the manufacturer's instructions, and close the lid. When smoke appears, place the poultry roaster with the chicken over **roasting/indirect medium heat**, close the lid and cook until the juices run clear and an instant-read thermometer inserted into the thickest part of the thigh (not touching the bone) registers 70–74°C/160–165°F, 45 minutes– 1 hour. After the first 15 minutes of cooking time, drain and add the remaining wood chips to the charcoal or smoker box. After 30 minutes of cooking time, wearing insulated barbecue mitts or oven gloves, swivel the poultry roaster with the chicken 180 degrees to ensure even cooking. If the neck and wings begin to brown too quickly, cover them with foil. If using a charcoal grill, replenish the charcoal as needed to maintain a steady temperature.

7   Remove the poultry roaster with the chicken from the grill and place on a heatproof surface. Use a large spoon to collect and transfer the majority of the cooking juices from the roaster to a fat separator; set aside for the fat and juices to separate. Let the chicken rest for 10 minutes (the internal temperature will rise 5–10 degrees during this time). Lift the chicken from the roaster and cut into serving pieces. Drizzle with the reserved, degreased cooking juices. Serve warm.

TIPS
BEER CAN CHICKEN

1

Use any beer you like. The flavour is almost impossible to taste in the chicken, but it helps keep the chicken moist. Any 350-ml/12-fl oz can works well for chickens in the range of 1.6–2.3kg/3½–5lb. A bigger chicken requires a 475-ml/16-fl oz can. Let the beer come to room temperature before cooking so it will get hot faster on the grill.

2

Tent the top. In this preparation the chicken's neck and wings tends to brown first. If they get dark too soon, loosely tent that area of the bird with aluminium foil. Nonstick foil works well here.

3

Balancing a chicken on a can may not be for everyone. If you have visions of your chicken falling over and beer spilling into your grill, you could invest in a dedicated poultry roaster for the same results more safely. It allows a chicken to stand upright over a small container you fill with beer, attached to a sturdy pan, so the chicken and beer remain steady from start to finish.

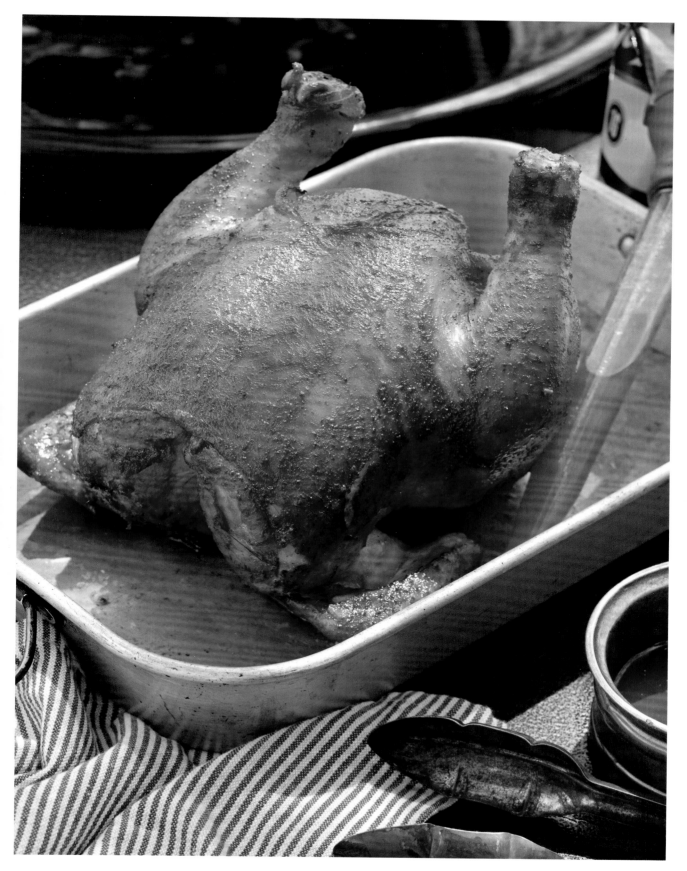

ROTISSERIE CHICKEN
BRINED IN HERBS AND BUTTERMILK

SERVES: 4 | PREP TIME: 25 MINUTES | BRINING TIME: 8–24 HOURS | GRILLING TIME: ABOUT 1¼ HOURS
SPECIAL EQUIPMENT: ROTISSERIE, KITCHEN STRING, LARGE DISPOSABLE FOIL TRAY, INSTANT-READ THERMOMETER

BRINE

1.5 litres/2½ pints buttermilk
5 tablespoons hot pepper sauce
4 tablespoons sea salt
4 tablespoons granulated sugar
12 garlic cloves, finely chopped
2 tablespoons chopped
    oregano leaves
1 tablespoon thyme leaves

3 tablespoons chopped rosemary
    leaves
1 whole chicken, about 2.3kg/5lb,
    neck, giblets, wing tips and excess
    fat removed
2 tablespoons extra-virgin olive oil

It seems to me that we are now living in the United States of Rotisserie Chicken. It's ubiquitous. You see it in warehouse stores, in supermarkets and in fast-casual restaurants. We the People love it, especially when the flesh is moist and the skin is crispy. For top-notch results, start with an organic, air-chilled chicken, which you can buy from specialist suppliers. They are more expensive, but well worth it for their savoury depths of taste. An easy, herby brine with buttermilk will add a nice bit of tangy richness to the natural flavour. Cook your chicken as close to 200°C/400°F as possible, and after it is done, allow it to rest for about 10 minutes before you cut into it.

1   Combine the brine ingredients, including 2 tablespoons of the rosemary, and stir until the salt and sugar are dissolved. Place the chicken, legs up, into a large, resealable plastic bag and pour in the brine, making sure to fill the chicken's cavity so all the brine will fit in the bag. Squeeze the air out of the bag and seal tightly. Place the bag in a large bowl to prevent any leakage. Refrigerate for 8–24 hours.

2   Place a large disposable foil tray underneath the cooking grate to catch the drippings. You may have to crush the foil tray a bit, but that's okay. Or, if you are using a charcoal grill, place the foil tray on the charcoal grate between the two piles of charcoal. Then prepare the grill for rotisserie cooking over indirect medium heat (as close to 200°C/400°F as possible).

3   Remove the chicken from the bag and discard the brine. Pat the chicken dry, inside and outside, with kitchen paper. Truss the chicken with kitchen string, securing the legs and wings.

4   Combine the remaining rosemary with the oil and brush it all over the chicken. Slide one pronged fork on to the spit, with the tines facing inwards, about 25cm/10 inches from the end of the spit. Secure the fork, but don't tighten it thoroughly yet. Slide the spit through the centre of the chicken and gently push it on to the fork tines so that

they are deep inside the chicken. Add the other pronged fork to the spit, with the tines facing inwards, and slide it down until they are firmly in the chicken. Secure the fork, but don't tighten it yet. Wearing insulated barbecue mitts or oven gloves, place the pointed end of the spit into the rotisserie motor. If necessary, adjust the chicken so that it is centred on the spit. Tighten both forks into place and turn on the motor.

5   Grill the chicken over **roasting/indirect medium heat** for about 1¼ hours, with the lid closed, until an instant-read thermometer inserted into the thickest part of the thigh (not touching the bone) registers 70–74°C/160–165°F. Before checking the temperature, turn off the rotisserie motor. If the skin is not nicely browned at the end of the cooking time, turn on the infra-red burner for medium heat (if your grill has one). With the rotisserie still rotating, cook the chicken for a few minutes longer, watching *very* carefully so the chicken doesn't burn.

6   Turn off the rotisserie motor. Wearing insulated barbecue mitts or gloves, carefully remove the spit from the grill. Gently loosen the forks and slide the chicken off the spit. Transfer to a carving board and allow to rest for 10 minutes (the internal temperature will rise 5–10 degrees during this time). Cut the chicken into serving pieces. Serve warm.

HONEY-GLAZED POUSSINS

SERVES: 2-4 | **PREP TIME:** 20 MINUTES | **GRILLING TIME:** 30-40 MINUTES
SPECIAL EQUIPMENT: 1 LARGE HANDFUL HICKORY WOOD CHIPS, POULTRY SHEARS

350g/12oz honey
4 tablespoons unseasoned rice vinegar
2 tablespoons soy sauce
1 canned chipotle chilli in adobo sauce, deseeded and finely chopped
2 poussins, each 450g/1lb, neck, giblets and wing tips removed
Sea salt

This little recipe for shiny glazed poussins highlights a few classic elements of American barbecue: simple but bold flavours, a strategic use of smoke and vigilance about the use of fire. Moving the poussins off the flame after a brief period of browning and basting gives you succulent meat with a glistening sheen. The final touch of a little salt sprinkled over the top brightens all the tastes involved.

1   Soak the wood chips in water for at least 30 minutes.

2   Prepare the grill for direct and indirect cooking over medium heat (180-230°C/350-450°F).

3   Combine the honey, vinegar, soy sauce and chipotle chilli and stir until the honey dissolves. Reserve 5 tablespoons to use as a dipping sauce.

4   Set the poussins, with the breast side facing down, on a work surface. Using poultry shears, cut along both sides of the backbone and discard. Spread the birds open like a book and use a large, sturdy knife to cut through the middle of the breast. The breastbone will stay attached to one of the halves.

5   Drain and add the wood chips to the charcoal or to the smoker box of a gas grill, following the manufacturer's instructions, and close the lid. When smoke appears, grill the poussins, skin side down, over **grilling/direct medium heat** for about 5 minutes, with the lid closed, until well browned. Baste with the honey mixture, turn and continue cooking, skin side up, for 5 minutes more. (Resist the urge to move the birds unless you see big flare-ups underneath. This will allow the sweet glaze to caramelise as the skin browns.)

6   Baste the poussins again, move them over **roasting/indirect medium heat**, close the lid and continue cooking for 20-30 minutes more until the meat is firm to the touch and opaque all the way to the centre, brushing often with the honey mixture. Remove from the grill, season generously with sea salt and allow to rest for 5 minutes. Serve the poussins warm with the reserved honey mixture for dipping.

SMOKED TURKEY PASTRAMI ON RYE

SERVES: 6–8 | PREP TIME: 15 MINUTES | REFRIGERATION TIME: 24–48 HOURS | COOKING TIME: ABOUT 2 HOURS
SPECIAL EQUIPMENT: SPICE MILL, WATER SMOKER, 3 LARGE HANDFULS CHERRY WOOD CHUNKS, INSTANT-READ THERMOMETER

RUB

1 tablespoon black peppercorns
1 tablespoon coriander seeds
2 teaspoons yellow mustard seeds
2 tablespoons light brown sugar
1 tablespoon sea salt
2 teaspoons paprika
1 teaspoon ground cumin

1 boneless turkey breast (with skin),
    1.1–1.4kg/2½–3lb
1 tablespoon extra-virgin olive oil
Sliced rye bread
Lettuce leaves
Tomato slices
Mayonnaise
New York-style deli mustard

Classic pastrami, like the ragged, fatty slices you get piled high on rye in a Jewish deli, comes from the brisket (chest area) of a cow. Because that thick, muscular slab of beef is smoked with low heat to break down its connective tissues, my friend Meathead Goldwyn of Amazingribs.com has declared that America's oldest, continually operated barbecue restaurant is Katz Deli, which opened in New York City in 1888. Traditionally the beef is cured in a brine, seasoned with spices such as coriander, black pepper, mustard seed and paprika, and then put into a smoker to transform before it is steamed and sliced. In this recipe I have applied similar techniques and seasonings to a turkey breast because, let's face it, that normally bland cut really benefits from an earthy, peppery burst of flavour and the quintessential dark crust of old-world pastrami.

1   In a small frying pan over a medium heat, stir and shake the peppercorns, coriander and mustard seeds for 3–4 minutes until lightly toasted and fragrant. Transfer to a small bowl and cool for 5 minutes. Pour into a spice mill and pulse 15–20 times until coarsely ground. Transfer back to the small bowl, add the remaining rub ingredients and mix well.

2   Brush the turkey breast with the oil and season evenly with the rub. Wrap tightly in a double layer of clingfilm, place on a plate and refrigerate for 24–48 hours.

3   Prepare the smoker for indirect cooking with very low heat (110–140°C/225–275°F). When the temperature reaches 110°C/225°F, add the wood chunks to the charcoal.

4   Cook the turkey breast, skin side up, over ***roasting/indirect very low heat*** for about 2 hours, with the lid closed, until an instant-read thermometer inserted into the thickest part of the breast registers 70°C/160°F. Remove the turkey from the smoker and allow to rest for 20 minutes, uncovered (the internal temperature will rise 5–10 degrees during this time). Cut the turkey into slices and make sandwiches with rye bread, lettuce, tomato, mayonnaise and mustard.

STATE FAIR TURKEY LEGS

SERVES: 6 | PREP TIME: 15 MINUTES | BRINING TIME: 12 HOURS | COOKING TIME: 1¾–2 HOURS
SPECIAL EQUIPMENT: WATER SMOKER, 2 LARGE HANDFULS CHERRY OR APPLE WOOD CHUNKS, INSTANT-READ THERMOMETER

BRINE

1 litre/1¾ pints water
600g/1lb 5oz demerara sugar
370g/13oz sea salt
1 tablespoon celery seeds
1 tablespoon coriander seeds
1 tablespoon cumin seeds
1 tablespoon yellow mustard seeds
1 litre/1¾ pints ice cubes

6 turkey drumsticks, each
    340–450g/12–16lb
2 tablespoons rapeseed oil

SAUCE

150ml/5fl oz tomato ketchup
2 teaspoons black treacle
2 teaspoons cider vinegar
2 teaspoons Worcestershire sauce
1 teaspoon mild chilli powder
1 teaspoon garlic granules
½ teaspoon freshly ground black
    pepper
½ teaspoon ground cumin

Every August, Des Moines, Iowa, is overrun with turkeys! Well, actually, with turkey legs. Brined and barbecued, they're a signature dish of the state fair, an 11-day event that highlights the best produce, livestock and home crafts from this agriculturally rich state. Don't skip the 12-hour brine. That and the gentle heat of a smoker are crucial for breaking down the tight turkey tendons and yielding tender meat dripping with juices. Have a crunchy, summery salad with a creamy dressing and some grilled corn on the cob to accompany this American classic.

1   In a large saucepan, combine all the brine ingredients except the ice cubes. Cook over a high heat for about 5 minutes until the salt and sugar are dissolved, whisking constantly. Add the ice and stir until it melts. Submerge the turkey drumsticks in the cool brine. Cover and refrigerate for 12 hours. If any parts of the drumsticks are not completely submerged, reposition them occasionally to make sure they all get enough time in the brine.

2   Prepare the smoker for indirect cooking with very low heat (130–150°C/250–300°F).

3   Remove the drumsticks from the brine, pat dry with kitchen paper and brush them all over with the oil. Discard the brine.

4   Add the wood chunks to the charcoal and, when smoke appears, cook the drumsticks over **roasting/indirect very low heat** for

1¼–1½ hours, with the lid closed, until well browned and an instant-read thermometer inserted into the thickest part of the meat (not touching the bone) registers 74°C/165°F. Meanwhile, make the sauce.

5   In a small saucepan, combine the sauce ingredients. Bring to a simmer over a medium heat and then lower the heat and simmer for about 2 minutes, stirring occasionally.

6   After the internal temperature of the drumsticks has reached 74°C/165°F, brush them all over with the sauce. Continue cooking over **roasting/indirect very low heat** for 20–30 minutes more, with the lid closed, until the internal temperature reaches 80–82°C/175–180°F. Remove the drumsticks from the smoker and allow to rest for 15 minutes (the internal temperature will rise 5–10 degrees during this time). Serve warm.

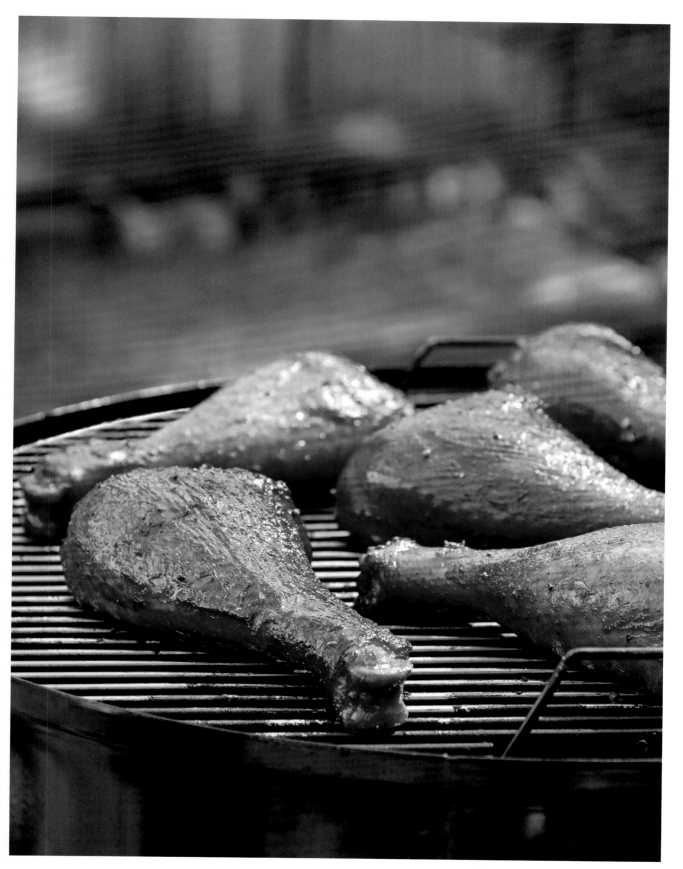

SMOKED TURKEY
WITH HERB GRAVY

SERVES: 8–10 | PREP TIME: 20 MINUTES, PLUS ABOUT 4 HOURS FOR THE STOCK | CHILLING TIME: 12–16 HOURS
COOKING TIME: 4½–5½ HOURS | SPECIAL EQUIPMENT: WOODEN SKEWER; KITCHEN STRING; 1 PIECE DOUBLE-THICK MUSLIN, ABOUT 75CM/30 INCHES LONG; WATER SMOKER; 3 LARGE HANDFULS PECAN, APPLE OR HICKORY WOOD CHUNKS; INSTANT-READ THERMOMETER

1 whole turkey, about 6kg/13lb, thawed if frozen

STOCK
1.4kg/3lb turkey wings, preferably chopped with a cleaver into 5–7.5-cm/2–3-inch chunks, plus reserved tail, fat, giblets and neck from the turkey
1 tablespoon vegetable oil
1 small onion, chopped
1 small carrot, chopped
1 small celery stalk with leaves, chopped
250ml/8fl oz dry white wine
4 sprigs flat-leaf parsley
1½ teaspoons sea salt
½ teaspoon dried thyme
½ teaspoon black peppercorns
1 bay leaf

RUB
2 tablespoons sea salt
2 teaspoons dried sage
1 teaspoon dried marjoram
1 teaspoon dried rosemary
1 teaspoon dried thyme
1 teaspoon freshly ground black pepper

Vegetable oil
1 onion, very coarsely chopped
½ small orange, very coarsely chopped
4 sprigs flat-leaf parsley
2 bay leaves, coarsely crumbled

GRAVY
Melted unsalted butter, as needed (up to 60g/2oz)
65g/2¼oz plain flour
1 teaspoon finely chopped thyme leaves
1 teaspoon finely chopped rosemary leaves
Sea salt
Freshly ground black pepper

Because the drippings from a barbecued turkey can sometimes be too smoky to make gravy, here I make the gravy separately with a homemade stock prepared earlier with oven-roasted turkey wings and giblets. The charcoal also gives off smoke and flavour, so resist the temptation to add extra wood chunks.

1 Pat the turkey dry, inside and outside, with kitchen paper. Pull any fat from inside the body cavity near the tail end. Remove the giblets and neck (discard the liver). Using a heavy knife or poultry shears, cut the neck into 5-cm/2-inch chunks. Save the fat, giblets and neck. Preheat the oven to 200°C/400°F/gas mark 6. Place the turkey wings fat, giblets and neck in a large roasting tin, and then roast until well browned, about 1 hour, turning the pieces once.

2 In a large saucepan over a medium-high heat, warm the oil. Add the onion, carrot and celery. Cook for about 3 minutes until softened and lightly browned, stirring occasionally. Add the turkey pieces to the pan and set the roasting tin aside. Pour enough cold water into the saucepan to just barely cover the ingredients. Bring to the boil, skimming off any foam that rises to the surface. Add the remaining stock ingredients. Reduce the heat to low and simmer until the stock is full-flavoured, about 2 hours, skimming occasionally. Strain the stock through a sieve into a bowl. Allow to stand for 5 minutes so that the fat separates. Skim and discard the fat. Return the stock to the pan and boil over a high heat for 15–20 minutes until reduced to 1 litre/1¾ pints.

3 Meanwhile, heat the roasting tin over a high heat until the fat is sizzling. Pour the fat from the tin into a small bowl. Return the tin to the heat. Add 250ml/8fl oz water and bring to the boil, scraping up all the browned bits in the pan. Cook for about 1 minute until reduced to 125ml/4fl oz. Transfer these deglazed drippings to a separate, small bowl. Cool, cover and refrigerate the stock, fat and deglazed drippings for up to 2 days.

4 While the stock is cooking, combine the rub ingredients. Brush the turkey with 2 tablespoons oil and season evenly, inside and outside, with the rub. Tuck the wing tips behind the turkey's back. Carefully coat the turkey all over with a little oil to keep the herbs moist. Place the turkey on a wire rack set over a rimmed roasting tray and refrigerate, uncovered, for 12–16 hours.

5 Stuff the onion, orange, parsley and bay leaves into the turkey body and neck cavities. Using a wooden skewer, pin the neck skin to the back skin to enclose the seasoning mixture. Tie the ends of the drumsticks together with kitchen string. Let the turkey stand at room temperature for 1 hour before cooking. Meanwhile, rinse the muslin under cold running water. Wring it out, put it in a bowl and saturate it with 2 tablespoons oil.

6 Prepare the smoker for indirect cooking with very low heat (110–130°C/225–250°F). When the temperature reaches 110°C/225°F, add the wood chunks to the charcoal.

7 Brush the bottom of the turkey again with oil. Wrap the moistened muslin around it and smoke over **roasting/indirect very low heat** for 3½ hours, with the lid closed. Discard the muslin and tent the breast area loosely with aluminium foil. Continue smoking for 1–2 hours more, with the lid closed, until the turkey is golden brown and an instant-read thermometer inserted in the thickest part of the thigh (not touching the bone) reaches 77–80°C/170–175°F, checking the temperature every 30 minutes.

8 Remove the turkey from the smoker. Tilt the body cavity over a measuring jug to catch any juices that have accumulated. Add enough stock to measure 1 litre/1¾ pints. Allow the turkey to rest for 30 minutes (the internal temperature will rise 5–10 degrees during this time).

9 In a saucepan over a medium heat, warm the turkey fat. Measure it and add enough melted butter to make 125ml/4fl oz. Return the fat mixture to the saucepan. Whisk in the flour and allow to bubble for 2–3 minutes over a medium heat until the flour is cooked and light golden brown. Whisk in the stock mixture, deglazed drippings, thyme and rosemary. Simmer, reduce the heat to medium-low and cook for 5–8 minutes until slightly thickened, stirring often. Season with salt and pepper.

10 Carve the turkey, discarding the ingredients in the body cavity. Serve warm with the gravy.

5
SEAFOOD

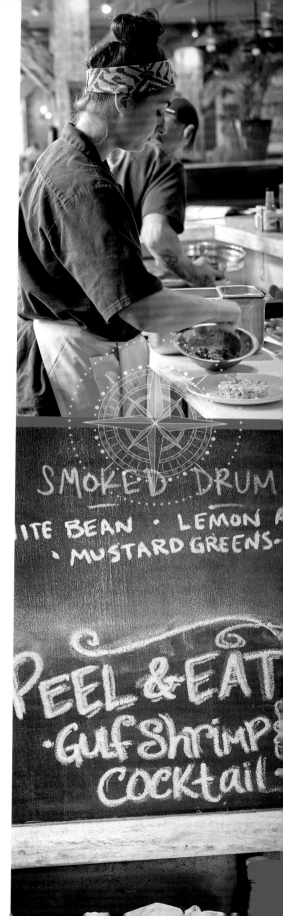

CEDAR-PLANKED SALMON
WITH PICKLED FENNEL SALAD AND HORSERADISH CREAM

SERVES: 4 | PREP TIME: 30 MINUTES | GRILLING TIME: 15–20 MINUTES
SPECIAL EQUIPMENT: 1 UNTREATED CEDAR PLANK, ABOUT 30CM/12 INCHES LONG AND 18CM/7 INCHES WIDE

PICKLING LIQUID
250ml/8fl oz dry white wine or vermouth
175ml/6fl oz white wine vinegar
2 tablespoons granulated sugar
2 teaspoons fennel seeds
8 juniper berries
2 small garlic cloves, crushed

Sea salt
½ large fennel bulb, cored and cut into 2.5-cm/1-inch strips
½ small head radicchio, cored and cut into 5-cm/2-inch strips
2 tablespoons prepared horseradish
1½ teaspoons finely chopped dill
125ml/4fl oz crème fraîche or soured cream
Freshly ground black pepper
1 centre-cut salmon fillet (with skin), about 900g/2lb and 2.5cm/ 1 inch thick, pin bones removed
Extra-virgin olive oil
1 small bunch watercress, torn into small sprigs

One chef who inspires me is Edward Lee, a Korean American who grew up in Brooklyn, trained in chichi French kitchens, and now runs his own restaurants in the South. He has a special way of weaving together the threads of his eclectic background and exploring the boundaries of barbecue. 'Nothing cuts the intensity of smokiness like a sharp pickle,' he writes in his first cookbook. 'Together they are harmonious, the perfect yin and yang.' That's why pickles show up so often with barbecue, including this recipe that skips the traditional dill pickles for a vegetable salad with pickled fennel and radicchio. After all, this is new American barbecue.

1 Soak the cedar plank in water for at least 1 hour.

2 In a small, non-reactive saucepan combine the pickling liquid ingredients, including 2½ tablespoons salt. Bring to the boil over a medium heat, add the fennel strips and simmer for 3–4 minutes until tender but not mushy. Using a slotted spoon, transfer the fennel strips to kitchen paper to dry. Add the radicchio to the simmering pickling liquid and cook for 1½ minutes only, just until wilted. Using a slotted spoon, transfer the radicchio to kitchen paper to dry.

3 Whisk the horseradish, dill and crème fraîche and season lightly with salt and generously with pepper.

4 Prepare the grill for direct cooking over medium heat (180–230°C/350–450°F).

5 Cut the salmon fillet into four equal portions, cutting down to, but not all the way through the skin. Brush the salmon with oil and season evenly with salt and pepper.

6 Drain the cedar plank. Place it over **grilling/ direct medium heat** and close the lid. When the plank begins to smoke and char, turn it over. Place the salmon, skin side down, on the plank. Grill over **grilling/direct medium heat**, with the lid closed, until cooked to your desired doneness, 15–20 minutes for medium rare. Carefully transfer the salmon on the plank to a heatproof surface. Slide a spatula between the skin and flesh and transfer individual portions of the salmon to serving plates.

7 In a bowl, combine the pickled vegetables, watercress and 1½ tablespoons oil and toss gently until evenly coated. Serve the salmon warm with the salad and horseradish cream.

Before cooking fish on a cedar plank, start the plank smoking. Submerge it in water for at least 1 hour, drain it and set it over the fire until you smell smoke. Then turn it over and lay the fish on top. If the plank ever catches fire, put out the flames with a spray bottle filled with water. Cedar is the classic pairing with salmon, but if you can find fruitwood or mesquite planks, try one of those for an interesting variation.

SALMON
IN TOMATO-SMOKED SAUSAGE BROTH

SERVES: 4 | **PREP TIME:** 25 MINUTES
GRILLING TIME: 16–18 MINUTES

BROTH
500ml/18fl oz low-sodium chicken
   stock
150ml/5fl oz dry white wine or
   vermouth
2 teaspoons white wine vinegar
3 sprigs thyme
3 garlic cloves, smashed and peeled
½ teaspoon ground cumin
½ teaspoon hot chilli-garlic sauce,
   such as Sriracha
¼ teaspoon sea salt
¼ teaspoon smoked paprika

3 vine-ripened tomatoes, about
   340g/12oz total, cored, each cut
   crossways in half, seeds scraped away
3 cooked smoked pork sausages, each
   75–115g/3–4oz
Extra-virgin olive oil
Sea salt
Freshly ground black pepper
565g/1¼lb salmon fillet (with skin),
   about 2cm/¾ inch thick, pin
   bones removed
¼ teaspoon smoked paprika
4 large slices artisan bread, each
   about 1cm/½ inch thick
Handful fresh coriander

One reason that salmon is such a popular fish for grilling is because you can taste the flavours of fire in the fish after just a few minutes on the hot grate. This recipe echoes those flavours in a warm, savoury broth made quickly with grilled smoky sausages and charred tomatoes. I like the way the broth keeps the fish moist and tender in the bowl.

1   In a small saucepan, combine the broth ingredients. Bring to a simmer over a medium heat, and then reduce the heat to low. Cover and simmer gently for 15 minutes to infuse the broth with flavour. Remove from the heat and keep covered.

2   Prepare the grill for direct cooking over medium-high heat (220–230°C/425–450°F).

3   Brush the tomato halves and sausages with oil and season the tomato halves with ¼ teaspoon salt and ¼ teaspoon pepper. Grill the tomatoes and sausages over *grilling/direct medium-high heat*, with the lid closed, until the tomatoes are slightly charred and the sausages are deep brown in spots, about 5 minutes for the tomatoes and about 8 minutes for the sausages, turning occasionally. Remove from the grill to cool slightly.

4   Lightly brush the salmon with oil and season with ¼ teaspoon salt, ¼ teaspoon pepper and ¼ teaspoon paprika. Lightly brush the bread slices with oil. Grill the salmon, skin side down, over *grilling/direct medium-high heat* for 8–10 minutes, with the lid closed, until opaque in the centre, (do not turn). During the last minute of grilling time, toast the bread over direct heat, turning once.

5   Reheat the broth, if necessary, and discard the thyme and large chunks of garlic. Dice the tomatoes and cut the sausages crossways into 5mm/¼-inch thick slices. Divide the tomatoes, sausages and salmon among four shallow bowls. Ladle the broth on top and garnish with coriander. Serve warm with the grilled bread slices on the side.

GRILLED SALMON BLT SANDWICHES

SERVES: 2 | **PREP TIME:** 15 MINUTES
GRILLING TIME: 5–6 MINUTES

Here I have taken a classic American sandwich on a road trip up the West Coast, picking up luscious avocado and fresh salmon along the way. Grilling skinless fish can be a little tricky because the skin usually helps to hold the flesh together, so be sure the cooking grates are really hot and clean, and don't fiddle too much with the fish. Turn the fillets just once. Also, brushing the fish generously with oil before you start helps prevent sticking.

4 thick-cut bacon rashers
2 skinless salmon fillets, each
    140–175g/5–6oz and about 1cm/
    ½ inch thick, pin bones removed
Extra-virgin olive oil
⅛ teaspoon sea salt
⅛ teaspoon freshly ground black
    pepper
4 slices sourdough bread from a
    crusty loaf
1 small avocado, mashed
Mayonnaise
2 leaves romaine lettuce
1 beefsteak tomato, cut crossways into
    4 thin slices

1. Prepare the grill for direct cooking over high heat (230–290°C/450–550°F).

2. In a large frying pan over a medium heat on the hob, fry the bacon for 10–12 minutes until crisp, turning occasionally. Transfer the bacon to a plate lined with kitchen paper.

3. Brush the salmon fillets on both sides with oil and season evenly with the salt and pepper. Brush one side of each slice of bread with oil.

4. Grill the fillets over **grilling/direct high heat** for about 3 minutes, with the lid closed, until you can lift them off the cooking grates without sticking. Turn the fillets over and continue grilling to your desired doneness, 2–3 minutes more for medium rare. During the last 30 seconds of grilling time, toast the bread over direct heat on the oiled side only. Remove from the grill and allow the salmon to rest for 2–3 minutes.

5. To build the sandwiches, generously spread the non-grilled side of two bread slices with avocado and the other two slices with mayonnaise. Then add tomato slices, lettuce, bacon and salmon. Serve immediately.

SMOKED TUNA PROVENÇAL SLIDERS

SERVES: 4–6 (MAKES 12 SLIDERS) | **PREP TIME:** 35 MINUTES | **GRILLING TIME:** 15–20 MINUTES
SPECIAL EQUIPMENT: 3 LARGE HANDFULS APPLE, CHERRY OR OAK WOOD CHIPS

This recipe elevates regular ole tuna salad to the nth degree by combining aromatic wood-smoked fish with Provençal favourites such as olives, capers and garlic. The sliders can be wrapped individually in clingfilm and refrigerated for a few hours before serving; in fact, you may prefer them that way, giving the flavours a chance to mingle. If, instead, you're serving them straightaway, insert a cocktail stick into the centre of each sandwich to keep all the ingredients neatly stacked inside the rolls.

150ml/5fl oz mayonnaise
1 large garlic clove, crushed
450g/1 lb tuna steaks, about 2.5cm/
    1 inch thick, patted dry
Extra-virgin olive oil
Sea salt
Freshly ground black pepper
2 tablespoons fresh lemon juice
1 teaspoon Dijon mustard
1 teaspoon anchovy paste
3 tablespoons finely chopped
    Kalamata olives
2 tablespoons capers, rinsed
12 slider buns or rolls, split, some of
    the interior bread pulled out from
    each side
3 ripe plum tomatoes, thinly sliced
3 large hard-boiled eggs, thinly sliced
40g/1½oz baby rocket

1   Soak the wood chips in water for at least 30 minutes.

2   Prepare the grill for indirect cooking over medium-low heat (about 180°C/350°F).

3   To make aioli, mix the mayonnaise and garlic. Cover and set aside while smoking the tuna.

4   Lightly brush the tuna on all sides with oil and season evenly with ¼ teaspoon salt and ¼ teaspoon pepper. Drain and add the wood chips to the charcoal or to the smoker box of a gas grill, following the manufacturer's instructions, and close the lid. When smoke appears, grill the tuna over ***roasting/indirect***

medium-low heat for 15–20 minutes, with the lid closed, until it has a light golden patina and is just turning opaque throughout. Remove from the grill and break the tuna into 1-cm/½-inch pieces.

5   In a large bowl, whisk the lemon juice, mustard, anchovy paste, ¼ teaspoon salt and ¼ teaspoon pepper. Gradually whisk in 3 tablespoons oil. Add the tuna, olives and capers and mix well.

6   Spread the cut side of each roll lightly with aioli. Top with tomatoes, tuna salad, eggs and rocket. Serve immediately, or wrap individually and refrigerate for a few hours.

SEARED TUNA
WITH OLIVE-CAPER VINAIGRETTE

SERVES: 4 | **PREP TIME:** 15 MINUTES
GRILLING TIME: 3–4 MINUTES

1½ teaspoons finely grated lemon zest
3 tablespoons fresh lemon juice
½ teaspoon anchovy paste
¼ teaspoon mustard powder
Sea salt
1 garlic clove, crushed
⅛ teaspoon crushed chilli flakes
Freshly ground black pepper
Extra-virgin olive oil
50g/2oz Kalamata olives,
    finely chopped
2 tablespoons capers, drained
1 teaspoon finely chopped thyme
    leaves
4 tuna steaks, preferably sushi grade,
    each about 175g/6oz and 2.5cm/1
    inch thick
175g/6oz baby rocket
4 large hard-boiled eggs, each cut
    into quarters

With its meaty texture, tuna takes especially well to a searing-hot grate and the marks add a nicely charred flavour. You can serve the tuna warm, but when the weather is warm, serve it chilled for a light meal that you can make ahead.

1   Prepare the grill for direct cooking over high heat (230–290°C/450–550°F).

2   In a bowl, whisk the lemon zest and juice, anchovy paste, mustard powder, ¼ teaspoon salt, garlic, chilli flakes and ⅛ teaspoon pepper. Gradually whisk in 4 tablespoons olive oil. Add the olives, capers and thyme and mix to create the vinaigrette.

3   Lightly brush the tuna steaks on both sides with oil, season evenly with 1 teaspoon salt and ½ teaspoon pepper and then grill over ***grilling/direct high heat***, with the lid open, until cooked to your desired doneness, 3–4 minutes for rare, turning once. Remove from the grill and allow to rest for about 3 minutes. Cut each tuna steak across the grain into 1-cm/½-inch thick slices, and then cut into bite-sized pieces.

4   Divide the rocket among four serving plates and top with tuna, eggs and vinaigrette. Serve while the tuna is still warm.

Most of the tuna in supermarkets today is sold in fairly thin slices, and the quality is such that you need to cook it all the way through for safe eating. Occasionally it's worth seeking out sushi-grade tuna for something special. It is particularly wonderful if the tuna 'steaks' are cut thick enough that you can sear the outside for flavour and appearance while leaving the centres raw. The colour contrast is gorgeous and the taste of the seared surfaces with the raw flesh is dynamite.

SWORDFISH STEAKS
WITH QUICK TOMATO-ANCHOVY SAUCE

SERVES: 4 | **PREP TIME:** 15 MINUTES, PLUS ABOUT 20 MINUTES FOR THE SAUCE | **GRILLING TIME:** 6-7 MINUTES
SPECIAL EQUIPMENT: CHARCOAL GRILL, ALL-NATURAL LUMP CHARCOAL , 4-6 LARGE HANDFULS HICKORY WOOD CHUNKS

SAUCE

1 tablespoon extra-virgin olive oil
1 onion, finely chopped
4 garlic cloves, finely chopped
3 anchovy fillets packed in olive
    oil, finely chopped
½ teaspoon crushed chilli flakes,
    or to taste
340g/12oz small cherry tomatoes
75g/3oz Kalamata olives,
    coarsely chopped
125ml/4fl oz dry white wine
1 tablespoon capers, rinsed

4 swordfish steaks (with skin), each
    175–225g/6–8oz and about
    2.5cm/1 inch thick
1 tablespoon extra-virgin olive oil
¾ teaspoon sea salt
½ teaspoon freshly ground black
    pepper

The sharp, pungent flavours of this sauce balance really well with charred fish and shellfish. The anchovies melt into the sauce, adding to the umami-rich flavours, while the chilli flakes give a nice kick of heat. Swordfish is dry when overcooked, so don't walk away from the steaks, and be sure to adjust your cooking time according to their thickness.

1 In a large, heavy frying pan over a medium heat, warm 1 tablespoon oil. Add the onion and sauté for about 2 minutes until it begins to soften, stirring occasionally. Add the garlic, anchovies and chilli flakes. Sauté until fragrant, about 1 minute, stirring often. Add the tomatoes, olives, wine and capers. Bring to the boil, and then reduce the heat to medium-low. Partially cover the pan and simmer for 8–10 minutes until the tomatoes begin to break down, breaking up some of the tomatoes with the back of a spoon and stirring occasionally. Uncover the pan and continue to cook for 5–7 minutes more until the sauce thickens, stirring occasionally. Remove from the heat and cover to keep warm.

2 Prepare the charcoal grill with all-natural lump charcoal for direct cooking over high heat (230–290°C/450–550°F) and add the wood chunks.

3 Lightly brush the swordfish steaks on both sides with 1 tablespoon oil and season evenly with the salt and pepper. When the wood chunks have burnt down to embers, grill the swordfish over *grilling/direct high heat* for 6–7 minutes, with the lid closed, until just opaque in the centre and still juicy, turning once. Remove from the grill and serve warm with the sauce.

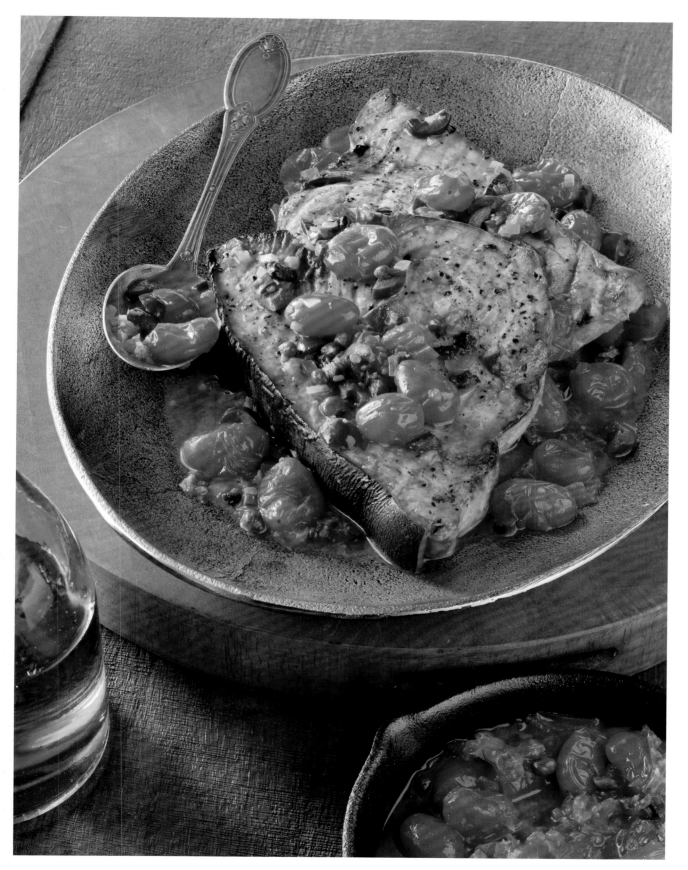

BLACKENED SEA BASS TACOS
WITH GRILLED PINEAPPLE SALSA

SERVES: 4 | **PREP TIME:** 20 MINUTES | **GRILLING TIME:** ABOUT 15 MINUTES
SPECIAL EQUIPMENT: 30CM/12-INCH CAST-IRON FRYING PAN

SALSA

1 pineapple, peel removed
1 tablespoon rapeseed oil
¼ small red onion, finely chopped
2 tablespoons fresh lime juice
2 tablespoons finely chopped fresh
    coriander
½ teaspoon sea salt
¼ teaspoon ground cumin

RUB

1 tablespoon paprika
1 teaspoon garlic powder
1 teaspoon dried oregano, crumbled
1 teaspoon sea salt
½ teaspoon ground cumin
¼ teaspoon freshly ground black
    pepper
⅛ teaspoon ground cayenne pepper

675g/1½lb skinless red snapper or sea
    bass fillets, about 1cm/½ inch thick
25g/1oz unsalted butter
8 flour or corn tortillas (15cm/
    6 inches)
2 limes, each cut into 4 wedges

One of the titans of American cooking, Paul Prudhomme of New Orleans, revolutionised regional cooking in the 1980s by highlighting Cajun food as a distinct style worthy to stand beside any other cuisine. Blackened redfish was the dish that launched his revolution. Here's a variation of that dish you can do on the grill, with the blackened snapper wrapped inside tortillas and topped with a salsa.

1 Prepare the grill for direct cooking over medium-high heat (200–230°C/400–450°F).

2 Cut the pineapple across into six 1-cm/½-inch thick slices (don't cut out the core). You may not need all of the pineapple. Brush the pineapple slices on both sides with the oil.

3 Grill the pineapple slices over **grilling/direct medium-high heat** for 5–8 minutes, with the lid closed, until lightly charred and softened, turning once. Remove from the grill, cut out the core and discard. Coarsely chop the pineapple and place in a bowl. Add the remaining salsa ingredients to the pineapple and stir until evenly combined.

4 Mix the rub ingredients. Season the fish fillets evenly on both sides with the rub.

5 In a 30-cm/12-inch cast-iron frying pan over **grilling/direct medium-high heat**, melt the butter. Before the butter begins to brown, add the fillets to the pan (see caption and photo below) and cook over **grilling/direct medium-high heat** for 5 minutes, with the lid closed. Using a metal spatula, turn the fillets over and continue cooking for 2–3 minutes more until the flesh barely begins to flake when poked with the tip of a knife. Remove the pan from the grill. Break the fish into large chunks.

6 Warm the tortillas over direct heat for about 10 seconds on each side. Fill the tortillas with equal amounts of the fish and top with the salsa. Serve straightaway with the lime wedges.

When chef Paul Prudhomme introduced America to blackened redfish (also called red drum), it grew so popular that it had to be protected from overfishing. Red snapper works well with this technique, as do sea bass and mahi mahi. Turn the fish away from you so that any splattering butter does not burn you.

ZITI AND SMOKED TROUT
WITH PEAS AND CREAM

SERVES: 4 | **PREP TIME:** 20 MINUTES | **GRILLING TIME:** ABOUT 10 MINUTES
SPECIAL EQUIPMENT: 1 LARGE HANDFUL PECAN OR APPLE WOOD CHIPS, WIDE SPATULA

2 whole trout, each about 225g/8oz, butterflied
1 tablespoon extra-virgin olive oil
Sea salt
Freshly ground black pepper
340g/12oz dried ziti or penne
50g/2oz unsalted butter, cut into small chunks
2 small shallots, chopped
250ml/8fl oz dry white wine, such as Chardonnay
250ml/8fl oz whipping cream
150g/5oz shelled fresh peas or frozen peas (do not thaw)
50g/2oz Parmesan cheese, finely grated
1 teaspoon finely grated lemon zest
2 tablespoons finely chopped dill

This warm pasta supper gets a burst of flavour from home-smoked trout, which is milder and tenderer than what you usually find in supermarkets. It is very nice served on a summer evening with a glass of cold beer or a crisp wine.

1 Soak the wood chips in water for at least 30 minutes.

2 Prepare the grill for indirect cooking over medium heat (180–230°C/350–450°F).

3 Rub the skin of the trout with the oil and season the flesh with ¼ teaspoon salt and ¼ teaspoon pepper. Drain and add the wood chips to the charcoal or to the smoker box of a gas grill, following the manufacturer's instructions, and close the lid. When smoke appears, grill the trout over **roasting/indirect medium heat** for about 10 minutes, with the lid closed, until the flesh is opaque and flakes easily (do not turn). Remove from the grill and cool for a few minutes. Remove the flesh from the trout, discarding the head, tail, skin and bones. Break the flesh into large, bite-sized pieces.

4 Bring a large saucepan of salted water to the boil on the hob for the pasta, and cook according to the packet instructions. Drain.

5 Preheat a large frying pan over a high heat for 3–4 minutes. Add the butter to the pan to melt. Add the shallots and cook for about 3 minutes until softened but not browned, stirring often. Add the wine and cream. Bring the sauce to a full boil, stirring occasionally, and then boil for 2 minutes to thicken slightly. The sauce should still be a bit soupy. Add the peas and cook for 1 minute, stirring occasionally. Add the pasta. Toss well until heated through and coated with the sauce, about 1 minute. Stir in the cheese, lemon zest, 1 teaspoon salt and ¼ teaspoon pepper and cook for about 1 minute until hot and bubbling. At the last moment, add the trout pieces to the pan and mix everything very gently to combine the ingredients. Garnish with dill. Serve immediately.

If the prospect of grilling fish makes you a little nervous, raise your confidence with a wide spatula like this one. Its offset neck lets you get under the fish easily, especially if you slide the front edge of the spatula in the same direction as the bars of the cooking grate. The wide blade supports the fish as you take it off the grill and move it to a baking tray.

NEW ORLEANS'
SEAFOOD BARBECUE

When fire meets meat, barbecue happens. What also often happens is a lively debate about the correct sauce and the best choice of wood or charcoal. Then there is the question of whether the meat should be beef or pork, or both. At Pêche Seafood Grill, the answer is neither. With a multifunctional, wood-fired grill, chef Ryan Prewitt and his team are fashioning a new, idiosyncratic style of barbecue that is more surf than turf, and miles from what you might expect of seafood in New Orleans.

'We wanted to open a seafood restaurant that put the focus on the quality of the Gulf seafood,' Prewitt told me just before lunch service at the restaurant. Whole pompano straight from the Gulf and grilled over oak and pecan coals was the daily special. It wasn't fried, doused in butter or topped with crab and crawfish like you'd find elsewhere in town, but covered in a relish of red onions, flat-leaf parsley and fresh cucumber. There is a smoky essence in the tender, mild white fish, and a brightness in the garnish that you don't often get with barbecue. Heck, it might even be considered healthy.

Prewitt seems a natural with seafood as he discusses the finer points of Champagne Bay versus Caminada Bay oysters (both from the Louisiana shore), and the James Beard Foundation agreed. They named him Best Chef: South (May 2014), but seafood wasn't his first love. Being a Memphis boy, he was all about pork barbecue growing up.

Prewitt moved to New Orleans four weeks before Katrina hit, having landed a position with chef Donald Link at a white-linen restaurant called Herbsaint, where Link was getting international acclaim for the way he put a Southern spin on French and Italian dishes. It all fell into place when Prewitt's wife got into graduate school at Tulane. 'Our fate was sealed,' he revealed. Hurricane or not, New Orleans was his new home, and opening a new restaurant with Donald Link was always his goal. They just didn't know what kind of restaurant. 'The idea developed concurrently with a period where we were travelling with a lot of barbecue guys,' Prewitt recalls. He and Link were part of the Fatback Collective –

a sort of barbecue dream team made up of chefs, writers and farmers – and they competed in his hometown at the biggest whole hog competition on the planet, Memphis in May. Prewitt was hooked, and knew he wanted to keep cooking with fire.

The idea and passion coalesced on a trip to Uruguay. 'Seeing the way they cooked and how they used fire was a completely different view of it than I had previously had,' said Prewitt. 'There were no smokers or other contraptions to harness the fire. They would just build bonfires and cook over it. They'd build walls of fire so hot you could put a pot next to it and it would boil,' he told me while sweating beside the mini-inferno blazing within his kitchen's grill. It might not be a wall of fire, but it's no joke. Soon after the restaurant opened, a cook fainted from dehydration while manning the grill. Now they work the grill in pairs.

In addition to the house speciality of whole fish, there's a seasonal menu and a more fluid daily menu. Wood-grilled sardines (one of the few items not from the Gulf) were fresh enough to bring in as a daily special. They showed their deep grill marks under a garnish of bacon jam and celery hearts. The fire made for some sweet and smoky fish with a nice char.

At the raw bar, they whip up an order of smoked tuna dip from Gulf-caught tuna smoked in a designated chamber within the wood grill. Chunks of smoked drum are tossed with pickled sweet potatoes and sesame seeds. The flavours of smoke

with pickled vegetables are familiar, but the combination is exhilarating. The same can be said for what sounds like a simple side dish of corn, but the wood grill makes it anything but simple. The whole cobs are grilled with their husks still on until the kernels are cooked. The husks and kernels are then removed from the cobs, and a rich, smoky stock is made with the charred husks and the cobs. That all gets mixed back into the corn along with chilli oil and Grana Padano cheese. The depth of the stock and umami from the corn and cheese make this dish taste more like barbecue than any vegetable I can remember.

Lovers of more traditional barbecue are also taken care of at Pêche Seafood Grill. Chicken with Alabama white sauce is on the regular menu, but, of course, it is reimagined into something more fitting for the rustic elegance of the restaurant. Rather than the usual half chicken, they grill boneless thighs on wood skewers, and then coat them with the tangy white sauce. It's like a barbecue hors d'oeuvre that you can't stop eating.

The twist on the barbecue paradigm is refreshing, but, as with all great barbecue, it's best when it isn't overcomplicated. 'The idea is that we have the wonderful cooking medium and this thoughtfully sourced product. Put them together and give them just a nudge in the right direction,' Chef Prewitt says modestly, but he and his staff provide a lot more than a nudge, and the direction they are going is both familiar and uncharted.

PRAWN COBB SALAD
WITH SMOKED TOMATO-BUTTERMILK DRESSING

SERVES: 4–6 | **PREP TIME:** 25 MINUTES | **CHILLING TIME:** 1 HOUR | **MARINATING TIME:** 1 HOUR | **GRILLING TIME:** 28–50 MINUTES
SPECIAL EQUIPMENT: 2 LARGE HANDFULS APPLE, CHERRY OR PECAN WOOD CHIPS; 8 METAL OR BAMBOO SKEWERS; 2 SMALL DISPOSABLE FOIL TRAYS; PERFORATED GRILL PAN

2 spring onions
2 large tomatoes, each about 175g/
    6oz, cut crossways in half
Extra-virgin olive oil
285g/10oz cherry tomatoes
Sea salt
Freshly ground black pepper
1 garlic clove, coarsely chopped
125ml/4fl oz buttermilk
75ml/3fl oz mayonnaise
2 tablespoons coarsely chopped
    dill
1 tablespoon cider vinegar
¼ teaspoon smoked paprika
675g/1½lb tiger prawns, peeled and
    deveined, tails left on or removed
1 tablespoon fresh lemon juice
2 romaine lettuce hearts, cut into
    bite-sized pieces
2 large avocados, diced
5 bacon rashers, fried and crumbled
115g/4oz feta cheese, crumbled
4 large hard-boiled eggs, each cut into
    4 wedges (optional)

According to American culinary folklore, the Cobb salad came together for the first time one night in 1937 at the hands of Bob Cobb, the hungry owner of a Hollywood restaurant. He gathered this and that from the restaurant's walk-in refrigerator and snatched some crispy bacon from the chef. Since then cooks have swapped various ingredients in and out. My own variation features grilled prawns in place of the typical chicken or turkey, and a creamy dressing based on smoked tomatoes.

1   Soak the wood chips and skewers (separately) in water for at least 30 minutes.

2   Prepare the grill for indirect cooking over medium heat (180–230°C/350–450°F).

3   Coarsely chop the white and light green parts of the spring onions (you will use them in the dressing), and thinly slice and reserve the dark green tops for garnish.

4   Place the tomato halves, cut side up, in a small disposable foil tray and drizzle with oil. Place the cherry tomatoes in another small disposable foil tray, drizzle with oil and season with salt and pepper. Drain and add two handfuls of the wood chips to the charcoal or to the smoker box of a gas grill, following the manufacturer's instructions, and close the lid. When smoke appears, place the two foil trays with the tomatoes over ***roasting/indirect medium heat*** and close the lid. Cook the tomato halves for 25–45 minutes until very tender and beginning to brown around the edges, and cook the cherry tomatoes for 12–25 minutes until the skins begin to split. Remove from the grill as they are done, and allow to cool completely.

5   Using a small spoon, scoop the seeds from the tomato halves and discard them. Cut out and discard the stalk ends. In a blender, purée the tomato halves with the white and light green spring onion and garlic. Add the buttermilk, mayonnaise, dill, vinegar, paprika, ¾ teaspoon salt and ¼ teaspoon pepper and process until smooth. Transfer the dressing to a bowl.

6   Place the prawns in a large, resealable plastic bag and add the lemon juice, 1 tablespoon oil and 2 tablespoons of the dressing. Press the air out of the bag and seal tightly. Turn the bag to distribute the marinade and refrigerate for 1 hour. Also cover and refrigerate the remaining dressing for 1 hour.

7   Prepare the grill for direct cooking over medium-high heat (200–230°C/400–450°F).

8   Remove the prawns from the bag, leaving any marinade still clinging to them, and discard the remaining marinade. Thread the prawns on to skewers, and then grill over ***grilling/direct medium-high heat*** for 3–5 minutes, with the lid closed, until firm to the touch and just turning opaque in the centre, turning once.

9   Whisk the dressing until smooth and pourable. In a large bowl, toss the lettuce with about half of the dressing and transfer to a large platter. Top with rows of cherry tomatoes, prawns, avocado, bacon, feta and eggs (if using), and garnish with the reserved dark green spring onion tops. Serve immediately with the remaining dressing.

PRAWNS AND GRITS

SERVES: 4 | **PREP TIME:** 15 MINUTES, PLUS ABOUT 20 MINUTES FOR THE GRITS | **GRILLING TIME:** 6–8 MINUTES
SPECIAL EQUIPMENT: 1 LARGE HANDFUL APPLE WOOD CHIPS

115g/4oz unsalted butter
1 litre/1¾ pints water
Sea salt
150g/5oz grits or polenta
75g/3oz white Cheddar cheese,
     finely grated
1 garlic clove, crushed
1 teaspoon hot pepper sauce
¼ teaspoon freshly ground black
     pepper
675g/1½lb tiger prawns, peeled and
     deveined, tails removed
3 spring onions (white and light green
     parts only), finely chopped

This Low Country classic is not typically cooked on a grill, but the sweet apple wood smoke does enhance the prawns. In another departure from tradition, brown butter gives the grits (or polenta) a warm, nutty flavour, and also serves as a simple sauce.

1   Soak the wood chips in water for at least 30 minutes.

2   Prepare the grill for direct cooking over medium heat (180–230°C/350–450°F).

3   In a saucepan over a medium-low heat on the hob, melt the butter. Cook for 3–4 minutes until brown bits form on the bottom of the pan, swirling the pan occasionally (see caption and photo below). Remove from the heat and transfer the browned butter to a small glass or other microwave-safe bowl.

4   In the same saucepan used for the butter, combine the water and 1½ teaspoons salt and bring to the boil over a medium-high heat; use a whisk to scrape up the brown bits from the bottom of the pan. Gradually whisk in the grits. Reduce the heat to low and continue cooking for 15–20 minutes until the mixture thickens and the grits are very tender, stirring occasionally. Remove the grits from the heat and stir in the cheese and 3 tablespoons of the browned butter. Keep warm over a low heat.

5   In a large bowl, whisk 1 tablespoon of the browned butter, the garlic, hot sauce, ½ teaspoon salt and the pepper. Add the prawns and toss to coat.

6   Drain and add the wood chips to the charcoal or to the smoker box of a gas grill, following the manufacturer's instructions, and close the lid. When smoke appears, grill the prawns over **grilling/direct medium heat** for 6–8 minutes, with the lid closed, until firm to the touch and just turning opaque in the centre, turning once.

7   If the browned butter has solidified, melt it, covered, in a microwave oven.

8   Divide the grits among four warm plates. Top the grits with the prawns and the remaining brown butter, and garnish with the spring onions. Serve immediately.

After the butter melts, it will foam up a bit. When the foam subsides, brown specks will appear on the bottom of the pan. These specks are the milk solids in the butter browning and developing nutty aromas. When the butter looks like this, remove the pan from the heat and transfer the butter to a small bowl to prevent the milk solids from burning.

GRILLED SCALLOPS
WITH CAULIFLOWER PURÉE AND CRISPY KALE

SERVES: 4 | **PREP TIME:** 30 MINUTES
GRILLING TIME: 5–8 MINUTES

6 large leaves cavolo nero kale
Extra-virgin olive oil
Sea salt
1 head cauliflower, about 900g/2lb,
    cored, florets coarsely chopped
350ml/12fl oz chicken stock
1 small garlic clove
25g/1oz Pecorino cheese, finely grated
40g/1½oz unsalted butter
Freshly ground black pepper
16 large scallops, patted dry
2 teaspoons finely grated lemon zest

When cooking scallops be sure to pat them completely dry before oiling them. They hold a lot of water, and sometimes they are soaked in a phosphate solution that makes them look whiter and absorb even more water. To avoid that phosphate solution, look for dry-packed scallops. Get the biggest scallops you can for this recipe.

1   Prepare the grill for direct cooking over medium heat (180–230°C/350–450°F).

2   Brush the kale leaves with oil and season with ¼ teaspoon salt. Grill over *grilling/direct medium heat* for 2–3 minutes, with the lid closed, until lightly charred and crisp, turning once and watching closely to prevent burning. Remove from the grill and, when cool enough to handle, remove and discard the tough ribs and tear the leaves into shards.

3   Place the cauliflower and stock in a large saucepan on the hob. Bring the stock to the boil, and then reduce the heat to medium-low. Cover the pan and simmer for 18–20 minutes until the cauliflower is very tender when pierced with a knife. Using a slotted spoon, transfer the cauliflower to the bowl of a food processor. Add 4 tablespoons of the hot stock and the garlic. Process until the cauliflower is smooth. Add the cheese, butter, 1 teaspoon salt and ½ teaspoon pepper and pulse to blend. The purée should be smooth and hold its shape when lifted with a spoon. Cover and keep warm.

4   Increase the temperature of the grill to high heat (230–290°C/450–550°F).

5   Remove and discard the small, tough side muscle that might be left on each scallop. Lightly brush the scallops on both sides with oil and season evenly with ¾ teaspoon salt and ½ teaspoon pepper. Grill the scallops over *grilling/direct high heat* for 3–5 minutes, with the lid closed, until lightly browned and just opaque in the centre, turning once.

6   Divide the cauliflower puree among serving plates. Using the back of a spoon, spread the purée slightly. Arrange the scallops over the purée and distribute the kale shards around the scallops. Garnish with the lemon zest and serve immediately.

SMOKED MUSSELS
WITH BEER, SHALLOTS AND GARLIC

SERVES: 4 | **PREP TIME:** 20 MINUTES | **GRILLING TIME:** 18-32 MINUTES | **SPECIAL EQUIPMENT:** 2 LARGE HANDFULS OAK, APPLE OR CHERRY WOOD CHIPS, LARGE GRILLPROOF ROASTING TIN OR DISPOSABLE FOIL ROASTING TRAY

150ml/5fl oz mayonnaise
2 tablespoons whole-grain
    Dijon mustard
50g/2oz unsalted butter, cut into
    tablespoons
2 shallots, chopped
4 garlic cloves, chopped
2 bottles (each 350ml) wheat beer,
    amber beer or pale ale
6 large sprigs fresh thyme
1.8kg/4lb live mussels, scrubbed
    and debearded
1 teaspoon sea salt
½ teaspoon freshly ground black
    pepper
3 tablespoons roughly chopped
    flat-leaf parsley leaves

Meat-loving barbecue purists may scoff at this idea, but early American barbecue actually included a fair amount of shellfish, especially in New England. Mussels were sometimes steamed in wine over a wood fire, but here's a modern take. Try this recipe with a mild-flavoured wheat beer. An amber lager or pale ale also works well. To avoid the chore of debearding the mussels, look for prepared cultivated varieties. Don't forget to serve lots of crusty bread for mopping up the savoury broth.

1 Soak the wood chips in water for at least 30 minutes.

2 Prepare the grill for direct and indirect cooking over medium-low heat (about 180°C/350°F).

3 Mix the mayonnaise and mustard, and then divide evenly among four small ramekins. Cover and set aside while cooking the mussels.

4 Put the butter, shallots and garlic into a large grillproof roasting tin. Drain and add one handful of the wood chips to the charcoal or to the smoker box of a gas grill, following the manufacturer's instructions, and close the lid. When smoke appears, place the tin with the butter, shallots and garlic over **roasting/indirect medium-low heat**, close the lid and cook for 8–10 minutes until the butter is melted and the shallots are tender, stirring occasionally. Add the beer and thyme and cook for 5–7 minutes until the mixture is steaming.

5 Drain and add the remaining wood chips to the charcoal or smoker box. Move the roasting tin over direct heat, and then add the mussels. Cook the mussels, uncovered, over **grilling/ direct medium-low heat** for 5–15 minutes, with the grill lid closed, until the mussels open, stirring occasionally. As each mussel opens, use tongs to transfer it to a large bowl; cover and keep them warm as you wait for the remaining mussels to open. Discard any unopened mussels and the thyme sprigs.

6 Season the cooking liquid with the salt and pepper. Divide the mussels among four deep soup bowls and ladle in the cooking liquid. Garnish with the parsley. Serve hot with the mayonnaise-mustard dip.

COAL-ROASTED CLAMS
WITH BLISTERED CHILLIES AND LINGUINE

SERVES: 4 | **PREP TIME:** 25 MINUTES | **GRILLING TIME:** 7–10 MINUTES
SPECIAL EQUIPMENT: CHARCOAL GRILL, ALL-NATURAL LUMP CHARCOAL, PERFORATED GRILL PAN

4 small red cherry chillies (pimiento chillies)
2 tablespoons extra-virgin olive oil
3 large garlic cloves, chopped
¼ teaspoon crushed chilli flakes
250ml/8fl oz dry white wine
4 tablespoons fresh lemon juice
1 teaspoon sea salt
900g/2lb live clams, scrubbed
450g/1lb dried linguine or spaghetti
4 tablespoons chopped flat-leaf parsley
50g/2oz unsalted butter, softened
2 teaspoons finely grated lemon zest
Freshly ground black pepper

How's this for a new way to cook clams? Roast them right over lump charcoal. This technique is a contemporary version of an old Native American tradition called a clambake, which involves digging a pit in the sand and cooking shellfish buried among wood embers, hot stones and steaming blankets of seaweed. In this recipe I've added the charred flavours and fairly mild spiciness of blistered (not blackened) red cherry peppers. If you prefer your food hotter, use jalapeño chillies instead, or add a little more crushed chilli flakes to the dish.

1   Prepare the charcoal grill with all-natural lump charcoal for direct cooking over medium heat (180–230°C/350–450°F).

2   Grill the red cherry chillies over **grilling/direct medium heat** for 3–5 minutes, with the lid closed, until blistered, not blackened, all over, turning as needed. Remove from the grill and, when cool enough to handle, cut the peppers lengthways in half, discard the stems and seeds, and cut crossways into thin slices. Set aside.

3   In a large, deep frying pan over a medium heat, warm the oil. Add the garlic and chilli flakes and sauté until fragrant, about 1 minute. Add the wine, lemon juice and salt. Bring to the boil, and then reduce the heat to medium-low and simmer for 5 minutes. Remove from the heat and cover.

4   Arrange the clams in a single layer on a perforated grill pan. Wearing insulated barbecue mitts or oven gloves, remove the cooking grate from the grill, and then place the pan with the clams directly on the coals (the coals should be covered with ash, glowing red, with no black remaining). Close the lid and grill the clams for 4–5 minutes until they open. Carefully transfer the pan from the grill to a heatproof surface. Discard any unopened clams. Transfer the clams with any of the juices in the shells to the frying pan with the wine mixture.

5   Bring a large saucepan of salted water to a rolling boil. Add the linguine and cook until it's about 1 minute short of al dente. Drain the linguine, reserving 125ml/4fl oz of the pasta water. Add the linguine, red cherry chillies, 2 tablespoons of the parsley, the butter and lemon zest to the frying pan (add some of the reserved pasta water if liked). Place the frying pan over a medium-high heat and toss the pasta until coated with the sauce and heated through. Season with pepper. Serve warm, garnished with the remaining parsley.

This is a case where it's best to cook entirely with all-natural lump charcoal. The chemicals and processed coal sometimes added to briquettes could get into the clams, so use lump charcoal that is nothing more than pieces of hardwood that have been burned down to charcoal in a low-oxygen environment.

The smaller and tenderer varieties of clam (about an 2.5cm/1 inch wide or less) work best for this recipe.

6

SIDES

HASSELBACK POTATOES
WITH GARLIC BUTTER AND PARMESAN

SERVES: 6 | **PREP TIME:** 45 MINUTES
GRILLING TIME: 1 HOUR 5 MINUTES– 1 HOUR 10 MINUTES

6 King Edward potatoes, each about
    340g/12oz, scrubbed and dried
75g/3oz unsalted butter
6 garlic cloves, smashed and peeled
1½ teaspoons sea salt
¾ teaspoon freshly ground black
    pepper
50g/2oz Parmesan cheese, finely
    grated
2 tablespoons finely chopped flat-leaf
    parsley

Hasselback potatoes have been dazzling guests at American barbecues during the last few years, although we cannot claim them as our own. The brilliant idea for these accordion-looking potatoes came from the chefs at Restaurant Hasselbacken in Stockholm, Sweden.

1   Prepare the grill for indirect cooking over medium-high heat (200–230°C/400–450°F).

2   So that each potato will lie flat on the cooking grate, cut off a very small piece (5mm/¼ inch or less) on the widest side of each potato, which will now be the bottom side. Then, using a very sharp knife, starting 2.5cm/1 inch from the end, cut slits crossways into each potato, 3–5mm/⅛–¼ inch apart, stopping just before you cut through so that the slices stay connected at the bottom.

3   In a small frying pan over a medium heat, melt the butter. Add the garlic and cook for 1½–2 minutes until lightly browned, stirring occasionally. Remove the pan from the heat and add the salt and pepper. Fan out the layers of each potato enough that you can get some butter and seasonings inside the layers. Brush the potatoes, including the bottoms, with half of the butter mixture.

4   Grill the potatoes over ***roasting/indirect medium-high heat***, with the lid closed, for 30 minutes. Brush the potatoes with the remaining butter mixture, making sure some of the butter drips down inside the slices. Continue grilling for 30 minutes more, with the lid closed, until the potatoes are almost cooked through. Top the potatoes evenly with the cheese and cook for 5–10 minutes more until the cheese is melted and slightly browned and the potatoes are crisp on the outside and tender on the inside. Garnish with the parsley and serve hot.

Making all those slices takes work, but creamy potato centres and crispy edges are so worth the time and effort. A helpful trick to keep you from slicing all the way through the potato is to put two chopsticks on either side of each spud to act as a guide and stop your knife from going too far, but as you get near the tapered ends, ignore the chopsticks and just be careful not to cut all the way through the potatoes.

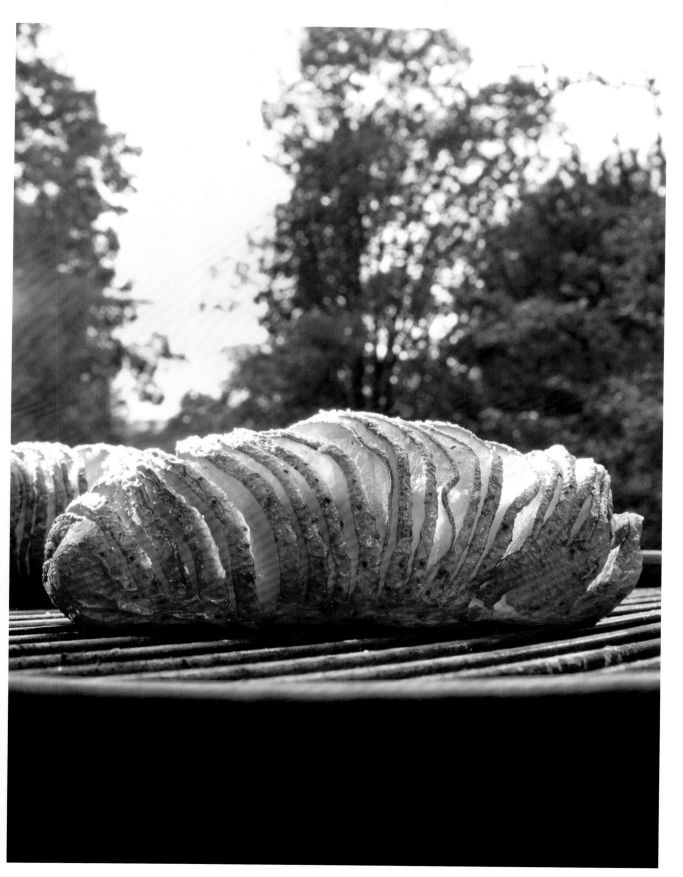

STUFFED POTATOES
WITH CHEDDAR, HORSERADISH AND CRISPY BACON

SERVES: 4 | PREP TIME: 20 MINUTES
GRILLING TIME: 1¼–1½ HOURS | SPECIAL EQUIPMENT: PERFORATED GRILL PAN

4 King Edward potatoes, each about
340g/12oz, scrubbed and dried

FILLING
2 thick-cut bacon rashers
75g/3oz mature Cheddar cheese,
    finely grated
125ml/4fl oz soured cream
3 spring onions, trimmed and thinly
    sliced
3 tablespoons peeled, finely grated
    fresh horseradish or 2 teaspoons
    prepared horseradish
25g/1oz unsalted butter, softened
1½ teaspoons sea salt
¾ teaspoon freshly ground black
    pepper

25g/1oz unsalted butter, melted
25g/1oz Parmesan cheese, finely
    grated

What's not to love about stuffed potatoes – especially when they are loaded with cheese and bacon? The extra kick from fresh horseradish adds a peppery bite to the rich filling. Alternatively, you could go with a Tex-Mex stuffing with chorizo, soured cream and roasted chillies, or maybe a vegetarian version with blue cheese and fresh thyme.

1   Prepare the grill for indirect cooking over medium heat (180–200°C/350–400°F).

2   Pierce the potatoes in several places with a fork, and then grill over **roasting/indirect medium heat** for 1–1¼ hours, with the lid closed, until tender. Remove from the grill and allow to stand until cool enough to handle.

3   Meanwhile, in a frying pan over a medium-high heat, fry the bacon until browned and crisp. Transfer to a plate lined with kitchen paper to drain. When cool enough to handle, crumble the bacon into small pieces. Mash together all the filling ingredients, setting aside about 2 tablespoons of the sliced spring onions for garnish.

4   Increase the temperature of the grill to high heat (as close to 230°C/450°F as possible).

5   Cut off a 1-cm/½-inch slice, lengthways, from the top of each potato and discard. Being careful not to tear the skin and leaving a thin layer of flesh intact, gently scoop out the potato flesh. Add the flesh to the filling mixture and, using a fork, stir and mash to blend (the filling will be a little lumpy).

6   Carefully spoon the filling back into the potato skins, dividing equally. Brush a thin film of butter on the inside of a perforated grill pan, place the potatoes on the pan and brush the skins with the remaining melted butter (see top photo, facing page). Distribute the Parmesan over the filling.

7   Cook the potatoes on the grill pan over **roasting/indirect high heat** for 8–10 minutes, with the lid closed, until the cheese is melted and the tip of a knife inserted deep into the centre of each potato comes out piping hot. Garnish with the reserved sliced spring onions.

VARIATIONS
Tex-Mex (left photo): Mix the potato flesh with 175g/6oz cooked and crumbled chorizo; 115g/4oz Mexican cheese blend; 4 tablespoons soured cream; 1 roasted, chopped poblano chilli; 2 tablespoons chopped fresh coriander; and 1 tablespoon thinly sliced spring onion. Vegetarian (right photo): Mix the potato flesh with 50g/2oz crumbled blue cheese, 125ml/4fl oz soured cream, 2 tablespoons each finely chopped thyme and flat-leaf parsley and ¼ teaspoon each salt and pepper.

ROASTED SALAD POTATOES
WITH MINT GREMOLATA

SERVES: 4–6 | PREP TIME: 20 MINUTES
GRILLING TIME: 40–45 MINUTES | SPECIAL EQUIPMENT: LARGE CAST-IRON GRIDDLE

A cast-iron griddle opens up a world of new recipe possibilities on the grill. Here is one way to use the griddle – cooking halved salad potatoes slowly, encouraging them to turn crisp and brown evenly without burning. Check them once or twice during cooking and move them around on the griddle as needed.

GREMOLATA
50g/2oz flat-leaf parsley
40g/1½oz mint
2 tablespoons extra-virgin olive oil
2 teaspoons finely grated lemon zest
1 garlic clove, chopped
¼ teaspoon sea salt

900g/2lb salad potatoes, each cut
   lengthways in half
2 tablespoons extra-virgin olive oil
1½ teaspoons sea salt
½ teaspoon freshly ground black
   pepper
1 garlic clove, crushed

1   In the bowl of a food processor, pulse the parsley and mint until coarsely chopped. Add the remaining gremolata ingredients and pulse until finely chopped. Transfer the gremolata to a large bowl.

2   Prepare the grill for indirect cooking over medium heat (as close to 200°C/400°F as possible) and preheat a large cast-iron griddle.

3   Combine the potatoes, oil, salt, pepper, and garlic and turn to coat. Arrange the potatoes, cut side down, on the griddle and cook over *roasting/indirect medium heat* for 40–45 minutes, with the lid closed, until tender, crisp and golden brown, checking occasionally and moving the potatoes around on the griddle to prevent over-browning. Transfer the potatoes to the large bowl with the gremolata and toss to combine. Serve immediately.

SIDES

246

BABY POTATO SALAD
WITH BASIL VINAIGRETTE

SERVES: 4–6 | **PREP TIME:** 20 MINUTES | **GRILLING TIME:** ABOUT 40 MINUTES
SPECIAL EQUIPMENT: 2 LARGE HANDFULS HICKORY WOOD CHIPS, PERFORATED GRILL PAN

Incorporating a touch of smoke gives a regular potato salad a terrific new quality. While the potatoes are hot, toss them with the vinaigrette so that it soaks into the porous flesh. Then enjoy this salad warm or at room temperature.

VINAIGRETTE
30g/1oz thinly sliced fresh basil leaves
2 tablespoons water
1 tablespoon white wine vinegar
2 teaspoons Dijon mustard

Extra-virgin olive oil
Seat
Freshly ground black pepper
900g/2lb baby red potatoes, each about
   3cm/1¼in in diameter, cut in half
1 medium red onion, cut into
   0.5-cm/¼-inch thick half-moons,
   broken apart
2 medium ribs of celery, diced
Fresh basil leaves

1. Soak the wood chips in water for at least 30 minutes.

2. Prepare the grill for indirect cooking over medium-high heat (200–230°C/400–450°F) and preheat a perforated grill pan.

3. Whisk the vinaigrette ingredients, including 4 tablespoons oil, ½ teaspoon salt and ¼ teaspoon pepper, until emulsified.

4. Put the potato halves in a large saucepan and cover them by about 5cm/2 inches with cold, salted water. Cover the pan and bring to the boil over a high heat, and then remove the lid and cook for 5 minutes. Drain the potatoes well and transfer them to a bowl. Add the onion, 2 tablespoons oil, ¾ teaspoon salt and ¼ teaspoon pepper and toss to coat evenly.

5. Drain and add half of the wood chips to the charcoal or to the smoker box of a gas grill, following the manufacturer's instructions, and close the lid. When smoke appears, add the potatoes and onion to the grill pan, close the lid and cook over **roasting/indirect medium-high heat** for about 40 minutes until tender, stirring once or twice. After 20 minutes, drain and add the remaining wood chips to the charcoal or smoker box.

6. Transfer the potato and onion mixture to a bowl, and then add the celery. Whisk the dressing again and add just enough of it to coat the ingredients lightly. Serve warm or at room temperature, garnished with basil.

Q39

smoldering since 2003

BBQ · Wood Fired Grill · Bar

BARBECUE CROSSROADS
IN KANSAS CITY

Kansas City earned its reputation in the early 1800s as a crossroads town at the confluence of the Kansas River, the Missouri River and the Santa Fe Trail. As the country's border pushed westward, Kansas City transformed itself from a fur trading outpost on the frontier to a perfectly centred national marketplace, as well as a magnet for an interesting mix of people, merchandise, music (primarily blues and jazz) and meat. Livestock ranchers from all over the central and western US quickly recognised Kansas City's commercial importance and, within decades, hundreds of thousands of animals (cows, pigs and sheep) had arrived at Kansas City's stockyards by boat, cattle drive, railway, truck and water.

Kansas City's expansive barbecue menu mirrors the inclusiveness of its stockyards, and unlike other barbecue hot spots around the country, Kansas Citians are not devoted to barbecuing one particular meat in one particular way. Beef, chicken, fish, mutton and pork, cooked using a variety of woods and techniques, all belong on the city's barbecue plate.

Tradition is a key ingredient in Kansas City barbecue, and legendary restaurants like Arthur Bryant's Barbeque, Gates Bar-B-Q and Rosedale Bar-B-Q still bring smiles to the city's longtime residents who take pride in their city's pork spareribs and 'burnt ends' (succulent cubes of fat-crowned meat chopped off the charred end of a beef brisket). Recently the barbecue competition circuit has pushed the restaurant culture to greater heights thanks, in part, to the stratospheric growth of the Kansas City Barbecue Society (KCBS). With its numerous contests held around the country and its annual American Royal World Series of Barbecue, held right in Kansas City, the KCBS has inspired a number of successful competitors to open restaurants. At these trophy-decorated destinations, diners munch on superlative barbecue from a core menu that tracks the KCBS competition categories. Joe's Kansas City Bar-B-Que (formerly Oklahoma Joe's) was started inside a gas station by the highly decorated Slaughterhouse Five competition team, and it may be the best example of this trend.

Chef Rob Magee, the creative force behind the Q39 restaurant, is a Culinary Institute of America graduate who cooked in upscale hotels before entering the barbecue competition circuit. Chef Magee is convinced that his hotel training gives him a decided edge in taking barbecue 'to the next level'. Talk with Chef Magee about his signature barbecue sauces, and your conversation will be peppered with technique-drenched words like sweating, simmering, straining, puréeing and flavour profiles. 'My sauce doesn't taste like anybody else's sauce', Magee says. 'It's more complex; it's more layered in flavours … it's not just one note.' Magee separates Q39 from local barbecue joints by insisting on cooking from scratch for the entire evolving menu and a full staff of waiters and bartenders because he senses that customers today are looking for 'something new and special'.

Could that 'something special' and possibly the future of barbecue, be a plate piled high with vegetables? The folks at Char Bar Smoked Meats & Amusements think so, and so they use fire creatively to flavour fruits and vegetables. Their cooks char Brussels Sprouts, aubergine and grapefruit; blister grapes; roast beetroot; and smoke corn and tropical jackfruit. The smoked jackfruit anchors the restaurant's sandwich 'The JackKnife' – this flavourful selection comes with an eclectic mix of provolone or cheddar cheese, sliced avocado and fried jalapeño chillies that will make you forget, albeit temporarily, about meat.

Today, Kansas City is a 'melting pit' of traditional, experimental and innovative approaches to barbecue. I'd expect nothing less from a crossroads town.

MANGO-RADISH-JICAMA SLAW
WITH CORIANDER-LIME DRESSING

Making beautiful, moist matchsticks from a gnarly root of jicama does require a few steps. Use a sharp knife or vegetable peeler to remove the brownish skin. Cut the jicama in half. Lay the flat (cut) sides down so they don't wobble on the board. Then make thin slices. Stack a few slices in a pile and cut them into skinny matchsticks.

SERVES: 6-8
PREP TIME: 1 HOUR

This refreshing anytime slaw is a great alternative to cabbage-based slaws. The sweetness of the mango balances wonderfully with the tanginess of the lime and the pepperiness of the radishes. Jicama is a juicy, crunchy tuber vegetable. If you can't find it, try crunchy apples instead. Feel free to prep the ingredients hours ahead, but don't toss them all together until you are ready to serve.

DRESSING
125ml/4fl oz mayonnaise
2 teaspoons finely grated lime zest
4 tablespoons fresh lime juice
4 tablespoons finely chopped fresh
    coriander
2 tablespoons granulated sugar
1½ teaspoons sea salt

2 ripe mangoes, peeled and cut into
    matchsticks
1 jicama, about 450g/1lb, peeled and
    cut into matchsticks
10 large radishes, cut into matchsticks
3 spring onions (white and light green
    parts only), thinly sliced

1   In a large serving bowl, whisk the dressing ingredients until smooth.

2   Add the mangoes, jicama, radishes and spring onions to the serving bowl with the dressing and stir until well combined. Allow to stand for 10 minutes before serving.

FENNEL AND CABBAGE COLESLAW
WITH BLUE CHEESE

SERVES: 4–6
PREP TIME: 25 MINUTES

This unorthodox slaw manages to deliciously up-end most of the standard assumptions about coleslaw. Red and green cabbage join up with fennel in a tart, vinegar-centric dressing with only a little mayo, and a sprinkling of blue cheese adds a rich, tangy finish.

DRESSING
4 tablespoons extra-virgin olive oil
4 tablespoons cider vinegar
2 tablespoons mayonnaise
1 tablespoon Dijon mustard
1 teaspoon sea salt
½ teaspoon freshly ground black
    pepper
½ teaspoon granulated sugar

1 fennel bulb
250g/9oz green cabbage, shredded
225g/8oz red cabbage, shredded
25g/1oz roughly chopped flat-leaf
    parsley
40g/1½oz blue cheese, crumbled

1   In a large serving bowl, whisk the dressing
    ingredients until smooth.

2   Trim the stalks of the fennel down to the
    bulb, reserve and chop the fronds, and discard
    the stalks. Cut the bulb into quarters, remove
    the thick triangular-shaped core, and then
    cut the fennel crossways as thinly as possible.

3   Add the fennel, green and red cabbage and
    parsley to the dressing in the serving bowl
    and toss to mix evenly. Allow to stand at
    room temperature for 5 minutes, toss again,
    and then top with the blue cheese. Serve
    right away.

CRUNCHY, TANGY COLESLAW

SERVES: 8–10 | **PREP TIME:** 30 MINUTES
STANDING TIME: 45 MINUTES

Coleslaw might just be barbecue's best accompaniment. The fresh, tangy and crunchy combination plays well against tender meat cooked for hours. It works every time. Well, actually, it doesn't work when the slaw turns watery because the dressing forces the vegetables to leach their natural moisture. The secret to perfectly crunchy coleslaw is to first salt the cabbage to remove excess water, and then rinse off any excess salt so the dressing isn't overwhelmed.

1 head green cabbage, about 1.4kg/
   3lb
2 tablespoons sea salt
3 carrots

DRESSING
4 tablespoons white balsamic vinegar
2 tablespoons wholegrain
   Dijon mustard
2 tablespoons mayonnaise
2 tablespoons granulated sugar
1 teaspoon Worcestershire sauce
½ teaspoon freshly ground black
   pepper

1 Cut the cabbage through the core into quarters. Cut out and remove the hard, white core from each section. Set the quarters, cut side down, on a chopping board and cut crossways into very thin strips. Place the cabbage in a very large bowl, add the salt and toss well. Set aside at room temperature for 45 minutes.

2 To remove the excess salt, add cool water to completely cover the cabbage. Stir well, and then drain in a colander set in the sink. Repeat this process twice to remove all the salt, then squeeze the cabbage dry one handful at a time.

3 Using the grater blade of a food processor or the large holes of a box grater, grate the carrots.

4 In a large bowl, whisk the dressing ingredients. Add the cabbage and carrots and toss to coat evenly. Serve right away.

BROCCOLI SLAW

For a colourful alternative to broccoli, use purple or yellow cauliflower. Combine it with the grated carrot, thin strips of red pepper, golden sultanas and toasted flaked almonds. Add some curry powder and/or mango chutney to the dressing.

SERVES: 4–6 | **PREP TIME:** 20 MINUTES
CHILLING TIME: 1–3 HOURS

Don't throw away tough broccoli stems. Run them through the grater attachment of a food processor, along with some carrots, and toss them in a tangy dressing. Add roasted almonds for a nice, salty crunch. A handful of dried cranberries is good for sweetness. Set the colourful mixture aside a few hours before your barbecue and you are good to go with a fresh new slaw that has nothing to do with cabbage.

DRESSING
1 small sweet onion
3 tablespoons cider vinegar
75ml/3fl oz mayonnaise
1 teaspoon Dijon mustard
1 teaspoon prepared horseradish
1 teaspoon granulated sugar
1 teaspoon sea salt
½ teaspoon freshly ground black pepper

450g/1lb broccoli stalks, outer
   layer peeled
2 carrots
140g/5oz roasted, salted almonds,
   coarsely chopped
40g/1½oz dried cranberries

1 Using the grater blade of a food processor or the large holes of a box grater, grate the onion, and then put it and all its juice in a large bowl. Add the vinegar, stir to combine and allow to stand for a few minutes. Then add the remaining dressing ingredients and mix well.

2 Using the grater blade of a food processor or the large holes of a box grater, grate the broccoli stalks and carrots. To the bowl with the dressing add the broccoli, carrots, almonds and cranberries. Mix well. Refrigerate for at least 1 hour or up to 3 hours to allow the flavours to develop.

MACARONI AND CHEESE
WITH PARMESAN CRUMBS

SERVES: 6–8 | **PREP TIME:** 25 MINUTES | **GRILLING TIME:** 20–25 MINUTES
SPECIAL EQUIPMENT: 30-CM/12-INCH CAST-IRON FRYING PAN

50g/2oz unsalted butter
30g/1oz plain flour
2 teaspoons mustard powder
1½ teaspoons onion powder
850ml/1½ pints full-fat milk
115g/4oz mature cheddar cheese,
   coarsely grated
115g/4oz processed cheese spread,
   diced
225g/8oz Monterey Jack or similar
   spicy cheese and provolone
   cheese, coarsely grated
1 teaspoon sea salt
½ teaspoon freshly ground black
   pepper
450g/1lb dried short-cut macaroni

TOPPING
100g/3½oz panko breadcrumbs
75g/2oz Parmesan cheese, finely
   grated
40g/1½oz unsalted butter, melted

With lots of crunchy, cheesy topping, this recipe is purposely on the mild side so that kids of all ages can enjoy it. If you prefer a bit more of a kick, use a spicy cheese. You may also like to use Gruyère cheese in place of some of the Cheddar. One final tip: if your main course is not heavily smoked, try adding apple wood chips to the grill to work some subtle smokiness into this comforting side dish.

1   Prepare the grill for indirect cooking over medium-low heat (180–200°C/350–400°F).

2   In a 30-cm/12-inch cast-iron frying pan over a medium heat, melt the butter. Whisk in the flour and let the mixture bubble for about 1 minute without browning (it should smell like baked pastry). Whisk in the mustard powder and onion powder. Gradually whisk in the milk and bring to the boil, whisking often until the sauce is smooth. Reduce the heat to low and simmer for about 3 minutes until all of the raw flour taste is gone, whisking often. Remove the sauce from the heat. Add the cheeses all at once and whisk until they have melted. Season with the salt and pepper.

3   Meanwhile, bring a large saucepan of salted water to the boil for the macaroni, and cook according to the packet instructions, removing the pasta when it is al dente (do not overcook the macaroni, as it will cook more in the sauce). Drain the macaroni well and add it to the frying pan. Stir into the sauce and mix well.

4   Combine the topping ingredients, then distribute evenly over the macaroni.

5   Place the pan with the macaroni and cheese over *roasting/indirect medium-low heat*, close the lid and cook for 20–25 minutes until the sauce is bubbling and the crumbs are lightly browned. Remove from the grill and allow to rest for 5 minutes. Serve warm.

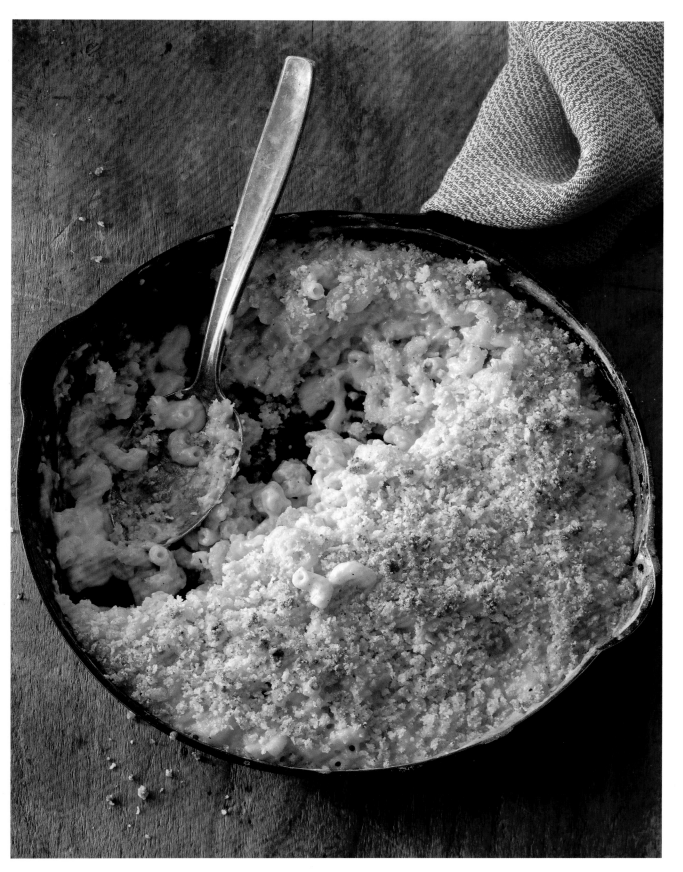

CREAMY CHIPOTLE MACARONI SALAD
WITH GRILLED CORN AND TOMATOES

SERVES: 8–10 | **PREP TIME:** 20 MINUTES
GRILLING TIME: 8–10 MINUTES

You can serve this colourful salad right after you make it, but chilling it overnight will allow the spicy, smoky flavours to permeate the macaroni. Slice the basil and add it just before serving because it can turn black at the edges a few minutes after it is cut.

DRESSING
125ml/4fl oz mayonnaise
125ml/4fl oz soured cream
2 canned chipotle chillies in adobo
   sauce, deseeded and chopped
2 teaspoons adobo sauce (from the can)
1½ teaspoons sea salt

340g/12oz dried short-cut macaroni
4 corn on the cobs, husked
2 teaspoons extra-virgin olive oil
2 peppers, 1 red and 1 green, finely
   chopped
340g/12oz cherry tomatoes, each
   cut in half
3 spring onions (white and light green
   parts only), thinly sliced
25g/1oz basil, thinly sliced

1   Prepare the grill for direct cooking over high heat (230–290°C/450–550°F).

2   In a large serving bowl, combine the dressing ingredients.

3   Bring a large saucepan of salted water to the boil. Add the macaroni and cook according to the packet directions until al dente; drain, rinse under cold water, and drain again. Transfer the macaroni to the serving bowl with the dressing and toss to combine.

4   Brush the corn all over with the oil, and then grill over **grilling/direct high heat** for 8–10 minutes, with the lid closed, until browned in spots and tender, turning occasionally. Remove from the grill and, when cool enough to handle, cut the kernels off the cobs. Add the corn, peppers, tomatoes and spring onions to the bowl with the macaroni and mix well. Refrigerate until ready to serve. Just before serving, gently mix in the basil.

SESAME-PEANUT NOODLE SALAD
WITH ROASTED LEMON JUICE

SERVES: 6-8 | **PREP TIME:** 20 MINUTES
GRILLING TIME: 10-15 MINUTES | **CHILLING TIME:** 2-8 HOURS

This is for those barbecue days when you want to make a noodle salad ahead of time and know that you have a winner waiting in the wings. Grilling the lemons helps to release a lot of tangy, fragrant juice.

2 lemons, each cut crossways in half
Vegetable oil
370g/13oz Chinese egg noodles, soba,
   or dried wholewheat spaghetti
115g/4oz creamy peanut butter
4 tablespoons soy sauce
2 tablespoons toasted sesame oil
1 shallot, finely chopped
1 tablespoon peeled, grated fresh ginger
2 teaspoons honey
½ teaspoon hot chilli-garlic sauce,
   such as Sriracha
3 large spring onions (white and light
   green parts only), thinly sliced
3 tablespoons finely chopped fresh
   coriander
1 tablespoon toasted sesame seeds

1 Prepare the grill for indirect cooking over medium heat (180-230°C/350-450°F).

2 Lightly brush the cut side of the lemons with oil, and then grill, cut side down, over *roasting/indirect medium heat* for 10-15 minutes, with the lid closed, until fragrant and marked by the grill (do not turn). Remove from the grill and allow to cool.

3 Bring a large saucepan of salted water to the boil. Add the noodles and cook according to the packet instructions until al dente; drain, rinse under cold water and drain again.

4 In a large bowl, combine the peanut butter, soy sauce, sesame oil, shallot, ginger, honey and chilli-garlic sauce. Squeeze the roasted lemons through a sieve into the peanut butter mixture and whisk until smooth. Add the noodles and mix gently with tongs until all the noodles are coated.

5 Cover and refrigerate until chilled, at least 2 hours or up to 8 hours. Serve chilled or at room temperature, garnished with the spring onions, coriander and sesame seeds.

COURGETTE-PEA PAPPARDELLE
WITH GRILLED ONION AND FETA

SERVES: 4–6 | **PREP TIME:** 25 MINUTES
GRILLING TIME: 10–12 MINUTES

15g/½oz dill sprigs, finely chopped
15g/½oz basil leaves, finely chopped
2 tablespoons fresh lemon juice
2 teaspoons Dijon mustard
¼ teaspoon crushed chilli flakes
Sea salt
Freshly ground black pepper
Extra-virgin olive oil
2 green courgettes, ends trimmed
2 yellow courgettes, ends trimmed
1 red onion, cut crossways into
    8-mm/⅓-inch slices
225g/8oz dried pappardelle pasta
100g/3½oz frozen petits pois, thawed
3 tablespoons crumbled feta

Grilled onion imparts a sweet, earthy quality to this colourful, summery pasta that could easily hold its own as a main course or live happily alongside barbecued chicken or ribs.

1   In a large serving bowl, combine the dill, basil, lemon juice, mustard, chilli flakes, ½ teaspoon salt, and ½ teaspoon pepper. Slowly whisk in 175ml/6fl oz oil to make a vinaigrette.

2   Prepare the grill for direct cooking over medium-high heat (200–230°C/400–450°F).

3   Using a sharp vegetable peeler, shave the courgettes lengthways into long, thin strips. Once you reach the seedy core, stop and leave the core whole. Turn over and repeat with the other side, again stopping at the seedy core. Transfer the strips to the serving bowl with the vinaigrette and toss. Discard the cores.

4   Lightly brush the onion slices with oil and generously season with salt and pepper. Grill the onion over **grilling/direct medium-high heat** for 10–12 minutes, with the lid closed, until softened and nicely charred, turning once or twice.

5   Meanwhile, cook the pasta according to the packet instructions until al dente. Drain the pasta well, reserving 125ml/4fl oz of the pasta water, and set aside.

6   Roughly chop the onion slices and add to the serving bowl. Add the pasta and toss well to combine, adding a little pasta water if needed. Top with the peas and feta, season with salt and pepper and gently toss. Serve right away.

To mimic the shape of the pasta, trim off the ends, and then shave the courgettes with a vegetable peeler. Run the blade lengthways down each vegetable until you see lots of little seeds. Then turn the vegetable over and do the same on the other side.

NOT YOUR GRANDMA'S SUCCOTASH

SERVES: 6 | **PREP TIME:** 25 MINUTES | **GRILLING TIME:** ABOUT 25 MINUTES
SPECIAL EQUIPMENT: LARGE GRILLPROOF FRYING PAN

In its purest form, succotash is a simple corn and bean combination that originated with the Native Americans of the North-east. This version brings succotash up to date by adding ripe tomatoes, fragrant basil and umami-rich cheese. Edamame stand in for the usual butter beans. If you wish, the courgettes, corn and red pepper could be grilled and prepped a few hours before the final cooking.

2 small courgettes, ends trimmed,
    each cut lengthways in half
Extra-virgin olive oil
2 corn on the cobs, husked
1 red pepper
25g/1oz unsalted butter
370g/13oz onions, chopped
2 tablespoons finely chopped jalapeño
    chilli
2 garlic cloves, finely chopped
225g/8oz frozen shelled edamame
    (soya beans), thawed
2 ripe plum tomatoes, about 255g/9oz
    total, cored, deseeded and cut into
    2-cm/¾-inch dice
1 teaspoon sea salt
¼ teaspoon freshly ground black pepper
50g/2oz Parmesan cheese, finely
    grated
2 tablespoons finely chopped basil
2 tablespoons fresh lemon juice

1 Prepare the grill for direct cooking over medium-high heat (220–240°C/425–475°F).

2 Lightly brush the courgettes with oil. Grill the courgettes, corn and red pepper over **grilling/direct medium-high heat**, with the lid closed, until the courgettes are crisp-tender, the corn is browned in spots and tender, and the pepper is blackened and blistered all over, turning as needed. The courgettes will take 5–7 minutes, and the corn and pepper will take 10–12 minutes. Remove from the grill as they are done. Place the pepper in a bowl and cover with clingfilm to trap the steam. Allow to stand for about 10 minutes.

3 Adjust the temperature of the grill to medium-low heat (180–200°C/350– 400°F).

4 Remove the pepper from the bowl and discard the charred skin, stalk and seeds. Cut the pepper and courgettes into 2-cm/¾-inch pieces. Cut the corn kernels from the cobs.

5 In a large grillproof frying pan over **grilling/direct medium-low heat**, melt the butter. Add the onions and cook for for 8–9 minutes, with the lid closed, until golden and tender, stirring occasionally. Stir in the chilli and garlic and cook until fragrant, about 1 minute. Add the courgettes, corn and pepper and mix well. Add the edamame, tomatoes, salt and pepper and cook for about 5 minutes, with the lid closed, until heated through, stirring occasionally. Remove from the grill. Stir in the cheese, basil and lemon juice. Serve warm.

BORRACHO BEANS

SERVES: 6–8 | **PREP TIME:** 15 MINUTES | **GRILLING TIME:** 1–1½ HOURS | **SPECIAL EQUIPMENT:** CHARCOAL GRILL, LARGE (6-LITRE/10-PINT) CAST-IRON CASSEROLE, 2 LARGE HANDFULS HICKORY OR OAK WOOD CHUNKS

At Texas barbecue restaurants you'll sometimes find a big pot of beans like this simmering on the pit alongside the meat, picking up traces of aromatic smoke. So called because they're cooked with so much beer (the word borracho means 'drunken' in Spanish), these beans make a nice alternative to traditional baked beans. I think you will find them some of the most flavourful beans you've ever eaten.

6 bacon rashers, cut into 1cm/½-inch pieces
1 large onion, about 340g/12oz, finely chopped
2 garlic cloves, finely chopped
2 teaspoons mild chilli powder
1 teaspoon ground cumin
175ml/6fl oz water
1 bottle (350ml/12fl oz) pilsner
3 cans (each 14oz) pinto beans, rinsed and drained
2 cans (each 400g/14oz) chopped tomatoes in juice
1 teaspoon sea salt
4 tablespoons coarsely chopped fresh coriander
3 tablespoons pure maple syrup
1 teaspoon cider vinegar

1 Prepare the charcoal grill for direct and indirect cooking over medium heat (180–230°C/350–450°F).

2 In a large grill-proof cast-iron casserole over *grilling/direct medium heat*, fry the bacon for 5–7 minutes, with the grill lid closed, until browned and crisp, stirring occasionally. Add the onion and cook until golden, about 5 minutes, stirring occasionally. Add the garlic, chilli powder and cumin and cook for 1 minute, stirring frequently. Add the water, lager, beans, tomatoes and salt and stir well. Close the grill lid and bring the mixture to the boil, which should take about 15 minutes.

3 Add the wood chunks to the charcoal. When smoke appears, slide the casserole over *roasting/indirect medium heat* and simmer the beans for 40 minutes–1 hour, uncovered, with the grill lid closed, until the cooking liquid is reduced by about half, stirring occasionally. Remove from the grill and stir in the coriander, syrup and vinegar. Serve warm.

SWEET AND STICKY BBQ BEANS

SERVES: 8 | PREP TIME: 30 MINUTES | GRILLING TIME: 35–45 MINUTES
SPECIAL EQUIPMENT: 2 HANDFULS HICKORY, APPLE OR CHERRY WOOD CHIPS; 6-LITRE/10-PINT GRILLPROOF CAST-IRON CASSEROLE

These bacon-flavoured beans dripping with treacle are a great side for hot dogs, hamburgers or smoked meat. If you want to gild the lily, sprinkle about 300g/10oz chopped barbecued beef brisket (preferably the burnt ends) over the beans during the last five minutes or so of cooking time. While the beef makes this is a very rich side dish, barbecue lovers will go weak in the knees at every bite.

4 thick-cut bacon rashers,
    coarsely chopped
1 tablespoon vegetable oil
400g/14oz onions, chopped
2 garlic cloves, chopped
250ml/8fl oz ketchup-style chilli
    sauce
150ml/5fl oz tomato ketchup
75ml/3fl oz black treacle
4 tablespoons light brown sugar
2 tablespoons spicy brown mustard
2 tablespoons Worcestershire sauce
1 tablespoon cider vinegar
1 teaspoon hot pepper sauce
2 cans (each 400g/14oz) haricot
    beans, rinsed and drained
2 cans (each 400g/14oz) pinto beans,
    rinsed and drained

1 Soak the wood chips in water for at least 30 minutes.

2 Prepare the grill for indirect cooking over medium-low heat (170–190°C/325–375°F).

3 In a large grillproof cast-iron casserole over a medium heat, fry the bacon in the oil for 8–10 minutes until browned and crisp, stirring occasionally. Using a slotted spoon, transfer the bacon to kitchen paper to drain, leaving the drippings in the pan. Add the onions to the drippings and cook for 8–10 minutes until golden brown, stirring occasionally. Add the garlic and stir until fragrant, about 30 seconds. Add the remaining ingredients, except the beans, and mix well with a wooden spatula. Scrape up any browned bits on the bottom of the pan and bring the mixture to a simmer. Stir in the beans and bring to the boil.

4 Drain and add half of the wood chips to the charcoal or to the smoker box of a gas grill, following the manufacturer's instructions, and close the lid. When smoke appears, place the casserole, uncovered, over **roasting/indirect medium-low heat**, close the grill lid and cook the beans for 15 minutes. Drain and add the remaining wood chips to the charcoal or smoker box, and continue cooking for 20–30 minutes more, with the grill lid closed, until the sauce is thickened and the top of the beans is glazed. Remove from the grill and allow to stand for 5 minutes. Garnish the beans with the reserved bacon pieces and serve warm.

GREEK WHITE BEANS

SERVES: 6–8 | **PREP TIME:** 15 MINUTES | **GRILLING TIME:** 40–50 MINUTES
SPECIAL EQUIPMENT: 1½–2-LITRE/2½–3½-PINT GRILLPROOF GRATIN DISH OR 20-CM/8-INCH CAST-IRON FRYING PAN

Instead of the usual sweet profile of American baked beans, this dish is tangy and tomato-y, too. With the feta cheese, oregano and fresh dill, there is a certain Greek feeling here that makes this a welcome accompaniment to a leg of lamb or smoked beef ribs.

1 large onion, cut crossways
    into 8-mm/⅓-inch slices
2 ripe tomatoes, cored and cut
    lengthways in half
Extra-virgin olive oil
Sea salt
Freshly ground black pepper
6 spring onions, ends trimmed
2 cans (each 400g/14oz) cannellini
    beans, rinsed and drained
115g/4oz feta cheese, crumbled
1 teaspoon dried oregano
25g/1oz dill, chopped
70g/2½oz panko breadcrumbs

1 Prepare the grill for direct and indirect cooking over medium-high heat (200–230°C/400–450°F).

2 Lightly brush the onion slices and tomato halves with oil and season liberally with salt and pepper. Grill the onion and the tomatoes over **grilling/direct medium-high heat** for 10–15 minutes, with the lid closed, until softened and nicely charred, turning once or twice. Remove the onion and tomatoes from the grill and, when cool enough to handle, roughly chop.

3 Finely chop the spring onions and set aside 2 tablespoons for the breadcrumb topping. Combine the remaining spring onions, onion, tomatoes, beans, feta, oregano, 4 tablespoons of the dill, 1 teaspoon salt and ½ teaspoon pepper. Mix well and transfer to a 1.5–2-litre/2½–3½-pint grillproof gratin dish.

4 Combine the breadcrumbs with the reserved spring onions, the remaining dill, 2 tablespoons oil and a pinch of salt. Distribute the dill crumbs on top of the bean mixture.

5 Place the gratin over **roasting/indirect medium-high heat**, close the lid and cook for 30–35 minutes until warmed through and golden. Remove from the grill and allow to rest for 10 minutes before serving.

GRILL-ROASTED LEEKS
WITH HAZELNUT CHIMICHURRI

SERVES: 4 | **PREP TIME:** 25 MINUTES
GRILLING TIME: 16–20 MINUTES

CHIMICHURRI
40g/1½oz hazelnuts, toasted
20g/¾oz flat-leaf parsley
4 tablespoons oregano leaves
2 tablespoons red wine vinegar
1 garlic clove, chopped

Extra-virgin olive oil
Sea salt
Freshly ground black pepper
8 leeks, each about 2.5cm/1 inch
    thick, tough outer leaves discarded
175g/6oz yellow cherry tomatoes,
    each cut in half

Sometimes it's fun to live on the edge. Charring leeks right up to the point where they turn black is exciting because there is always a chance that you will completely burn them. No worries. If that happens, you can peel away the burnt leaves and eat the rest. The biggest pay-off here is that the interiors of the leeks will soften and turn smoky, especially if you are cooking over charcoal. The nutty and slightly tart chimichurri adds texture and vibrancy to the sweet leeks, making a remarkable side dish.

1   In the bowl of a food processor, pulse the hazelnuts to coarsely chop. Add the remaining chimichurri ingredients, including 75ml/3fl oz oil, ½ teaspoon salt and ⅛ teaspoon pepper, and process until almost smooth (some texture will still remain). Transfer to a small bowl.

2   Prepare the grill for direct and indirect cooking over medium heat (180–230°C/350–450°F).

3   Remove the dark green tops from the leeks, cutting about 5cm/2 inches above the point where the leaves begin to darken. Trim just enough of each root end to remove the stringy parts, but leave enough of each root end so that the layers remain attached. Cut each leek lengthways in half. Rinse the leeks under water, opening up the layers to remove any dirt. Pat dry, and then lightly coat with oil and season with ¾ teaspoon salt and ½ teaspoon pepper.

4   Grill the leeks over **grilling/direct medium heat** for 4–6 minutes, with the lid closed, until charred on all sides, turning as needed. Then move the leeks over **roasting/indirect medium heat** and continue grilling for 12–14 minutes more, with the lid closed, until tender, turning once or twice and peeling away any burnt leaves. Transfer the leeks to a serving platter. Spread the chimichurri over the leeks and top with the tomatoes. Serve warm.

POT LIKKER SPRING GREENS

SERVES: 8 | **PREP TIME:** 1 HOUR, PLUS ABOUT 1 HOUR TO COOK THE STOCK
SPECIAL EQUIPMENT: 12–16-LITRE/21–28-PINT STOCKPOT

STOCK
1 litre/1¾ pints chicken stock
675g/1½lb smoked ham hocks or
    turkey wings, sawed by the
    butcher into large pieces
1 litre/1¾ pints water
370g/13oz onions, chopped
6 garlic cloves, smashed and peeled

1 tablespoon vegetable oil
450g/1lb onions, chopped
3 garlic cloves, finely chopped
1.8kg/4lb spring greens, thick stems
    removed
2 tablespoons granulated sugar
2 teaspoons sea salt
½ teaspoon crushed chilli flakes
Hot pepper sauce
Cider vinegar

Nothing sets off a plate of barbecue more than a heap of tender greens nicely seasoned with smoked meat. Ham is traditional, but smoked turkey has become a new favourite. A tasty cooking liquid makes the difference between good greens and those that are truly great, so go ahead and start it beforehand to give the meat extra time to release its flavour. The final broth (called pot likker) is so mouthwatering that it is often served with the greens for sopping up with a hunk of corn bread.

1   In a 4-litre/7-pint saucepan, combine the chicken stock, ham hocks and water. Bring to the boil over a high heat. Skim off any foam that rises to the top. Add the chopped onions, garlic and additional water, as necessary, to cover the solids. Reduce the heat to medium-low and simmer for about 1 hour until the stock is reduced to about 1.5 litres/2½ pints. Strain the stock through a sieve placed over a bowl. Discard the onion and garlic and reserve the ham hocks.

2   In a 12–16-litre/21–28-pint stockpot over a medium heat, warm the oil. Add the chopped onions and cook for 7–8 minutes until they begin to brown and brown bits form on the bottom of the pot, stirring occasionally. Add the chopped garlic and sauté for 1 minute, stirring frequently. Pour in the stock, add the reserved ham hocks and bring to a simmer.

3   In the meantime, fill a sink with cold water and add the spring greens. Agitate the greens well to loosen any grit. In batches, lift a handful of greens from the water and shake off the excess water. Roll up the greens into a thick

cylinder and, using a large knife, cut the greens crossways into strips about 1cm/½ inch wide. Add them to the stockpot and stir well until the greens wilt. Stir in the sugar, salt and chilli flakes. If needed, add enough water to barely cover the ingredients. Bring to the boil over a high heat. Reduce the heat to low, cover and simmer for about 30 minutes until the greens and the meat on the ham hocks are all very tender, stirring occasionally. Transfer the ham hocks to a plate. Remove the stockpot from the heat and cover to keep the greens warm.

4   When the ham hocks are cool enough to handle, but still warm, dice the meat into small pieces, discarding the skin, fat and bones. Stir the meat into the greens.

5   Using a slotted spoon, transfer the greens to a serving bowl and add enough of the cooking liquid (called pot likker) to moisten the greens without making them soupy. Serve warm, with hot sauce and vinegar for sprinkling on the greens and the remaining pot likker on the side.

If you have a side burner, fire it up to simmer the greens and ham hocks in a large pot while you make the rest of your meal on the grill. These greens are really rich, so one or two spoonfuls will be plenty alongside some barbecued meat and a piece of corn bread.

NAAN
WITH GARLIC-HERB BUTTER

SERVES: 4–8 | **PREP TIME:** 30 MINUTES | **RISING TIME:** ABOUT 45 MINUTES
GRILLING TIME: ABOUT 4 MINUTES PER BATCH | **SPECIAL EQUIPMENT:** PIZZA STONE, SILICONE BASTING BRUSH

175ml/6fl oz warm water
(40–46°C/105–115°F)
10g packet (¼oz) fast-action
dried yeast
Pinch granulated sugar
75ml/3fl oz plain Greek yogurt, at
room temperature
Rapeseed oil
Sea salt
1 teaspoon ground white pepper
350g/12oz strong white flour, plus
more as needed
115g/4oz unsalted butter
3 tablespoons mixed chopped
fresh herbs
2 teaspoons finely chopped garlic

Probably one of the first foods humans cooked over fire (hot stones), about two million years ago, was bread, so this isn't exactly a new thing; but, then again, how many of your neighbours these days are cooking flatbread outside on a pizza stone? It's time to wow the neighbourhood with naan hot off the grill. Pick any duo of fresh green herbs you like to season the melted butter seeping into the bread.

1   Pour the warm water into a large, warm bowl and sprinkle with the yeast and a pinch of sugar. Allow to stand for about 5 minutes, without stirring, until the yeast dissolves. Add the yogurt, 2 tablespoons oil, 1 teaspoon salt and the pepper; stir to combine. Add the flour and stir to form a soft dough (add another 70g/2½oz flour, if needed). Turn on to a clean, dry work surface; knead until smooth, about 8 minutes.

2   Grease the inside of a large bowl with oil. Shape the dough into a ball, set it in the bowl and turn the dough to coat all sides with oil. Cover with clingfilm and set aside in a warm, draught-free place until doubled in bulk, about 45 minutes.

3   Prepare the grill for direct cooking over medium heat (180–230°C/350–450°F) and preheat a pizza stone for 20 minutes, following the manufacturer's instructions.

4   In a small saucepan over a low heat, melt the butter. Stir in the herbs, garlic and 1 teaspoon salt. Set aside off the heat.

5   Punch down the dough and divide it into four equal balls. On a clean, dry work surface, stretch each ball by hand into an oval about 25cm/10 inches long and 8mm/⅓ inch thick. If the ovals fail to retain their dimensions once stretched to size, cover the dough with a tea towel and allow them to rest for 10–20 minutes before continuing. Transfer the ovals, not touching, to a lightly floured baking tray.

6   Using a silicone basting brush, brush off any crumbs that may be on the pizza stone. Place two ovals of dough on the pizza stone and lightly brush the tops with some of the herb butter. Grill the naan over **grilling/direct medium heat** (as close to 200°C/400°F as possible), with the lid closed, for 2 minutes. Turn the naan over, lightly brush with more herb butter and continue grilling for about 2 minutes more, with the lid closed, until puffy, lightly browned in places, and firm to the touch. Transfer the naan to a basket lined with a napkin and keep covered and warm. When the grill temperature returns to 200°C/400°F, continue as above, cooking the remaining pieces of dough in one more batch. Serve warm.

This dough draws nice flavours from yogurt. Take the yogurt out of the refrigerator for 20 minutes before using it so that it's not so cold that it slows down the action of the yeast. Knead and stretch the dough until the surface is smooth. Then let the dough double in size in an oiled bowl. Shape pieces of the risen dough into ovals for buttering and cooking.

BUTTERMILK SCONES
WITH HONEY BUTTER

MAKES: 10–12 SCONES | **PREP TIME:** 30 MINUTES
GRILLING TIME: 20–25 MINUTES | **SPECIAL EQUIPMENT:** 5-CM/2½-INCH ROUND PASTRY CUTTER

SCONES
375g/13oz plain flour, plus more for
    rolling the dough
1 tablespoon granulated sugar
2 teaspoons baking powder
1 teaspoon bicarbonate of soda
1 teaspoon sea salt
175g/6oz cold butter, cut into 1-cm/
    ½-inch cubes
325ml/11fl oz buttermilk (see
    page 272)

BUTTER
115g/4oz unsalted butter, softened
3 tablespoons honey, preferably clover

Flaky biscuits are delicious icons of American home cooking, including barbecue. Quickly prepared and 'baked' on a grill, they are excellent to serve as a barbecue side dish or to sandwich smoked meats. A key to perfect scones is gentle handling of the dough, so avoid strong kneading at all costs. Also, when you cut the scones from the dough, do not twist the cutter. Pull straight up!

1   Prepare the grill for indirect cooking over medium-high heat (200–230°C/400–450°F).

2   Sift the flour, the sugar, baking powder, bicarbonate of soda and salt into a large bowl. Add the butter cubes and stir to coat them with the flour mixture. Using a pastry blender or two knives, cut in the butter until the mixture resembles coarse crumbs with some pea-sized pieces of butter. Resist the temptation to use your hands because the colder the butter is, the flakier the scones will be. Pour in the buttermilk and, using your hands with your fingers spread apart, gently mix until the dough is moistened. Very lightly knead the dough in the bowl a few times, just until it holds together. If the dough is too moist to knead and it is sticking to your hands, add up to 2 tablespoons more flour, one tablespoon at a time, until the dough is just workable. Do not overwork the dough.

3   Turn the dough out on to a lightly floured work surface and dust the top of the dough with flour. Gently roll or pat the dough into a round 2–2.5cm/¾–1 inch thick. Using a 5-cm/2½-inch round pastry cutter, cut out scones, being sure not to twist the cutter. Set the scones on an ungreased baking sheet so they are not touching. Repeat the process, but push and pinch the dough, scraping into a cohesive mass without kneading for the remaining scone. Do this once because too much regathering makes tough scones.

4   Place the baking sheet with the scones over *roasting/indirect medium-high heat*, close the lid and cook for 20–25 minutes until the scones rise, are golden brown and a wooden skewer inserted into the centre comes out clean.

5   Meanwhile, in a small bowl using an electric mixer on high speed, beat the butter until creamy. Gradually beat in the honey. Cover and allow to stand at room temperature until the scones are ready to eat. Serve them warm with the honey butter.

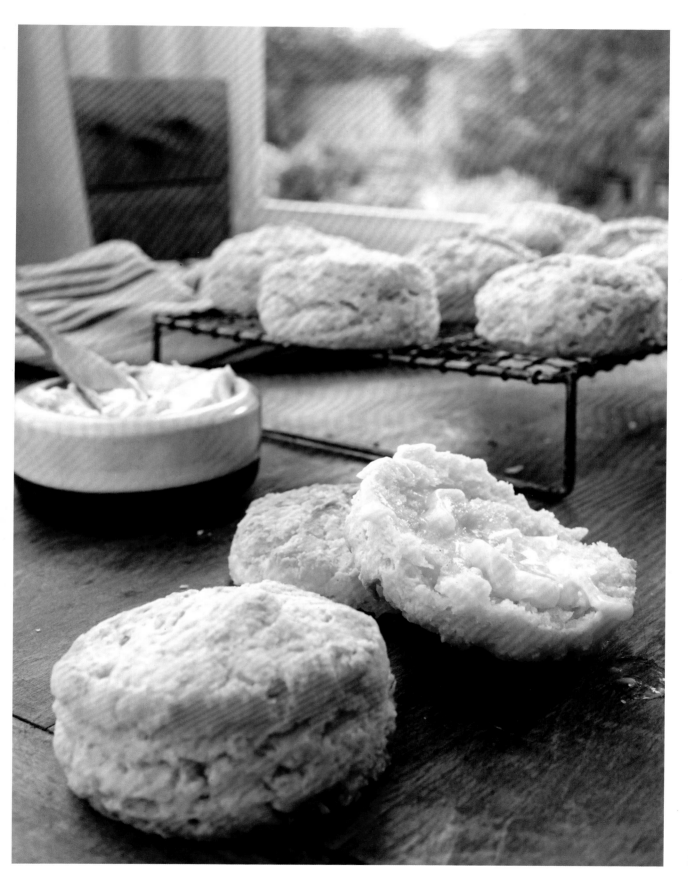

MOIST AND TENDER CORN BREAD

SERVES: 8 | **PREP TIME:** 15 MINUTES | **GRILLING TIME:** 20–25 MINUTES
SPECIAL EQUIPMENT: 23-CM/9-INCH CAST-IRON FRYING PAN OR GRILLPROOF ROUND CAKE TIN WITH
4–4.5-CM/1½–1¾-INCH HIGH SIDES

90g/3¼oz unsalted butter
250ml/8fl oz buttermilk (see below)
1 large egg
125g/4½oz plain flour
150g/5oz polenta, preferably stone
    ground with not too coarse a grind
75g/3oz granulated sugar
2 teaspoons baking powder
1 teaspoon bicarbonate of soda
¾ teaspoon sea salt

Like barbecued meats, corn bread can be prepared in many ways. It isn't unusual to find it thick or thin, sweet or savoury, served in wedges or cut into squares, plain or with additions – the variations seem endless. This one, with a moist and sweet crumb, is a real crowd-pleaser, and it can be prepared in minutes. If you prefer a less sweet corn bread, just reduce the sugar to 2 tablespoons. Change up the recipe a bit by adding small amounts of chopped fresh herbs, such as sage, thyme or rosemary. Or, for a savoury note, stir in some grated cheese, like mature Cheddar, and cooked, crumbled bacon.

1   Prepare the grill for indirect cooking over medium-high heat (200–230°C/400–450°F). Grease a 23-cm/9-inch cast-iron frying pan with 1 tablespoon of the butter.

2   Melt the remaining butter, and then add the buttermilk and egg and whisk until well blended. Sift the remaining ingredients into a separate large bowl. Make a well in the centre of the dry ingredients. Pour in the buttermilk mixture and stir with a rubber spatula just until the batter is moistened (the batter may be slightly lumpy). Pour the batter into the prepared pan and smooth the top.

3   Cook the corn bread over **roasting/indirect medium-high heat** for 20–25 minutes, with the lid closed, until golden brown and a wooden cocktail stick inserted in the centre comes out clean. Allow the corn bread to cool for 5 minutes. Cut into wedges and serve warm directly from the pan. The bread is very tender, and if turned out of the pan, it may break apart. Wrap any leftover corn bread tightly in clingfilm. Corn bread dries out quickly, so the sooner you wrap it, the longer it will stay moist.

If you don't have buttermilk, mix 250ml/8fl oz full-fat or semi-skimmed milk with 1 tablespoon cider vinegar or distilled white vinegar, and allow to stand for 5 minutes.

The corn bread is cooked just right when a cocktail stick inserted in the centre comes out clean with no wet batter attached.

ICED CINNAMON ROLLS

SERVES: 6–12 (MAKES 12 ROLLS) | **PREP TIME:** 40 MINUTES | **RISING TIME:** ABOUT 1½ HOURS
STANDING TIME: 1 HOUR TO OVERNIGHT | **GRILLING TIME:** ABOUT 1 HOUR | **SPECIAL EQUIPMENT:** STAND MIXER WITH PADDLE
AND DOUGH HOOK ATTACHMENTS, 25-CM/10-INCH CAST-IRON FRYING PAN OR GRILLPROOF BAKING TIN

DOUGH

300ml/10fl oz warm full-fat milk
    (38–43°C/100–110°F)
5 tablespoons granulated sugar
10g/¼oz fast-action dried yeast
1 teaspoon sea salt
3 large eggs, at room temperature
750g/1lb 10oz flour, plus more for
    dusting
115g/4oz unsalted butter, softened

FILLING

225g/8oz light brown sugar
4 teaspoons ground cinnamon
115g/4oz unsalted butter, softened

ICING

115g/4oz cream cheese, softened
3 tablespoons full-fat milk
225g/8oz icing sugar
1 teaspoon vanilla extract
⅛ teaspoon sea salt

Okay, I admit it...including cinnamon rolls in a barbecue book is a stretch. It begs the question, what is barbecue anyway? For a complete answer, read my introduction on pages 5–6. You might be surprised by what you learn. You might also be surprised by how amazingly good these cinnamon rolls are. That's another reason they are in this book.

1   In the bowl of a stand mixer, whisk 125ml/4fl oz of the milk, 1 tablespoon of the sugar and the yeast and allow to stand for about 5 minutes until frothy. Add the remaining milk, the remaining sugar, the salt and eggs and, using the paddle attachment with the mixer on low speed, beat for 1 minute. Change to the dough hook and add 675g/1lb1½ of the flour. Starting on low speed and working slowly up to medium, mix for about 3 minutes until the dough is fairly smooth. Reduce the speed to medium-low and add the butter and the remaining flour. Transfer the dough to a floured work surface and knead for about 2 minutes until the dough is soft, smooth and no longer sticky. Transfer the dough to an oiled bowl, cover and allow to rise in a warm place until doubled in bulk, about 1½ hours.

2   Combine the brown sugar and cinnamon. Press the dough down, and then turn out on to a lightly floured surface. Knead the dough two to three times, and then roll out into a 60-cm/24-inch long by 30-cm/12-inch wide rectangle. Spread the dough all over (do not leave a border) with 75g/3oz of the butter. Sprinkle evenly with the cinnamon sugar. Starting at the long side closest to you, tightly roll up the dough, and then pinch the seam closed. Cut the log of dough into twelve 5-cm/2-inch pieces. Generously grease the bottom and sides of a 25-cm/10-inch cast-iron frying pan with the remaining butter and arrange the rolls, cut side up, in a single layer. Cover with aluminium foil and allow to stand at room temperature for 1 hour, or refrigerate overnight. (If refrigerating, return to room temperature before proceeding.)

3   Prepare the grill for indirect cooking over medium heat (as close to 190°C/375°F as possible).

4   Place the pan with the rolls covered with foil over ***roasting/indirect medium heat***, close the lid and cook for 25 minutes. Wearing insulated barbecue mitts or oven gloves, rotate the pan 180 degrees, close the lid and cook for 10 minutes. Remove the foil from the pan and continue cooking for 20–30 minutes more until the dough is cooked through and the tops are lightly browned. Remove from the grill, set on a heatproof surface and allow to cool for 10 minutes. Meanwhile, make the icing.

5   In a large bowl, stir the cream cheese and milk. Sift the icing sugar into the bowl and stir to combine. Add the vanilla and salt and whisk until smooth. Spread the icing over the top of the rolls and allow to stand for 10 minutes. Using a thin-edged knife, cut between the seams of the rolls and transfer to a platter or wire rack. Serve warm or at room temperature.

7
SEASONINGS

SAUCES

SWEET CAROLINA MUSTARD SAUCE

MAKES ABOUT 350ML/12FL OZ

In a saucepan, mix 250ml/8fl oz American mustard; 4 tablespoons unsweetened apple juice; 2 tbsp each brown sugar, honey and black treacle; 1½ tsp each garlic granules, onion flakes and mild chilli powder; and ½ tsp each ground black pepper and drinking chocolate powder. Simmer for 5 minutes over a medium heat, stirring often.

NORTH CAROLINA VINEGAR SAUCE

MAKES ABOUT 725ML/1¼ PINTS

Place a saucepan over a medium-high heat and add 500ml/18fl oz distilled white vinegar, 250ml/8fl oz ketchup, 4 tablespoons light brown sugar, 1 tbsp Worcestershire sauce, 2 tsp sea salt and ½ tsp ground cayenne pepper. Bring to the boil and cook for 8–10 minutes until the sugar is dissolved and the sauce is reduced to a ketchup-like consistency.

SWEET AND SMOKY KANSAS CITY SAUCE

MAKES ABOUT 500ML/18FL OZ

Fry 3 bacon rashers in a saucepan over a medium heat until most of the fat is rendered out. Eat the bacon. Leave 2 tbsp bacon fat in the pan; add 1 small finely diced onion and cook for 3–4 minutes until soft, stirring often. Add 3 chopped garlic cloves and cook for 1 minute, stirring to prevent burning. Whisk in 125ml/4fl oz each tomato ketchup, golden syrup and cider vinegar; 4 tablespoons each tomato purée and mild chilli powder; 2 tbsp light brown sugar; 1 tbsp each black treacle, liquid smoke and Worcestershire sauce; 1 tsp celery salt and ½ tsp sea salt. Simmer over a medium heat for 10–15 minutes, stirring occasionally. Cool. Pour the sauce into a blender and blend until smooth.

ALABAMA WHITE SAUCE

MAKES ABOUT 300ML/10FL OZ

Whisk 250ml/8fl oz mayonnaise, 4 tablespoons white wine vinegar, 2 tsp ground black pepper, ¾ tsp caster sugar and ¼ tsp sea salt until smooth.

CRANBERRY-GINGER BARBECUE SAUCE

MAKES ABOUT 725ML/1¼ PINTS

In a saucepan, combine 250ml/8fl oz tomato ketchup, 1 (250-ml/8-oz) can cranberry sauce, 125ml/4fl oz unsweetened apple juice, 75ml/3fl oz each cider vinegar and honey, 2 tbsp black treacle, 1 tbsp Worcestershire sauce, 1 tsp each mild chilli powder and ground ginger and ¼ tsp ground black pepper. Bring to a simmer over a medium heat and cook, until slightly thickened for about 5 minutes, stirring occasionally.

RED WINE BARBECUE SAUCE

MAKES ABOUT 350ML/12FL OZ

Melt 25g/1oz unsalted butter in a saucepan over a medium-low heat. Add 1 finely chopped shallot and cook for 2–3 minutes until softened, stirring often. Stir in 2 finely chopped garlic cloves and cook until fragrant, about 1 minute. Add 125ml/4fl oz red wine and increase the heat to medium-high. Boil for 1 minute. Then add 250ml/8fl oz tomato ketchup, 4 tbsp each balsamic vinegar and honey, 1 tbsp each Dijon mustard and soy sauce, 1½ tsp each finely chopped fresh thyme and rosemary leaves and ¼ tsp crushed chilli flakes. Bring to the boil, stirring often, and then reduce the heat to low and simmer, uncovered, for 20–25 minutes until the sauce thickens and is reduced to about 350ml/12fl oz, stirring occasionally.

MAKES ABOUT 500ML/18FL OZ

In a saucepan over a medium heat, warm 1 tbsp rapeseed oil. Add 1 tbsp finely chopped fresh ginger and 2 tsp finely chopped garlic and cook for 1 minute, stirring often. Add 250ml/8fl oz pineapple juice, 125ml/4fl oz each hoisin sauce and tomato ketchup, 2 tbsp each honey and unseasoned rice vinegar, ½ tsp each toasted sesame oil and chipotle chilli powder, and ¼ tsp sea salt. Cook for about 5 minutes, stirring occasionally. If liked, pour the sauce through a sieve to strain out the bits of ginger and garlic.

PINEAPPLE-HOISIN BBQ SAUCE

PEACHY DIPPING SAUCE

MAKES ABOUT 500ML/18FL OZ

Put the following ingredients in a large saucepan: 500ml/18fl oz chopped tomatoes in juice (from a can); 250ml/8fl oz peach jam; 75ml/3fl oz white wine vinegar; 2 tbsp black treacle; 1 tsp mustard powder; ½ tsp each onion powder, ground allspice and sea salt; and ¼ tsp each crushed chilli flakes, garlic powder and ground mace. Bring to a low boil over a medium-high heat, stirring often. Then reduce the heat to low and simmer, uncovered, for about 1 hour until thick and reduced to about 500ml/18fl oz, stirring often.

MAKES ABOUT 500ML/18FL OZ

Cut 2 bacon rashers into 1-cm/½-inch wide strips. Fry in a saucepan with 2 tsp oil over a medium heat for 3–5 minutes until crisp; transfer to kitchen paper and keep the bacon fat in the pan. Finely chop a small onion and add to the pan. Reduce the heat to medium-low and cook for 8–10 minutes until soft, stirring occasionally. Stir in 1 finely chopped garlic clove and cook for 1 minute. Then add 4 tbsp bourbon, increase the heat to medium-high and boil to reduce slightly, about 1 minute. Stir in 250ml/8fl oz tomato ketchup, 4 tbsp water, 3 tbsp each cider vinegar and black treacle, 2 tbsp brown sauce, 1 tbsp spicy brown mustard, 1 tsp liquid hickory smoke flavouring, and ½ tsp hot sauce. Bring to the boil over a medium-high heat, then reduce the heat to low and simmer, uncovered, for 20 minutes until the sauce thickens and is reduced to about 500ml/18fl oz, stirring occasionally. Remove from the heat and stir in the bacon.

KENTUCKY BOURBON BARBECUE SAUCE

SAUCES

No matter what you grill or what sort of regional styles you prefer, chances are very good that you will brush, ladle or drizzle some sort of sauce on your food. Without it, your meal could be missing an essential range of flavour, an important degree of texture or a beautiful boost of colour – or all three. Grilling sauces are usually pretty easy to make. Sometimes the prep is as simple as whisking a handful of ingredients, most of which are probably in your store cupboard or refrigerator already.

CHARRED POBLANO ROMESCO SAUCE

MAKES ABOUT 125ML/4FL OZ

2 poblano chillies, about 225g/8oz total
15g/½oz fresh coriander
4 tablespoons almonds, toasted
1 small jalapeño chilli, deseeded
    and chopped
3 tablespoons extra-virgin olive oil
1 tablespoon fresh lemon juice
1 teaspoon sea salt
2 garlic cloves
¼ teaspoon freshly ground black pepper
⅛ teaspoon granulated sugar

1 Prepare the grill for direct cooking over a high heat (230–290°C/450–550°F).

2 Grill the chillies over *grilling/direct high heat* for 10–12 minutes, with the lid closed, until blackened and blistered all over, turning occasionally. Place in a bowl and cover with clingfilm to trap the steam. Allow to stand for about 10 minutes. Remove and discard the charred skins, stems and seeds, and then coarsely chop the chillies.

3 In the bowl of a food processor, combine the chillies and the remaining ingredients and process until well blended but some texture still remains.

ESPRESSO BARBECUE SAUCE

MAKES ABOUT 250ML/8FL OZ

1 tablespoon extra-virgin olive oil
1 small onion, finely chopped
1 garlic clove, finely chopped
1 tablespoon mild chilli powder
1 teaspoon ground cumin
½ teaspoon paprika
125ml/4fl oz ketchup-style chilli sauce
125ml/4fl oz strong coffee
2 tablespoons light brown sugar
2 tablespoons balsamic vinegar

1 In a saucepan over a medium-low heat, warm the oil. Add the onion and cook for about 30 minutes until super soft and as dark as possible, stirring occasionally. Stir in the garlic and cook until fragrant, about 1 minute. Add the chilli powder, cumin and paprika and stir well. Add the chilli sauce, coffee, brown sugar and vinegar and bring to the boil over a medium-high heat. Reduce the heat to low and simmer, uncovered, for 15–20 minutes until the sauce thickens and is reduced to about 250ml/8fl oz, stirring occasionally.

BLACKBERRY-SAGE SAUCE

MAKES ABOUT 400ML/14FL OZ

15g/½ oz unsalted butter
2 tablespoons finely chopped shallot
350g/12oz fresh blackberries
4 tablespoons honey
2 tablespoons tomato ketchup
2 tablespoons balsamic vinegar
2 teaspoons chopped sage
1 teaspoon Worcestershire sauce
½ teaspoon freshly ground black pepper
⅛ teaspoon sea salt

1 In a saucepan over a medium heat, melt the butter. Add the shallot and cook for about 2 minutes until lightly browned, stirring often. Add 225g/8oz of the berries, the honey, ketchup, vinegar, sage, Worcestershire sauce, pepper and salt. Bring to the boil, and then reduce the heat to medium-low. Cook the sauce at a steady simmer until the juices have thickened slightly, about 10 minutes, stirring often and mashing some of the berries to release their juice. Remove from the heat. Purée the sauce in a blender (in batches) with a small opening in the lid to let the steam escape, and return to the saucepan. Stir in the remaining blackberries. Let the sauce cool until tepid and slightly thickened.

SWEET TREACLE BARBECUE SAUCE

MAKES ABOUT 400ML/14FL OZ

175ml/6fl oz tomato ketchup
125ml/4fl oz water
4 tablespoons light brown sugar
4 tablespoons black treacle
1 tablespoon Worcestershire sauce
1 tablespoon mild chilli powder
1 teaspoon sea salt
½ teaspoon freshly ground black pepper

1 In a saucepan, combine the ingredients. Bring to a gentle boil over a medium-high heat, stirring frequently. Reduce the heat to medium-low and simmer for 5–10 minutes until the sauce thickens slightly to a light syrupy consistency, stirring occasionally.

BLACK CHERRY BARBECUE SAUCE

MAKES ABOUT 400ML/14FL OZ

250ml/8fl oz tart black cherry juice
125ml/4fl oz tomato ketchup
4 tablespoons American mustard
2 tablespoons honey
1½ teaspoons mild chilli powder
1½ teaspoons dried thyme
1 teaspoon Worcestershire sauce
¾ teaspoon freshly ground black pepper
¼ teaspoon paprika
¼ teaspoon sea salt

1 In a saucepan, combine the ingredients. Bring to a simmer over a medium heat. Cook for 3–5 minutes, stirring occasionally.

HAZELNUT CHIMICHURRI

MAKES ABOUT 175ML/6FL OZ

40g/1½oz hazelnuts, toasted
20g/¾oz flat-leaf parsley
75ml/3fl oz extra-virgin olive oil
4 tablespoons oregano leaves
2 tablespoons red wine vinegar
½ teaspoon sea salt
1 garlic clove, chopped
⅛ teaspoon freshly ground black pepper

1 In the bowl of a food processor, pulse the hazelnuts to coarsely chop. Add the remaining ingredients and process until almost smooth (some texture will still remain).

KOGI SAUCE

MAKES ABOUT 175ML/6FL OZ

4 tablespoons *gochujang* (Korean fermented hot pepper paste)
4 tablespoons soy sauce
3 tablespoons granulated sugar
1 tablespoon toasted sesame oil
2 teaspoons unseasoned rice vinegar

1 Whisk the ingredients.

BUTTERMILK DRESSING

MAKES ABOUT 125ML/4FL OZ

4 tablespoons buttermilk
3 tablespoons soured cream
1 tablespoon fresh lemon juice
¼ teaspoon sea salt
¼ teaspoon freshly ground black pepper

1 Whisk the ingredients until smooth.

BLUE CHEESE DIP

MAKES ABOUT 350ML/12FL OZ

115g/4oz blue cheese, crumbled
125ml/4fl oz soured cream
4 tablespoons mayonnaise
2 tablespoons fresh lemon juice
½ teaspoon celery seeds
½ teaspoon sea salt
Several dashes hot pepper sauce

1 Combine the ingredients and mix well. If you like the dip a little thinner, stir in a little milk.

MARINADES

It's what's inside that counts – and that's flavour, where marinades are concerned. Letting food sit in a mixture of acidic liquid, oil, herbs and seasonings does wonders to kick-start items that might need a little boost, like leaner cuts of meat and even vegetables, in addition to keeping them moist on the grill. Bold ingredients work best – think garlic, rosemary, or soy sauce – to maximise the marinade's effect, and the right combinations can give your meal a regional or ethnic flair.

KOREAN BBQ MARINADE

6 garlic cloves
1 Granny Smith apple, cored and quartered
1 large onion, about 175g/6oz, quartered
1 piece fresh ginger, about 5cm/2 inches long, peeled and coarsely chopped
250ml/8fl oz soy sauce
115g/4oz light brown sugar
4 tablespoons rice wine or sherry
2 tablespoons toasted sesame oil
1 teaspoon freshly ground black pepper
½ teaspoon ground cayenne pepper

1   In a food processor, combine the garlic, apple, onion and ginger and process until finely chopped. Add the remaining ingredients and process until pureed and well blended.

JAMAICAN JERK MARINADE

1 Scotch bonnet or habanero chilli, deseeded
6 large spring onions, coarsely chopped
4 tablespoons vegetable oil
2 tablespoons each soy sauce, fresh lime juice, ground allspice berries and light brown sugar
1 tablespoon peeled, chopped fresh ginger
1 tablespoon coarsely chopped thyme leaves
1 teaspoon sea salt
½ teaspoon each freshly grated nutmeg
½ teaspoon ground cinnamon
2 garlic cloves, coarsely chopped

1   Wear rubber gloves to coarsely chop the chilli. In a blender, combine the ingredients. Purée, stopping to scrape down the inside of the jar as needed, and add a little water if the paste is too thick.

LITTLE ITALY MARINADE

250ml/8fl oz extra-virgin olive oil
4 tablespoons red wine vinegar
4 tablespoons fresh lemon juice
4 tablespoons finely chopped mint
4 tablespoons finely chopped parsley
2 tablespoons finely chopped dill
1½ teaspoons fennel seeds
2 teaspoons crushed garlic
2 teaspoons sea salt
½ teaspoon freshly ground black pepper

HOW LONG?

The time varies depending on the marinade strength and the food you are marinating. Don't overdo strong marinades. Also, an acidic marinade left on meat or fish too long, can turn the surface dry or mushy. Here are some guidelines.

TIME	TYPES OF FOOD
15–30 minutes	Small foods, such as shellfish, fish fillets, cubed meat for kebabs and tender vegetables
1–3 hours	Thin cuts of boneless meat, such as chicken breasts, pork fillets, chops, steaks and sturdy vegetables
2–6 hours	Thicker cuts of boneless or bone-in meat, such as leg of lamb, whole chickens and beef joints
6–12 hours	Big or tough cuts of meat, such as racks of ribs, whole hams, pork shoulders and turkeys

ROSEMARY-LEMON MARINADE

Freshly grated zest and juice of 2 lemons
4 tablespoons extra-virgin olive oil
2 tablespoons finely chopped rosemary leaves
2 teaspoons sea salt
4 garlic cloves, crushed
1 teaspoon smoked paprika
1 teaspoon freshly ground black pepper

CHINATOWN MARINADE

125ml/4fl oz hoisin sauce
125ml/4fl oz bourbon
4 tablespoons soy sauce
4 tablespoons honey
2 tablespoons toasted sesame oil
2 tablespoons peeled, chopped fresh ginger
1 tablespoon crushed garlic
2 teaspoons Chinese five spice
½ teaspoon ground white pepper

MOJO MARINADE

350ml/12fl oz fresh orange juice
125ml/4fl oz fresh lemon juice
125ml/4fl oz extra-virgin olive oil
1 onion, finely chopped
    in a food processor
20 peeled garlic cloves, finely chopped
    in a food processor
1 tablespoon dried oregano
1 tablespoon sea salt

SOUTH-EAST ASIAN MARINADE

4 tablespoons Vietnamese or Thai fish sauce
4 tablespoons fresh lime juice
2 tablespoons finely chopped shallot
2 tablespoons vegetable oil
1 tablespoon toasted sesame oil
2 garlic cloves, finely chopped

GO-TO FAVOURITE MARINADE

1 small onion, grated, with juice
4 tablespoons fresh lemon juice
3 tablespoons extra-virgin olive oil
3 tablespoons soy sauce
2 tablespoons Dijon mustard
1 teaspoon freshly ground black pepper

SWEET AND SIMPLE MARINADE

125ml/4fl oz soy sauce
4 tablespoons bourbon or Scotch
4 tablespoons honey
2 tablespoons tomato ketchup
2 tablespoons Dijon mustard
1 tablespoon cider vinegar
1 tablespoon extra-virgin olive oil
4 garlic cloves, crushed

INDIAN MARINADE

125ml/4fl oz full-fat yogurt
4 tablespoons extra-virgin olive oil
2 tablespoons fresh lemon juice
1 tablespoon peeled, finely grated
    fresh ginger
2 teaspoons ground cardamom
3 large garlic cloves, crushed
1 teaspoon ground coriander
1 teaspoon sea salt
1 teaspoon freshly ground black pepper

FIESTA MARINADE

125ml/4fl oz fresh orange juice
4 tablespoons fresh lime juice
4 tablespoons gold tequila
1 large jalapeño chilli, including seeds, finely
    chopped
3 tablespoons agave nectar
2 tablespoons soy sauce
2 teaspoons ground cumin
4 garlic cloves, crushed

SMOKY MARINADE

4 canned chipotle chillies in adobo sauce,
    chopped
4 tablespoons fresh lime juice
3 tablespoons tomato ketchup
2 tablespoons extra-virgin olive oil
1 tablespoon dark brown sugar
4 garlic cloves, crushed
2 teaspoons sea salt
1 teaspoon ground cumin
1 teaspoon mild chilli powder

BRINES

When it comes to making brines, the key is to use the right ratio of salt to water. Too much or too little salt can lead to major disappointments. Begin with 125–250g/4½–9oz of sea salt for each 4 litres/7 pints of water or other liquid. This level of saltiness creates a subtle background of flavour inside the meat. What happens is that the salt penetrates the meat and changes the structure of the protein so that the cells inside the meat are able to trap more moisture and flavour. Nature likes equilibrium, so the saltiness inside the meat rises until it is equal to the saltiness in the brine outside the meat. If you like, you can also add sugar to your brine, about the same amount as the salt, and the sugar will complement the saltiness and also caramelise nicely on the surface of the food. Then you can add whatever other flavours you like, including a variety of herbs and spices.

If your brine includes some acidic liquid, be sure to use a non-reactive container. This is a dish or bowl made of glass, plastic, stainless steel or china. A container made of aluminium, or some other metals, will react with acids and add a metallic flavour to food.

Whatever you brine should be completely submerged, covered with clingfilm and then refrigerated.

APPLE BRINE

1.5 litres/3½ pints chilled unsweetened apple juice
125g/4½oz sea salt
125ml/4fl oz soy sauce
7.5-cm/3-inch piece fresh ginger, peeled, thinly sliced
1 tablespoon dried rosemary
1 teaspoon black peppercorns
2 lemons, zest removed in wide strips with a vegetable peeler
2 bay leaves

1   In a saucepan, combine half of the apple juice, the salt, soy sauce, ginger, rosemary, peppercorns, lemon zest strips and bay leaves. Bring to a simmer over a medium heat, stirring occasionally. Pour into a large heatproof bowl set in a larger bowl of iced water. Allow to stand for about 30 minutes until chilled, stirring often. Stir the remaining chilled apple juice into the brine.

ITALIAN BRINE

500ml/18fl oz water
1 orange, quartered
1 lemon, quartered
1 small onion, quartered
4 tablespoons granulated sugar
4 tablespoons sea salt
4 sprigs oregano or thyme
2 teaspoons black peppercorns
4 sage leaves
2 garlic cloves, smashed and peeled
2 bay leaves
500ml/18fl oz dry white wine

1   Pour the water into a saucepan, and then add the orange and lemon quarters, simultaneously squeezing the juice into the water. Add the remaining ingredients except the wine. Cook over a medium-low heat, stirring to dissolve the sugar and salt. Remove from the heat and add the wine. Cool completely.

NORMANDY BRINE

500ml/18fl oz apple cider
75g/3oz dark brown sugar
75g/3oz sea salt
4 thyme sprigs
6 garlic cloves, smashed and peeled
1 tablespoon yellow mustard seeds
2 teaspoons black peppercorns
2 bay leaves, torn
500ml/18fl oz water

1   In a saucepan over a medium-low heat, combine all of the ingredients, except the water, whisking to dissolve the sugar and salt. Remove from the heat and add the water. Cool completely.

DEMERARA SUGAR BRINE

1 litre/1¾ pints water
600g/1lb 5oz demerara sugar
370g/13oz sea salt
1 tablespoon celery seeds
1 tablespoon coriander seeds
1 tablespoon cumin seeds
1 tablespoon yellow mustard seeds
1 litre/1¾ pints ice cubes

1   In a saucepan, combine all of the
    ingredients, except the ice cubes.
    Cook over a high heat until the salt
    and sugar are dissolved, whisking
    constantly. Remove from the heat
    and add the ice cubes.

BLACK CHERRY BRINE

1 litre/1¾ pints water
500ml/18fl oz tart black cherry juice
125g/4½oz sea salt
115g/4oz brown sugar
2 litres/3½ pints ice cubes

1   In a saucepan, combine all of the
    ingredients, except the ice cubes. Bring
    to the boil, mixing well to dissolve the
    salt and sugar. Remove from the heat
    and add the ice cubes.

BUTTERMILK-HERB BRINE

1.5 litres/2½ pints buttermilk
4 tablespoons sea salt
4 tablespoons granulated sugar
2 tablespoons chopped rosemary leaves
2 tablespoons chopped oregano leaves
1 tablespoon thyme leaves
12 garlic cloves, finely chopped
5 tablespoons hot pepper sauce

1   Combine the ingredients and stir until
    the salt and sugar are dissolved.

BEER BRINE

4 bottles (each 350ml/12fl oz) lager
225g/8oz light brown sugar
200g/7oz sea salt
3 tablespoons smoked paprika
1½ tablespoons dried thyme
1 tablespoon cracked black peppercorns
1 tablespoon garlic granules
1 tablespoon onion granules
½ teaspoon ground cayenne pepper
3 litres/5 pints ice water

1   Combine all of the ingredients, except
    the ice water, and whisk until the salt and
    sugar are dissolved. Add the ice water.

BOURBON BRINE

125ml/4fl oz bourbon
125ml/4fl oz water
4 tablespoons brown sugar
2 tablespoons sea salt
½ teaspoon crushed chilli flakes
250ml/8fl oz ice cubes

1   In a saucepan over a medium heat,
    combine the bourbon, water, sugar, salt
    and chilli flakes. Stir until the sugar and
    salt dissolve. Remove from the heat
    and add the ice cubes.

ALL-PURPOSE BRINE

500ml/18fl oz water
125g/4½oz sea salt
75g/3oz light brown sugar
1.5 litres/2½ pints ice cubes

1   In a saucepan, combine all of the
    ingredients, except the ice cubes.
    Bring to the boil over a high heat and
    whisk until the salt is dissolved. Add
    the ice cubes and let the brine cool
    to room temperature.

HOW LONG?

*The most deserving candidates for brining
are big, lean cuts of meat, such as pork
loins and whole turkeys, which you should
soak in a brine for several hours. But even
small items like pork chops, chicken pieces
and salmon fillets are bound to be juicier
and more flavourful if you brine them for
an hour or two. Here are some guidelines.*

TIME	TYPES OF FOOD
Up to 30 minutes	Small foods, such as shellfish, cubed meat for kebabs and vegetables
30 minutes–1 hour	Thin cuts of boneless meat, such as chicken breasts, fish fillets, pork fillet, chops and steaks
2–4 hours	Thicker cuts of boneless or bone-in meat, such as leg of lamb, whole chickens and beef joints
4–12 hours	Big or tough cuts of meat, such as racks of ribs, whole hams, pork shoulders and turkeys

RUBS

A rub is a mixture of spices, herbs and other seasonings (often including sugar) that can quickly give a boost of flavours to foods before grilling. These two pages provide some mighty good examples, but dare to be different. One of the steps towards developing your own style at the grill is to concoct a signature rub recipe or two. Only you will know exactly what ingredients are blended in your special jar of 'magic dust'.

A word about freshness: ground spices lose their aromas in a matter of months (eight to ten months maximum). If you have been holding on to a little jar of coriander for years, waiting to blend the world's finest version of curry powder, forget about it. Dump the old, tired coriander and buy some freshly ground. Better yet, buy whole coriander seeds and grind them yourself. Whatever you do, store your spices and spice rubs in airtight containers away from light and heat, to best preserve their flavours and fragrances.

ALL-PURPOSE RUB

2 tablespoons sea salt
2 tablespoons light brown sugar
2 tablespoons mild chilli powder
1 tablespoon paprika
2 teaspoons onion flakes
1 teaspoon ground cumin
1 teaspoon freshly ground black pepper

PORK RUB

2 teaspoons sea salt
1 teaspoon ground cumin
½ teaspoon freshly ground black pepper
½ teaspoon dried oregano
½ teaspoon light brown sugar
¼ teaspoon chipotle chilli powder

BEEF RUB

2 teaspoons sea salt
1 teaspoon garlic granules
1 teaspoon freshly ground black pepper
1 teaspoon smoked paprika
½ teaspoon ground coriander
½ teaspoon ground cumin

LAMB RUB

2 teaspoons sea salt
1 teaspoon paprika
1 teaspoon curry powder
1 teaspoon freshly ground black pepper
½ teaspoon onion granules
½ teaspoon anise seeds

POULTRY RUB

2 teaspoons sea salt
2 teaspoons dried thyme
1 teaspoon dried oregano
1 teaspoon onion flakes
1 teaspoon ground coriander
1 teaspoon freshly ground black pepper
½ teaspoon mild chilli powder

SEAFOOD RUB

2 teaspoons sea salt
1 teaspoon mild chilli powder
1 teaspoon garlic granules
½ teaspoon ground coriander
½ teaspoon celery seeds
½ teaspoon freshly ground black pepper

VEGETABLE RUB

1 teaspoon mustard powder
1 teaspoon onion flakes
1 teaspoon paprika
1 teaspoon sea salt
½ teaspoon garlic granules
½ teaspoon ground coriander
½ teaspoon ground cumin
½ teaspoon freshly ground black pepper

CAJUN RUB

1 tablespoon paprika
1 tablespoon light brown sugar
1 teaspoon garlic powder
1 teaspoon sea salt
½ teaspoon dried thyme
½ teaspoon dried oregano
½ teaspoon celery salt
½ teaspoon onion powder
½ teaspoon mustard powder

ASIAN RUB

2 tablespoons paprika
2 teaspoons sea salt
2 teaspoons ground coriander
2 teaspoons Chinese five spice
1 teaspoon ground ginger
½ teaspoon ground allspice
½ teaspoon ground cayenne pepper

KANSAS CITY RUB

115g/4oz light brown sugar
4 tablespoons smoked paprika
4 teaspoons sea salt
2½ teaspoons mild chilli powder
2½ teaspoons garlic powder
2½ teaspoons onion powder
1½ teaspoons coarsely ground black pepper
½ teaspoon ground cayenne pepper

CHIPOTLE SPICE RUB

2 teaspoons sea salt
1 teaspoon light brown sugar
1 teaspoon chipotle chilli powder
1 teaspoon ground cumin
1 teaspoon smoked paprika
½ teaspoon freshly ground black pepper
¼ teaspoon ground cayenne pepper

DEMERARA RIB RUB

4 tablespoons demerara sugar
2 tablespoons paprika
2 tablespoons mild chilli powder
4 teaspoons onion flakes
4 teaspoons sea salt
2 teaspoons ground ginger
2 teaspoons freshly ground black pepper

MOROCCAN RUB

2 teaspoons hot chilli powder
1 teaspoon sea salt
½ teaspoon freshly ground black pepper
½ teaspoon ground coriander
½ teaspoon ground cumin
½ teaspoon caraway seeds
¼ teaspoon garlic powder

GARLIC LOVERS' RUB

1½ teaspoons sea salt
1½ teaspoons garlic powder
1 teaspoon ground cumin
¾ teaspoon freshly ground black pepper
½ teaspoon mild chilli powder
½ teaspoon ground ginger
⅛ teaspoon ground cinnamon

PASTRAMI RUB

1 tablespoon black peppercorns
1 tablespoon coriander seeds
2 teaspoons yellow mustard seeds
2 tablespoons light brown sugar
1 tablespoon sea salt
2 teaspoons paprika
1 teaspoon ground cumin

1   In a small frying pan over a medium heat, stir and shake the peppercorns, coriander and mustard seeds for 3–4 minutes until lightly toasted and fragrant. Transfer to a small bowl and cool for 5 minutes. Pour into a spice mill and pulse 15–20 times until coarsely ground. Transfer back to the small bowl, add the remaining ingredients and mix well.

SMOKED PAPRIKA RUB

1 teaspoon smoked paprika
1 teaspoon light brown sugar
1 teaspoon sea salt
1 teaspoon onion flakes
½ teaspoon chipotle chilli powder

DALMATIAN RUB

4 tablespoons sea salt
3 tablespoons freshly ground black pepper
3 tablespoons demerara sugar (optional)

HOW LONG?

If you leave a rub on for a long time, the seasonings intermix with the juices in the meat and produce more pronounced flavours as well as a crust. This is good to a point, but a rub with a lot of salt or sugar will draw moisture out of the meat over time, making the meat tastier, yes, but also drier. So how long should you use a rub? Here are some guidelines.

TIME	TYPES OF FOOD
Up to 15 minutes	Small foods, such as shellfish, cubed meat for kebabs and vegetables
15–30 minutes	Thin cuts of boneless meat, such as chicken breasts, fish fillets, pork fillet, chops and steaks
30 minutes–1½ hours	Thicker cuts of boneless or bone-in meat, such as leg of lamb, whole chickens and beef joints
2–8 hours	Big or tough cuts of meat, such as racks of ribs, whole hams, pork shoulders and turkeys

8

RESOURCES

GRILLING }GUIDES

The following cuts, thicknesses, weights and grilling times are meant to be guidelines rather than hard and fast rules. Cooking times are affected by such factors as altitude, wind, outside temperature, and desired doneness. Two rules of thumb: grill steaks, fish fillets, boneless chicken pieces and vegetables using the direct method for the time given on the chart or to your desired doneness, turning once. Grill joints, whole poultry, bone-in chicken pieces, whole fish and thicker cuts using the indirect method for the time given on the chart or until an instant-read thermometer reaches the desired internal temperature. Let roasts, larger cuts of meat, and thick steaks and chops rest for 5–10 minutes before carving (the internal temperature of the meat will rise 5–10 degrees during this time).

▼ PORK

CUT	THICKNESS / WEIGHT	APPROXIMATE GRILLING TIME
Bratwurst, fresh	75g/3oz	20–25 minutes *grilling/direct medium heat*
Bratwurst, precooked	75g/3oz	10–12 minutes *grilling/direct medium heat*
Chop, boneless or bone in	2cm/¾ inch thick	6–8 minutes *grilling/direct medium heat*
	2.5cm/1 inch thick	8–10 minutes *grilling/direct medium heat*
	3–4cm/1¼–1½ inches thick	10–12 minutes: sear 6 minutes *grilling/direct medium heat*, grill 4–6 minutes *roasting/indirect medium heat*
Fillet	500g/1lb	15–20 minutes *grilling/direct medium heat*
Gammon, smoked, bone in	3.5kg/7lb	1½–2 hours *roasting/indirect medium-low heat*
Loin roast, bone in	1.5–2.5kg/3–5lb	1¼–1¾ hours *roasting/indirect medium heat*
Loin roast, boneless	1.75kg/3½lb	28–40 minutes: sear 8–10 minutes *grilling/direct high heat*, grill 20–30 minutes *roasting/indirect high heat*
Pork, minced	1cm/½ inch thick	8–10 minutes *grilling/direct medium heat*
Pork shoulder, boneless	2.5–3kg/5–6lb	5–7 hours *roasting/indirect low heat*
Pork shoulder, bone in	3kg/6lb	8–10 hours *roasting/indirect very low heat*
Ribs, baby back	700g–1kg/1½–2lb	3–4 hours *roasting/indirect low heat*
Ribs, country-style, bone in	2.5cm/1 inch thick	45–50 minutes *roasting/indirect medium heat*
Ribs, country-style, boneless	2.5cm/1 inch thick	12–15 minutes *grilling/direct medium heat*
Ribs, spareribs	1.25–1.75kg/2½–3½lb	3–4 hours *roasting/indirect low heat*

BEEF

CUT	THICKNESS / WEIGHT	APPROXIMATE GRILLING TIME
Beef, minced	2cm/¾ inch thick	8–10 minutes *grilling/direct medium-high heat*
Brisket, whole (untrimmed)	6–7kg/12–14lb	8–10 hours *roasting/indirect very low heat*
Fillet, whole	1.75–2kg/3½–4lb	35–45 minutes: sear 15 minutes *grilling/direct medium heat*, grill 20–30 minutes *roasting/indirect medium heat*
Kebab	4-cm/1½-inch cubes	6–7 minutes *grilling/direct high heat*
Rib roast (prime rib), boneless	2.5–3kg/5–6lb	1¼–1¾ hours *roasting/indirect medium heat*
Rib roast (prime rib), with bone	4kg/8lb	2–3 hours: sear 10 minutes *grilling/direct medium heat*, grill 2–3 hours *roasting/indirect low heat*
Short ribs	2–2.5kg/4–4½lb	6–7 hours *roasting/indirect low heat*
Sirloin, boneless	2–2.5kg/4–5lb	50 minutes–1 hour: sear 10 minutes *grilling/direct medium heat*, grill 40–50 minutes *roasting/indirect medium heat*
Skirt steak	0.5–1cm/¼–½ inch thick	4–6 minutes *grilling/direct high heat*
Steak: rump, sirloin, rib-eye, T-bone and fillet	2cm/¾ inch thick	4–6 minutes *grilling/direct high heat*
	2.5cm/1 inch thick	6–8 minutes *grilling/direct high heat*
	3cm/1¼ inches thick	8–10 minutes *grilling/direct high heat*
Top rump	1kg/2–2½lb	30–40 minutes: sear 10 minutes *grilling/direct medium heat*, grill 20–30 minutes *roasting/indirect medium heat*

LAMB

CUT	THICKNESS / WEIGHT	APPROXIMATE GRILLING TIME
	2cm/¾ inch thick	4–6 minutes *grilling/direct high heat*
Chop: loin or rib	2.5cm/1 inch thick	6–8 minutes *grilling/direct high heat*
	4cm/1½ inches thick	8–10 minutes *grilling/direct high heat*
Lamb, minced	2cm/¾ inch thick	8–10 minutes *grilling/direct medium-high heat*
Leg of lamb, boneless, rolled	1.25–1.5kg/2½–3lb	30–45 minutes: sear 10–15 minutes *grilling/direct medium heat*, grill 20–30 minutes *roasting/indirect medium heat*
Leg of lamb, butterflied	1.5–1.75kg/3–3½lb	30–45 minutes: sear 10–15 minutes *grilling/direct medium heat*, grill 20–30 minutes *roasting/indirect medium heat*
Rack of lamb	500–750g/1–1½lb	15–20 minutes: sear 5 minutes *grilling/direct medium heat*, grill 10–15 minutes *roasting/indirect medium heat*

POULTRY

CUT	THICKNESS / WEIGHT	APPROXIMATE GRILLING TIME
Chicken breast, bone in	*300–340g/10–12oz*	*23–35 minutes: 3–5 minutes* **grilling/direct medium heat,** *20–30 minutes* **roasting/indirect medium heat**
Chicken breast, boneless, skinless	*175–225g/6–8oz*	*8–12 minutes* **grilling/direct medium heat**
Chicken drumstick	*75–115g/3–4oz*	*26–40 minutes: 6–10 minutes* **grilling/direct medium heat,** *20–30 minutes* **roasting/indirect medium heat**
Chicken thigh, bone in	*140–175g/5–6oz*	*36–40 minutes: 6–10 minutes* **grilling/direct medium heat,** *30 minutes* **roasting/indirect medium heat**
Chicken thigh, boneless, skinless	*115g/4oz*	*8–10 minutes* **grilling/direct medium heat**
Chicken thigh, minced	*2cm/¾ inch thick*	*12–14 minutes* **grilling/direct medium heat**
Chicken, whole	*2–2.5kg/4–5lb*	*1¼–1½ hours* **roasting/indirect medium heat**
Chicken, whole leg	*300–340g/10–12oz*	*48 minutes–1 hour: 40–50 minutes* **roasting/indirect medium heat,** *8–10 minutes* **grilling/direct medium heat**
Chicken wing	*70–75g/2–3oz*	*35–43 minutes: 30–35 minutes* **roasting/indirect medium heat,** *5–8 minutes* **grilling/direct medium heat**
Poussin	*450g/1lb*	*50 minutes* **roasting/indirect high heat**
Duck breast, boneless	*300–340g/10–12oz*	*9–12 minutes: 3–4 minutes* **grilling/direct low heat,** *6–8 minutes* **roasting/indirect high heat**
Duck, whole	*2.75–3kg/5½–6lb*	*40 minutes* **roasting/indirect high heat**
Turkey breast, boneless	*1.1kg/2½lb*	*1–1¼ hours* **roasting/indirect medium heat**
Turkey, whole, not stuffed	*5–6kg/10–12lb*	*2½–3½ hours* **roasting/indirect medium-low heat**

USDA AND CHEF STANDARDS FOR DONENESS

> For optimal safety, the United States Department of Agriculture (USDA) recommends cooking red meat to 145°F (final temperature) and minced red meat to 160°F. The USDA believes that 145°F is medium rare, but virtually all chefs today believe medium rare is closer to 130°F. The chart at right compares chef standards with USDA recommendations. Ultimately, doneness decisions are your choice.

DONENESS	CHEF STANDARDS	USDA
PORK	*63°C/145°F*	*63°C/145°F*
Red Meat: Rare	*49–52°C/120°–125°F*	*n/a*
RED MEAT: Medium rare	*52–57°C/125°–135°F*	*63°C/145°F*
RED MEAT: Medium	*57–63°C/135°–145°F*	*70°C/160°F*
RED MEAT: Medium well	*63–68°C/145°–155°F*	*n/a*
RED MEAT: Well done	*68°C/155°F +*	*77°C/170°F*
Poultry	*70–74°C/160°–165°F*	*74°C/165°F*

SEAFOOD

TYPE	THICKNESS / WEIGHT	APPROXIMATE GRILLING TIME
Clam (discard any that do not open)	50–75g/2–3oz	6–8 minutes *grilling/direct high heat*
Fish, fillet or steak: halibut, red snapper, salmon, sea bass, swordfish and tuna	1cm/½ inch thick	6–8 minutes *grilling/direct high heat*
	2.5cm/1 inch thick	8–10 minutes *grilling/direct high heat*
	2.5–3cm/1–1¼ inches thick	10–12 minutes *grilling/direct high heat*
	450g/1lb	15–20 minutes *roasting/indirect medium heat*
Fish, whole	1–1.2kg/2–2½ lb	20–30 minutes *roasting/indirect medium heat*
	1.5kg/3lb	30–45 minutes *roasting/indirect medium heat*
Mussel (discard any that do not open)	25–50g/1–2oz	5–6 minutes *grilling/direct high heat*
Oyster	75–115g/3–4oz	5–7 minutes *grilling/direct high heat*
Prawn	40g/1½oz	2–4 minutes *grilling/direct high heat*
Scallop	40g/1½oz	4–6 minutes *grilling/direct high heat*

FRUIT

TYPE	THICKNESS	APPROXIMATE GRILLING TIME
Apple	whole	35–40 minutes *roasting/indirect medium heat*
	1-cm/½-inch slices	4–6 minutes *grilling/direct medium heat*
Apricot	halved lengthways	4–6 minutes *grilling/direct medium heat*
Banana	halved lengthways	3–5 minutes *grilling/direct medium heat*
Peach/Nectarine	halved lengthways	6–8 minutes *grilling/direct medium heat*
Pear	halved lengthways	6–8 minutes *grilling/direct medium heat*
Pineapple	1-cm/½-inch slices or 2.5-cm/1-inch wedges	5–10 minutes *grilling/direct medium heat*
Plum	halved lengthways	6–8 minutes *grilling/direct medium heat*
Strawberry	whole	4–5 minutes *grilling/direct medium heat*

⊙ VEGETABLE

TYPE	THICKNESS	APPROXIMATE GRILLING TIME
Artichoke hearts	whole	14–18 minutes: boil 10–12 minutes; cut in half and grill 4–6 minutes **grilling/direct medium heat**
Asparagus	1-cm/½-inch diameter	6–8 minutes **grilling/direct medium heat**
Aubergine	1-cm/½-inch slices	8–10 minutes **grilling/direct medium heat**
Beetroot	whole	1–1½ hours **roasting/indirect medium heat**
Carrot	2.5-cm/1-inch diameter	7–11 minutes: boil 4–6 minutes, grill 3–5 minutes **grilling/direct high heat**
Corn, husked		10–15 minutes **grilling/direct medium heat**
Corn, in husk		20–30 minutes **grilling/direct medium heat**
Courgette	1-cm/½-inch slices	4–6 minutes **grilling/direct medium heat**
Garlic	whole	45 minutes–1 hour **roasting/indirect medium heat**
Mushroom, button or shiitake	whole	8–10 minutes **grilling/direct medium heat**
Mushroom, portobello	whole	8–12 minutes **grilling/direct medium heat**
Onion	halved	35–40 minutes **roasting/indirect medium heat**
	1-cm/½-inch slices	8–12 minutes **grilling/direct medium heat**
Pepper	whole	10–12 minutes **grilling/direct medium heat**
Potato, new	halved	15–20 minutes **grilling/direct medium heat**
Potato	whole	45 minutes–1 hour **roasting/indirect medium heat**
	1-cm/½-inch slices	9–11 minutes **grilling/direct medium heat**
Spring onion	whole	3–4 minutes **grilling/direct medium heat**
Sweet potato	whole	45 minutes–1 hour **roasting/indirect high heat**
	1-cm/½-inch slices	12–15 minutes **grilling/direct medium heat**
Tomato	whole	8–10 minutes **grilling/direct medium heat**
	halved	6–8 minutes **grilling/direct medium heat**

INDEX

S

ACKNOWLDGEMENTS

There are so many people that made this book what it is. It took total dedication to excellence at stage after stage.

First, there was the idea that sprouted, believe it or not, in Germany (at the Frankfurt Book Fair) from the sharp minds of Stephanie Wenzel, Gabriella Hoffmann and other wonderful colleagues at Gräfe und Unzer. They saw the potential for a book in Europe about traditional American barbecue. Mike Kempster, Brooke Jones and Susan Maruyama at Weber broadened that vision to capture the evolving diversity of styles in new American barbecue. Thank you, Mike, Brooke and Susan, for your compelling ideas and your unwavering trust in me.

Charged with the mission of telling a comprehensive story, I interviewed dozens of pit masters, chefs, food writers and barbecue fanatics all over the land. I want to thank all of them, especially Doug Adams, Arthur Aguirre, Peter Botcher, Bryan Bracewell, Melissa and Pete Cookston, Steve Cruz, Ardie Davis, Greg and Gabrielle Denton, Ryan Farr, Aaron Franklin, Meathead Goldwyn, Craig and Gay Jones, Ray Lampe, Adam Perry Lang, Edward Lee, Chris Lilly, Amy Mills, Mike Mills, Wayne Mueller, Robert Moss, Sonny Orsini, Steven Raichlen, Barry Sorkin, Norman Van Aken, Daniel Vaughn, Lee Ann Whippen, Carolyn Wells and Doug Worgul. Each of them is a blazing star in the barbecue universe.

I also want to acknowledge the talented members of the 2015 Danish National Barbecue Team, who allowed me to watch them compete with impressive success at the Memphis in May World Championship Barbecue Cooking Contest. I salute you all: Per Svane Aastradsen, Jim Boland, Peter Bragh, Asger Hvam, Anders Jensen, Mads Bo Kristensen, Claus Hasse Olesen, Stig Pedersen, Michael Dahl Thomsen and the amazing Anne Jungersen Thomsen.

While working on the recipes and text, I was spoiled by some of the brightest, most creative culinarians in the country. My heartfelt gratitude goes to: Patty Ada, Lynda Balslev, Brigit Binns, Lena Birnbaum, David Bonom, Linda Carucci, Sarah Epstein, Suzy Farnsworth, Heather John Fogarty, Elizabeth Hughes, Allison Kociuruba, Adrian Miller, Marge Perry, Lesley Porcelli, Rick Rodgers, Cheryl Sternman Rule, Mic Stanfield, Kerry Trotter, Bruce Weinstein and Terri Wuerthner.

When it came time to photograph the recipes and all the techniques so important for making barbecue successfully, I relied on the endlessly skilled Tim Turner and his team. We couldn't have done all this without Brett Bulthuis, Mike Caviani, Ben Leikness, Josh Marrah, Meghan Ross and Donte Tatum. For the phenomenal food styling, we were fortunate to work with Lynn Gagné and Nina Albazi. The photography of restaurants featured in essays throughout the book was done beautifully by Michael Warren.

Throughout the book-making process, I turned time and again to the barbecue professionals at Weber. I can't thank these people enough for responding every time with genuine collaboration and professionalism: Kim Lefko, Suzanne Brown, Deanna Budnick, Mike Chavez, Marc Colavitti, Neal Conner, Larry Donahue, Kim Durk, Mark Fenne, Lexy Fricano, Heather Herriges, Melanie Hill, Matt Jost, Kevin Kolman, Jennie Lussow, Theresa Stahl, and the man who steers the entire company, Tom Koos.

The main reason this book is such fun to peruse is that Christina Schroeder led a team of creative wizards at rabble+rouser. Thank you, Marsha Capen, for giving every aspect of this book your acute editorial expertise. Shum Prats will forever have my admiration and respect for his brilliant design. Alyx Chapman also worked wonders with the graphics. Tamara McTavish and Teddy Sirotek stepped up whenever they were asked and performed like champions. Becky LaBrum pulled it all together in a clear, thorough index.

This is my first book with Houghton Mifflin Harcourt (HMH) as publisher, and I couldn't be happier with the partnership. Bruce Nichols, Natalie Chapman and Cindy Kitchel brought tremendous insights and editorial resources to this project. I am confident that the book will be sold far and wide because of dedicated HMH people, especially Laurie Brown, Maire Gorman, Lori Glazer, Brad Parsons, James Phirman, Rebecca Liss, Colleen Murphy and Allison Renzulli.

At home I am blessed to have a fabulous family that doesn't object when I set off for yet another research trip or when I walk in the front door with yet another immense brisket that will require barbecuing throughout the night. Thank you, Fran, Julia, James and Peter. I love you all.

An Hachette UK Company
www.hachette.co.uk

First published in Great Britain in 2016 by Hamlyn, a division of
Octopus Publishing Group Ltd
Carmelite House, 50 Victoria Embankment
London EC4Y 0DZ
www.octopusbooks.co.uk

ISBN 978-0-60063-413-3

A CIP catalogue record for this book is available from the British Library.
Printed and bound in China

10 9 8 7 6 5 4 3 2 1

AUTHOR
Jamie Purviance

MANAGING EDITOR
Marsha Capen
EDITORIAL, DESIGN AND PRODUCTION
rabble+rouser, inc.:
Chief Creative Officer: **Christina Schroeder**
Editorial Director: **Marsha Capen**
Creative Director: **Shum Prats**
Graphic Design: **Alyx Chapman**
Senior Producer: **Tamara McTavish**
Producer: **Teddy Sirotek**

FOOD PHOTOGRAPHER
Tim Turner
LIFESTYLE PHOTOGRAPHER
Michael Warren
PHOTOGRAPHY CREDIT
Jamie Purviance, pp. 56, 80, 81, 82, 160, 164, 186
PHOTO ASSISTANTS TO TIM TURNER
**Brett Bulthuis, Mike Caviani, Ben Leikness,
Josh Marrah, Donte Tatum**

LOCATION MANAGER
Meghan Ross
FOOD STYLING
Food Stylist: **Lynn Gagné**
Assistant Food Stylist: **Nina Albazi**
PROP STYLING
Christina Schroeder

COLOUR IMAGING AND IN-HOUSE PRE-PRESS
Weber Creative Services:
Deanna Budnick
Neal Conner
Mike Chavez

CONTRIBUTORS
**Patty Ada, Lynda Balslev, Brigit Binns, Lena Birnbaum,
David Bonom, Linda Carucci, Sarah Epstein, Suzy Farnsworth, Heather John
Fogarty, Elizabeth Hughes, Allison Kociuruba, Adrian Miller, Marge Perry, Lesley
Porcelli, Rick Rodgers, Cheryl Sternman Rule, Mic Stanfield, Kerry Trotter,
Bruce Weinstein, Terri Wuerthner**

INDEXER
Becky LaBrum

EDITORIAL DIRECTOR (OCTOPUS)
Eleanor Maxfield
SENIOR EDITOR (OCTOPUS)
Pauline Bache
SENIOR DESIGNER (OCTOPUS)
Jaz Bahra
PAGE LAYOUT (OCTOPUS)
Jeremy Tilston
PRODUCTION MANAGER (OCTOPUS)
Caroline Alberti

ROUND MOUNTAIN MEDIA
Consulting Global Publishing Director: **Susan J. Maruyama**

WEBER-STEPHEN PRODUCTS LLC
Executive Board Director: **Mike Kempster**
Chief Marketing Officer: **Kim Lefko**
Vice President Marketing, Global Marketing: **Brooke Jones**

HOUGHTON MIFFLIN HARCOURT
Vice President, Publisher: **Natalie Chapman**
Editorial Director: **Cindy Kitchel**
Managing Editor: **Marina Padakis Lowry**
Production Director: **Thomas Hyland**

SOURCES
The following books and websites were excellent sources of information for this book.

Cookston, Melissa. *Smokin' in the Boys' Room: Southern Recipes from the Winningest
Woman in Barbecue.* Andrews McMeel Publishing, LLC, 2014.

Engelhardt, Elizabeth S. D. *Republic of Barbecue: Stories Beyond
the Brisket.* University of Texas Press, 2009.

Franklin, Aaron, and Jordan Mackay. *Franklin Barbecue:
A Meat-Smoking Manifesto.* Ten Speed Press, 2015.

Goldwyn, Craig. www.amazingribs.com.

López-Alt, J. Kenji. *The Food Lab: Better Home Cooking Through Science.* W. W.
Norton & Company, Inc., 2015.

Moss, Robert F. *Barbecue: The History of an American Institution.* University Alabama
Press, 2010.

Raichlen, Steven. *BBQ USA: 425 Fiery Recipes from All Across America.* Workman
Publishing Company, Inc., 2003.

Vaughn, Daniel. www.tmbbq.com.